AMERICAN FOREIGN POLICY
SINCE WORLD WAR II

AMERICAN FOREIGN POLICY SINCE WORLD WAR II

Second Revised Edition

By JOHN W. SPANIER

FREDERICK A. PRAEGER, *Publishers*

New York • Washington • London

FREDERICK A. PRAEGER, *Publishers*
111 Fourth Avenue, New York, N.Y. 10003, U.S.A.
77-79 Charlotte Street, London W. 1, England

Published in the United States of America in 1965
by Frederick A. Praeger, Inc., Publishers

Third printing, 1966

The original edition of this book was published in 1960, and a revised
edition in 1962, by Frederick A. Praeger, Inc., Publishers. This new
edition has been extensively revised and brought up to date.

© 1960, 1962, 1965 by Frederick A. Praeger, Inc.

Library of Congress Catalog Card Number: 65-15649

Printed in the United States of America

PREFACE TO THE SECOND REVISED EDITION

My purpose in this book is to present an account of American foreign policy since 1945: from the breakdown of the wartime alliance with the Soviet Union, through the beginning of the cold war, to the uneasy *détente* of 1965, and including the various efforts—political, military, social, and economic—of the Truman, Eisenhower, Kennedy, and Johnson administrations to contain Communist expansion in Europe, Asia, the Middle East, Africa, and Latin America. However, this book is intended to be not merely a catalogue of events, but primarily an analysis of American policy in the post–World War II era. It is my hope that it will contribute both to a more profound understanding of the past and to a greater insight into the basic problems that currently face the United States in the international area—particularly, the two fundamental issues upon whose resolution American and free-world security (indeed, survival) depend. These two issues are the nature of our military strategy and the future of the underdeveloped countries.

The framework for my analysis is the traditional American approach to foreign affairs. This emphasis is deliberate. For as the United States moved through the late 1940's and the 1950's, it became increasingly evident that the American approach to foreign policy, with its intense distaste for "power politics," hindered an adequate response to the ideological, social, and strategic challenges of our age. The American penchant for separating war and peace into two mutually exclusive states of affairs and divorcing force from diplomacy hampered a union of power and policy; the resulting all-or-nothing military strategy tended to paralyze our diplomacy and make it difficult to respond to the continuous limited challenges presented by the Communists. American failure to understand social politics—i.e., the class struggle—has also proved to be a grave obstacle to our comprehension of the

v

social changes accompanying the "revolution of rising expectations" throughout the underdeveloped areas. Large-scale economic aid for capital development would not suffice to meet the aspirations of the new nations; economic progress must be attended by social transformation. The crisis of postwar American foreign policy was, in short, the crisis of American society, since the American approach to international politics was the product of both our experience and our predominantly middle-class culture. And the challenge for the 1960's is the need to re-examine and adjust this approach. Indeed, definite progress in this direction has already been made.

Before closing, I should like to express my gratitude to two people: Arnold Dolin, for his continued fine editing of the manuscript; and Sheila Coffey, who prepared the original index and was the person most responsible for this book. I should also like to thank Walter Lippmann and the *New York Herald Tribune* for allowing me to quote from one of Mr. Lippmann's superb series of articles published in early 1960 on national defense and America's loss of national purpose.

J. W. S.

Gainesville, Florida
May, 1965

CONTENTS

AMERICAN FOREIGN POLICY
SINCE WORLD WAR II

I. THE AMERICAN APPROACH
TO FOREIGN POLICY

Following World War I, the English geopolitician Halford MacKinder wrote: "Who rules East Europe commands the Heartland [largely Russia and China, plus Iran and Afghanistan]: Who rules the Heartland commands the World-Island [Eurasia and Africa]: Who rules the World-Island commands the World." Some years later, an American geopolitician, Nicolas Spykman, paraphrased MacKinder in a reply to his thesis: "Who controls the Rimland [the peripheral areas of the Eurasian continent] rules Eurasia; who rules Eurasia controls the destinies of the world."

No two maxims could have summed up the history of the post–World War II era more aptly. The Soviet Union and Communist China now occupy most of the Heartland; surrounding them along a 20,000-mile periphery lie the exposed and weaker Rimland nations—the Scandinavian and West European countries, Italy, Greece, Turkey, the Arab countries, Iran, Afghanistan, India, Burma, Thailand, Malaya, Indochina, and Korea (with Britain, Indonesia, and Japan lying just off the Eurasian continent). It is the Communists' aim to extend their control to these nations. This would leave the United States and the Americas—the Western Hemisphere—a lone island in a totalitarian sea. American security would then be, at best, very precarious and could be maintained only by the organization of our society as a "garrison state," a condition incompatible with any interpretation of the "American way of life." At worst, the United States would be at the mercy of the Soviet bloc controlling the Eurasian continent. The ability of the United States to ensure its own security—indeed, its survival—under these circumstances depends upon its capacity to establish a balance of power in Eurasia in order to prevent the Communists from expanding into the Rimland or neutralizing those nations.

As far back as the 1830's, a prophetic Frenchman, Alexis de Tocqueville, had foreseen this struggle which dominates our age:

> There are, at the present time, two great nations in the world which seem to tend toward the same end, although they started from different points: I allude to the Russians and the Americans. . . . The Anglo-American relies upon personal interest to accomplish his ends, and gives free scope to the unguided exertions and common sense of the citizens; the Russians centers all the authority of society in a single arm: the principal instrument of the former is freedom; of the latter is servitude. Their starting point is different, and their courses are not the same; yet each of them seems to be marked out by the will of Heaven to sway the destinies of half the globe.

Yet, the United States in 1945 could not have been less equipped to conduct this struggle and to assume the global responsibilities involved. American experience in foreign affairs, in comparison with that of the other great powers of the world, had been limited. Consequently, the United States was essentially a novice in the art she now had to practice—the art of "power politics." For over a century the nation had cut itself off from Europe and pursued a policy of isolationism, or what today would be called neutralism or nonalignment. Like the new nations of the post–World War II era, the United States, as the world's first new nation to emerge from colonial subjection, refused to involve herself in the quarrels of Britain, France, and the other European powers. "Europe has a set of primary interests, which to us have none, or a very remote relation. Hence she must be engaged in frequent controversies, the causes of which are essentially foreign to our concerns," said George Washington in his Farewell Address. Therefore, he continued, it would be unwise "to implicate ourselves, by artificial ties, in the ordinary vicissitudes of her politics, or the ordinary combinations and collisions of her friendships, or enmities: Our detached and distant situation invites and enables us to pursue a different course. . . . Why forego the advantages of so peculiar a situation? Why quit our own to stand upon foreign ground? Why, by inter-weaving our destiny with that of any part of Europe, entangle our peace and prosperity in the toils of European ambition, Rivalship, Interest, Humour or Caprice?" Why, indeed?

The republic was young, hardly yet conscious of its national identity. American nationalism had been aroused during the War of Independence. But once the British had been defeated and ejected, each of the thirteen colonies had become more interested in its own affairs than in those of the Confederation. The Confederation was a "league of states" in which loyalty to the states took precedence; it was a "firm league of friendship," not a united nation. For example, when Jefferson talked of "my country," he was referring to Virginia, not to the United States. The resulting interstate rivalries and conflicts, the absence of any effective central government, and the lack of an international status for the Confederation led to the formation of the "more perfect union." But once the colonial master who had formerly united the people in common opposition had been removed, how could this new union gain its sense of identity as a new nation? The answer given by the leaders of the young republic—and this answer is still given by the leaders of most of today's new nations—was to continue pursuing an anti-colonial policy. This is essential for a new nation's national cohesion. It was colonial subjugation that first kindled the spirit of revolt and awakened the people's sense of national consciousness. It is by continuing to "fight colonialism"—both the specific former colonial ruler and colonialism in general—that this feeling of nationalism is strengthened. Since it was Europe that colonized the world, the rejection of Europe is essential to the formation of the new nation's sense of identity. Therefore, it cannot realign itself with the old colonial master, even when its security is threatened. Whether this threat comes from the Holy Alliance or Communism, the newborn state cannot in most circumstances "stand up and be counted." It must remain independent, for only its assertion against Europe—or, as we say today, "the West"—will foster its growth of national consciousness.

Avoiding "foreign entanglements," as Jefferson called it, is also necessary for the young nation's "economic development." How will it become strong enough to defend the country against possible foreign attacks or assert its prestige against disrespectful, "neocolonial" treatment by the older nations of the world? How can it tie the various parts of the nations together into an effective union and subordinate local and regional loyalties to a primary national loyalty? And finally, how can it provide a better life and standard of living for its new citizens? These are the three vital questions that confront the leaders of all new states, for the government must prove to its people that the recently formed nation is worthy of their support and allegiance because it can furnish them with a secure and decent life. Hamilton, the father of American industrialism, was keenly aware of these needs, particularly the security of the nation. Industrialization thus became a necessity if the United States was to defend her national security, safeguard her independence, and gain the respect of those states who still considered her a colonial weakling and inferior. The continuing friction with Britain during the first years after independence made this clear. The British treated the young republic in an arrogant and high-handed fashion as if it were still a colony; they refused to vacate the Northwest frontier and impressed American sailors by stopping American ships on the high seas and simply taking the sailors off. Not surprisingly, the lesson of the War of 1812 (also known as the Second War of Independence) was the need for industrialization and strength. But the purpose of industrialization is to do more than augment national power; it is also to strengthen the still fragile political bonds of union with economic bonds. Industrialization, with its high degree of specialization and division of labor, welds together the many areas of a country and binds the people living therein into a closer union; once strangers to each other—hardly thinking of one another as countrymen and fellow nationals—they will be compelled to travel and communicate as the imperative of economic interdependence envelops the entire nation in one large market. The people thereby become "nationalized" as industrialization molds the consciousness of the new citizens and impresses upon them an awareness that they are members of one nation who will all have to work together if their common aspirations are to be fulfilled. Finally, it enables the new nation to raise its people's standard of living. This is the ultimate test of the new political order—its ability to confer economic benefits, or, more succinctly, its ability to "pay off." This is not to deny the importance of such other values as national independence and self-government. However, if man does not live by bread alone, he cannot survive without bread either; and the crucial issue therefore becomes the new order's capacity to furnish its citizens with at least the basic necessities of life, if not a degree of affluence and leisure. It was precisely the opportunities the American political and economic system afforded to its people to improve their material condition that drew the millions of immigrants to these shores. Freedom alone would not have proved such a powerful magnet. Indeed, it is doubtful that freedom can be established, let alone survive, in conditions of poverty. A degree of affluence and a reasonably equitable distribution of income seem to be prerequisites for the blossoming of a democracy, although they are not the sole prerequisites. In any case, the conclusion is clear: Economic development is vital if the new nation is to grow strong, united, and prosperous. In fact, the term "economic development" is a misnomer. It is the *political* results of this development that are essential to the future of the new state. Economic development might more appropriately be called "nation-building."

Granted that, in the American instance—as for new nations after 1945—the avoidance of foreign entanglements was thus a realistic policy, the subsequent American understanding of international relations proved to be unrealistic. For the priority of internal political and economic tasks, all of which were reinforced by the opening of the West and the subsequent transcontinental drive to the Pacific, led to the depreciation of the importance of foreign policy and the role that power plays in protecting the nation's interests. The ability of the United States to live in isolationism during the nineteenth century and a good part of the twentieth century was attributed, not to the nation's geographic distance from Europe or to the Royal Navy as the protector of the *Pax Britannica,* but to the nature of democracy. The United States was more than just the world's first "new nation"; it was also the world's first democracy and, as such, the first country in history that would devote itself to improving the lot of the common man, granting each individual the opportunity to enrich and ennoble his life. ("Give me your tired, your poor, your huddled masses yearning to be free," reads the inscription on the Statue of Liberty.) The more perfect union was to be an egalitarian society. European concepts of social hierarchy, nobility and titles, and bitter class struggles were not to be planted in its democratic soil. "Here the free spirit of mankind, at length, throws its last fetters off," exclaimed one writer. America was to be a "beacon lighting for all the world the paths of human destiny," wrote Emerson. From the very beginning of their national life, Americans believed strongly in their destiny—to spread, by example, the light of freedom to all men and to lead mankind out of the wicked ways of the Old World. The massive immigration of the nineteenth century—particularly after 1865—was to reinforce this sense of destiny. "Repudiation of Europe," as John Dos Passos once said, "is, after all, America's main excuse for being." Europe stood for war, poverty, and exploitation; America for peace, opportunity, and democracy. But the United States was not merely to be a beacon of a superior democratic domestic way of life. It was also to be an example of a morally superior democratic pattern of international behavior. The United States would voluntarily reject power politics as unfit for the conduct of its foreign policy. Democratic theory posits that man is a rational and moral creature, and that differences among men can be settled by rational persuasion and moral exhortation. Indeed, granted this assumption about man, the only differences that could arise would simply be misunderstandings; and since man is endowed with reason and a moral sense, what quarrels could not be settled, given the necessary good will? Peace—the result of harmony among men—was thus the natural or normal state.

Conversely, conflict was considered a deviation from this norm, caused primarily by wicked statesmen whose morality and reason had been corrupted by the exercise of uncontrolled authority. Power politics was an instrument of selfish and autocratic rulers—that is, men unrestrained by democratic public opinion—who loved to wield it for their own personal advantage. To them, war was a grand game. They could remain in their palatial homes, continuing to eat well and to enjoy the luxuries of life. They suffered none of the hardships of war. These hardships fell upon the ordinary people; it was they who had to leave their families to fight, to endure the higher taxes made necessary by the costs of war, possibly to see their homes destroyed and their loved ones maimed or killed. It was only the despot who thought of war as a sport, as a sort of "bully" fox hunt; the common man, who had to endure all the cruelties of war, was therefore by his very nature peaceful. The conclusion was clear: Undemocratic states were inherently warlike and evil; democratic nations, in which the people controlled and regularly changed their leaders, were peaceful and moral.

American experience seemed to support this conclusion. The United States was a democracy and she was at peace. Furthermore, peace seemed to be the normal state of affairs. It was therefore logical that democracy and peaceful behavior and intentions should be thought of as synonymous. Americans never asked themselves whether democracy was really responsible for the peace they enjoyed, or whether this peace they assumed to be a natural condition was the product of other forces. The constant wars of Europe appeared to provide the answer: European politics were power politics, and this was because of the undemocratic nature of European regimes. Americans were therefore relieved that they had long ago, at the time of the Revolutionary War, cut themselves off from Europe and its constant class conflicts and power politics. America had to guard her democratic purity and abstain from any involvement in the affairs of Europe lest she be soiled and corrupted. Nonalignment was therefore the morally correct policy which allowed the United States to quarantine herself from contact with Europe's hierarchical social structures and immoral international habits. At the same time, by confusing the results of geography and international politics with the supposed consequences of democracy, Americans could smugly enjoy a self-conferred moral superiority. It was the Monroe Doctrine, proclaimed in 1823, which first stressed, officially and explicitly, this ideological difference between the New and Old Worlds. It declared specifically that the American political system was "essentially different" from that of Europe, whose nations were constantly engaged in warfare. The implication was very clear: Democratic government equals peace, and aristocratic government—which was identified with despotism—means war.

But this association of peace with democracy was not the only reason for the American depreciation of power politics. Another was that the United States was an overwhelmingly one-class society in which almost all men shared the same set of middle-class, capitalistic, and democratic values or beliefs. America was unique among nations in this respect. The European countries were, by contrast, three-class societies. In addition to the middle class, they contained in their bodies politic an aristocratic class whose energies were devoted either to maintaining itself in power or to recapturing power in order to return to the glorious days of a feudal past. Moreover, European urbanization and industrialization during the nineteenth century gave birth to a proletariat which, because it felt that it did not receive a fair share of the national income, became a revolutionary class. The nations of the Old World were, in short, a composite of three elements: a reactionary aristocracy, a democratic middle class, and a revolutionary proletariat. Or, to put it another way, these nations had, in an intellectual as well as a political sense, a right, a center, and a left. The United States had only a center, both intellectually and politically. This country had never experienced a feudal past and therefore possessed no large and powerful aristocratic class on the right; and because it was, by and large, an egalitarian society, it also lacked a genuine left-wing movement of protest, such as socialism or Communism. America was, as De Tocqueville had said, "born free" as a middle-class, individualistic, capitalistic, and democratic society. We were not divided by the kind of deep ideological conflicts which in France, for instance, set one class of Frenchmen against another. No one class was ever so afraid of another that it preferred national defeat to domestic revolution—as in France in the late 1930's, when the bourgeoisie was so apprehensive of a proletarian upheaval that its slogan became "Better Hitler than Blum [the French Socialist leader]."

Americans are, in fact, in such accord on their basic values that whenever the nation is threatened from the outside, the public becomes fearful of internal disloyalty. It is one of the great ironies of American society that although Americans possess this unity of shared beliefs to a greater degree than any other people, their apprehension of external danger leads them, first, to insist upon a general and somewhat dogmatic reaffirmation of loyalty to the "American way of life," and then to a hunt for internal groups or forces that might betray this way of life. Disagreement tends to become suspect as disloyalty; men are accused of "un-American" thinking and behavior, and labeled "loyalty or security risks." Perhaps only a society so overwhelmingly committed to one set of values could be so sensitive to internal subversion and so fearful of internal betrayal; perhaps only a society in which two or more ideologies have long since learned to live together could genuinely tolerate diverse opinions. Who has ever heard of "un-British" or "un-French" activities? The United States has often been called a "melting pot" because of the many different nationality groups it comprises; but before each generation of immigrants has been fully accepted into American society, it has had to be "Americanized." Few Americans have ever accepted diversity as a value. American society has, in fact, taken great pride in destroying diversity through assimilation.

It was precisely this overwhelming agreement on the fundamental values of American society and Europe's intense class struggles that reinforced the American misunderstanding of the nature and functions of power on the international scene. Dissatisfied groups never developed a revolutionary ideology because the growing prosperity spread to them before they could translate their grievances against the capitalistic system into political action. America—politically secure and economically prosperous—therefore remained unaware of two important principles: that conflict is the natural offspring of clashing interests and groups, and that power plays a vital role in protecting, promoting, and compromising interests. By contrast, the European states, with their internal class struggles and external conflicts among themselves, never failed to appreciate the nature and role of power.

Politics did not, in any event, seem very important to Americans. The United States matured during the nineteenth century, the era of *laissez-faire* capitalism, whose basic assumption was that man was economically motivated. It was self-interest that governed the behavior of man; it might be referred to as "enlightened self-interest," but it was nevertheless self-interest. Each individual, seeking to maximize his wealth, responded to the demand of the free market. In an effort to increase his profit, he supplied the product the consumers wanted. The laws of demand and supply therefore transformed each person's economic selfishness into socially beneficial results. The entire society would prosper. The free market was thus considered the central institution that provided "the greatest good of the greatest number." Politics mattered little in this self-adjusting economic system based upon individuals' actions whose combined efforts resulted in the general welfare. The best government was the government that governed least. Arbitrary political interference with the economic laws of the market would only upset the results these laws were intended to produce. Private property, profit, the free market were thus the keys to assuring the happiness of mankind by providing him with abundance. Capitalism, in short, reflected the materialism of the age of industrialization.

To state the issue even more bluntly: Economics was good, politics was bad. This simple dichotomy came naturally to the capitalist middle class. Were the benefits of economic freedom not as "self-evident" as the truths stated in the Declaration of Independence? And had this economic freedom not been gained only by a long and bitter struggle of the European middle class to cut down the authority of the powerful monarchical state, and finally to overthrow it by revolution in France? The middle class, as it had grown more prosperous and numerous, had become increasingly resentful of paying taxes from which the aristocracy was usually exempt, of the restrictions placed upon trade and industry, of the absence of institutions in which middle-class economic and political interests were represented, of the class barriers to the social status that came with careers in the army and in the bureaucracy, and of the general lack of freedom of thought and expression. Since the middle class identified the power of the state with its own lack of freedom, its aim was to restrict this power. Only by placing restraints upon the authority of the state could it gain the individual liberty and, above all, the right to private enterprise it sought. Democratic philosophy stated these claims in terms of the individual's "natural rights" against the state. The exercise of political authority was thus equated with the abuse of that authority and the suppression of personal freedoms. The power of the state had therefore to be restricted to the minimum to ensure the individual's maximum political and economic liberties. It was with this purpose in mind that the American Constitution divided authority between the states and the Federal Government, and, within the latter, among the executive, legislative, and judicial branches. Federalism and the separation of powers were deliberately designed to keep all governments—and especially the national government—weak. Man's secular problems would be resolved not by the state's political actions but by the individual's own economic actions in society.

Again, both man's economic motivation and the benefits of a government that acts least were considered to be reflected in the American experience. Millions came to the United States from other lands to seek a better way of life. America was the earthly paradise where all men, no matter how poor or humble they had been in the old country, could earn a respectable living. A virgin and underdeveloped land, America presented magnificent opportunities for individual enterprise. First, there was the Western frontier with its rich soil; later, during the Industrial Revolution, the country's bountiful natural resources were exploited. The environment, technology, individual enterprise, and helpful governmental policies enabled the American people to become the "people of plenty." But to earn money was not only economically necessary in order to attain a comfortable standard of living; it was also psychologically necessary in order to gain social status and to earn the respect of one's fellow citizens.

Individual self-esteem is determined by the community in every society, for the individual can only judge his own worth by the standards of that society. In a class society, status can be easily recognized by certain upper-class traits, such as the clothes a man wears, the manners with which he conducts himself, and the way he pronounces his words. His education is, in fact, the key to his status. But in an egalitarian society, the successful man can be recognized only by his affluence; only the fact that he is richer than his peers, that he has more possessions, that he can afford to indulge in "conspicuous consumption" distinguishes him from other men. It follows logically that if material gain is the exclusive or at least principal sign of differentiation among men and if it confers upon them social respect and position, everyone will preoccupy himself with the pursuit and accumulation of the "almighty dollar." If men are judged primarily by their economic achievements, they will concentrate on "getting ahead." It is not surprising, therefore, that money comes closer to being the common standard of value in the United States than in any other country. For money is the symbol of power and prestige; it is the sign of success, just as failure to earn enough money is a token of personal failure. It has been said, not without some justice, that the American prefers two cars to two mistresses.

It was hardly surprising that in these circumstances the solution to international problems should be thought of in economic terms. Economics was identified with social harmony and the welfare of all men; politics was equated with conflict and war and death. Just as the "good society" was to be the product of free competition, so the peaceful international society would be created by free trade. An international *laissez-faire* policy would benefit all states just as a national *laissez-faire* policy benefited each individual within these states. Consequently, people all over the world had a vested interest in peace in order to carry on their economic relations. Trade and war were incompatible. Trade depended upon mutual prosperity (the poor do not buy much from one another). War impoverishes and destroys and creates ill-will among nations. Commerce benefits all the participating states; the more trade, the greater the number of individual interests involved. Commerce was consequently nationally and individually profitable and created a vested interest in peace. War, by contrast, was economically unprofitable and therefore obsolete. Free trade and peace, in short, were one and the same cause.

Thus the United States entered the twentieth century with a relative unawareness of the role that power plays in the relations among nations, even though as a highly industrialized and powerful nation she was at the turn of the century increasingly exerting a dominating influence in the Western Hemisphere. At no time was this attitude more vividly demonstrated than at the point of our entry into World War I and during the interwar period. It was Germany's unrestricted submarine warfare in early 1917 that brought us into that conflict; it was thus the German High Command's fatal decision that propelled the United States into the war. Yet, our security demanded this entry. The balance of power in the European battlefield was about to collapse: Britain and France were nearing financial exhaustion; Britain's food supply had reached near-starvation level because of the effectiveness of the German submarine campaign; the French Army had suffered such enormous casualties during a series of offensives that it had mutinied; and above all, the Czarist Empire was about to collapse, and this would allow the Germans to transfer some 2 million troops to the Western Front for their 1918 spring offensives. If the Western Allies had then been defeated, as seemed quite likely, the United States would have had to confront a Germany astride the whole continent, dominating European Russia, and in alliance with Austria-Hungary and the Ottoman Empire, extending her influence over the Balkans and the Middle East as far as the Persian Gulf. This would have posed a grave threat to American security, since Germany would have been in substantial control of the Heartland and the European Rimland. The United States, therefore, had good reason to ally herself with Britain and France to safeguard her own security before this menacing situation matured. But she did not—and would not have, if Germany had not launched its unrestricted submarine warfare in the spring of 1917.

The United States thus entered the war in a political vacuum. The American people were never aware of the power realities and security interests which made American participation in the war absolutely necessary. Rather, they believed they were fighting a war for freedom and democracy, conducting a crusade to destroy German despotism and militarism and to banish power politics forever. It is hardly surprising, therefore, that once the war had burned out this crusading spirit, the American public, still blissfully unaware of the relationship between American independence and the balance of power, should again wish to retire into its prewar isolationist state. The United States thus refused to help protect herself, although Britain and France had been exhausted by the four years of fighting and Germany remained second only to the United States as potentially the most powerful country in the world. We refused to face the responsibility that attended the possession of great power. Instead of playing our proper role in world affairs and attempting to preserve the international balance, thereby heading off the next war, we buried our head in the sand for more than twenty years. The result was that a renascent Germany—allied this time with Italy and Japan (plus the Soviet Union from 1939 to 1941)—once again sought to dominate the world. In December, 1941, Japan's attack on Pearl Harbor precipitated the American entry into World War II. Our ostrich policy had not prevented the waves of world politics from once more lapping our shores.

This American depreciation of power, so evident in these events, has meant that the United States draws a clear-cut distinction between war and peace in its approach to foreign policy. Peace is characterized by a state of harmony among nations; power politics, or war, is considered abnormal. In peacetime, one need pay little or no attention to foreign problems; indeed, to do so would divert men from their individual, materialistic concerns and upset the whole scale of social values. The effect of this attitude is clear: Americans turn their attention toward the outside world only with the greatest reluctance and only when provoked—that is, when the foreign menace has become so clear that it can no longer be ignored. Or, to state it somewhat differently, the United States rarely initiates policy; the stimuli which are responsible for the formulation of American foreign policy come from beyond America's frontiers.

Once Americans are provoked, however, and the United States has to resort to force, the employment of this force can be justified only in terms of the universal moral principles with which the United States, as a democratic country, identifies itself. Resort to this evil instrument, war, can be justified only by presuming noble purposes and completely destroying the immoral enemy who threatens the integrity, if not the existence, of these principles. American power must be "righteous" power; only its full exercise can ensure salvation or the absolution of sin. The national aversion to violence thus becomes transformed into a national glorification of violence, and our wars become ideological crusades to make the world safe for democracy—by democratizing it or by converting the authoritarian or totalitarian states into peaceful, democratic states and thereby banishing power politics for all time. Once that aim has been achieved, the United States can again withdraw into itself, secure in the knowledge that American works have again proved to be "good works." In this context, foreign affairs are an annoying diversion from more important domestic matters. But such diversions are only temporary, since maximum force is applied to the aggressor or warmonger to punish him for his provocation and to teach him that aggression is immoral and will not be rewarded. As a result, American wars are total wars—that is, wars aimed at the total destruction of the enemy.

Not only does the American approach to international politics consider peace and war as two mutually exclusive states of affairs; it also divorces force from diplomacy. In peacetime, diplomacy unsupported by force is supposed to preserve the harmony among states. But in wartime, political considerations are subordinated to force. Once the diplomats have failed to keep the peace with appeals to morality and reason, military considerations become primary. During war, the soldier is placed in charge. Just as the professional medical man has the responsibility for curing his patients of their several maladies, so the military "doctor" must control the curative treatment of the international society when it is infected with the disease of power politics. General Douglas MacArthur has aptly summed up this attitude: when diplomacy has failed to preserve the peace, he said, "you then go to force; and when you do that, the balance of control . . . is the control of the military. A theater commander, in any campaign, is not merely limited to the handling of his troops; he commands the whole area politically, economically, and militarily. . . . when politics fail, and the military take over, you must trust the military."

The United States, then, has traditionally rejected the concept of war as a political instrument and the Clausewitzian definition of war as the continuation of politics by other means. Instead, it has regarded war as a politically neutral operation which should be guided by its own professional rules and imperatives. The military officer is a nonpolitical man who conducts his campaign in a strictly military, technically efficient manner. And war is a purely military instrument whose sole aim is the destruction of the enemy's forces and of his despotic regime so that his people can be democratized.

War is thus a means employed to abolish power politics; war is conducted to end all wars. This same moralistic attitude which is responsible for our all-or-nothing approach to war—either to abstain from the dirty game of power politics or to crusade for its complete elimination—also militates against the use of diplomacy in its classical sense: to compromise interests, to conciliate differences, and to moderate and isolate conflicts. While, on the one hand, Americans regard diplomacy as a rational process for straightening out misunderstandings between nations, they are, on the other hand, extremely suspicious of diplomacy. If the United States is by definition moral, it obviously cannot compromise; for a nation endowed with a moral mission can hardly violate its own principles. That would constitute appeasement and national humiliation. The nation's principles would be transgressed, the nation's interests improperly defended, the national honor stained. For to compromise with the immoral enemy is to be contaminated with evil. Moreover, to reach a settlement with him, rather than wiping him out in order to safeguard our principles, would be a recognition of our weakness. This attitude toward diplomacy which, in effect, prevents its use as an instrument of compromise thus reinforces our predilection for war as a means of settling our international problems. For war allows us to destroy our evil opponent, while permitting us to keep our moral mission intact and unsullied by any compromises which could infect our purity.

The result of this depreciation of power and moralistic approach to foreign policy is the inability of the United States to relate military power to political objectives. Yet, only if the two are combined can a nation conduct an effective foreign policy. Diplomacy, as an instrument by which the nation's interests are guarded without resort to force, cannot achieve its aims unless it is supported by military strength. It is precisely this strength which safeguards a nation's interests and enables it to head off crises, instead of having to pay the terrible costs of war involved in actually applying this force once the threat has become clear. Power can be employed in administering pressure upon an opponent, forcing him to be conciliatory if he wishes to avoid a clash. Military strength, in short, can act as an incentive for an adversary to compromise; for if he is unwilling to be conciliatory, he is faced with the prospect of defeat in battle. A diplomacy unsupported by a proper military power and strategy thus spells impotence. Good intentions by themselves are insufficient and must be supplemented by power. It may be true, as some like to say, that right is might; but superior moral ideals, unsupported by a political and military strategy, inevitably lead to their self-defeat. Faith without works, as Christianity has taught us, is not enough.

In the past, American foreign policy has not been characterized by such a happy marriage between diplomacy and force. Even when the United States has been involved in foreign affairs, its policy has featured the divorce of political aims from military strategy. In peacetime, the United States has, at best, possessed a skeleton military establishment; and during hostilities, it has simply maximized its strength to achieve total defeat of the enemy. American diplomacy in peacetime has been paralyzed by a lack of strength; during war, purely military objectives have become paramount. The American approach to foreign policy has been an all-or-nothing affair, characterized by either complete abstention and impotence or total commitment and strength.

The situation which faced the United States in 1945, however, no longer allowed her to abstain from this struggle. The Soviet threat required a long-range policy which would effectively combine the political, military, and economic factors of power; above all, it demanded a permanent commitment. There could be no disengagement from this conflict if the United States wished to survive as a free nation. Engagement was the only course.

II. THE BEGINNING OF
THE COLD WAR

American Wartime Illusions

Before one of the wartime conferences between Prime
Minister Winston Churchill and President Franklin Roosevelt, an American Intelligence forecast of Russia's postwar
position in Europe concluded that the Soviet Union would
be the dominant power on the continent of Europe: "With
Germany crushed, there is no power in Europe to oppose her
tremendous military forces. . . . The conclusions from the
foregoing are obvious. Since Russia is the decisive factor in
the war, she must be given every assistance, and every effort
must be made to obtain her friendship. Likewise, since without question she will dominate Europe on the defeat of the
Axis, it is even more essential to develop and maintain the
most friendly relations with Russia."

The importance of this estimate lies less in its prediction
of the Soviet Union's postwar position—which was, after all,
fairly obvious—than in its reflection of American expectations about future Russo-American relations. American
policy-makers were apparently unable to conceive of the
Soviet Union, the acknowledged new dominant power in
Europe, replacing Nazi Germany as a grave threat to the
European and global balance of power. Yet, the United States
had already twice in this century been propelled into Europe's
wars at exactly those moments when Germany became so
powerful that she menaced—indeed, almost destroyed—this
balance. The lessons of history—specifically, the impact of
any nation's domination of Europe upon American security
—had not yet been absorbed. President Roosevelt and the
American Government did not aim at re-establishing a balance of power in Europe to safeguard the United States; they

expected this security to stem from mutual Russo-American goodwill, unsupported by any power considerations. This reliance upon mere goodwill and mutual esteem was to prove foolish at best and, at worst, might have been fatal.

Indeed, the expectation of a postwar "era of good feeling" between the Soviet Union and the United States was characteristic of the unsuspecting and utopian nature of American wartime thinking, which held that war was an interruption of the normal state of harmony among nations, that military force was an instrument for punishing the aggressor or war criminals, that those who cooperated with this country in its ideological crusade were equally moral and selfless, and that once the war was finished, the natural harmony would be restored and the struggle for power ended. The implication was clear: the United States need take no precautionary steps against its noble wartime allies in anticipation of a possible disintegration of the alliance and potential hostility among its partners. Instead, it was hoped that the friendly relations and mutual respect which American leaders believed had matured during the war would preserve the common outlook and purposes and guarantee an enduring peace.

These optimistic expectations of future Russo-American relations made it necessary, however, to explain away continuing signs of Soviet hostility and suspicion. Throughout the war, the Russians constantly suspected the United States and Britain of devious intentions. This was particularly true with regard to the Western delay in opening up a second front. When the front was postponed from 1942 to 1943 to 1944, Stalin, Russia's dictator, became very bitter. He brusquely rejected Allied explanations that sufficient invasion barges for such an enormous undertaking were not available; and he especially denounced Prime Minister Churchill for declaring that there would be no invasion until the Germans were so weakened that Allied forces would not have to suffer forbiddingly high losses. To Stalin, this was no explanation, for the Russians accepted huge losses of men as a matter of course. "When we come to a mine field," Marshal Zhukov explained to General Eisenhower after the war, "our infantry attacks exactly as if it were not there. The losses we get from personnel mines we consider only equal to those we would have gotten from machine guns and artillery if the Germans had chosen to defend that particular area with strong bodies of troops instead of with mine fields." It was no wonder, then, that the Russians should dismiss these Allied explanations and fasten instead upon a more reasonable interpretation which, to them, would account for American and British behavior. From the Marxist viewpoint, the Allies were doing exactly what they should be doing—namely, postponing the second front until the Soviet Union and Germany had exhausted one another. Then the two Western powers could land in France, march bloodlessly into Germany, and dictate the peace to both Germany and Russia. The Western delay was, in short, apparently seen as a deliberate attempt by the world's two leading capitalist powers to destroy both of their two major ideological opponents at one and the same time. Throughout the war, the Russians displayed again and again this almost paranoid fear of hostile Western intentions.

American leaders found a ready explanation for these repeated indications of Soviet suspicion. They thought of Soviet foreign policy not in terms of the internal dynamics of the regime and its enmity toward all non-Communist nations, but solely in terms of Russian reactions to Western policies. The Soviet attitude was viewed against the pattern of prewar anti-Soviet Western acts: the Allied intervention in Russia at the end of World War I in order to overthrow the Soviet regime, and, after the failure of that attempt, the establishment by France of the *cordon sanitaire* in Eastern Europe to keep the Soviet virus from infecting Europe; the West's rejection of Soviet efforts in the mid- and late 1930's to build an alliance against Hitler; and especially, the Munich agreement in 1938, which, by destroying Czechoslovakia, in effect opened Hitler's gateway to the East. In short, Western efforts to ostracize and ultimately destroy the Soviet Union, as well as attempts to turn the Hitlerian threat away from the West and toward Russia, were considered the primary reasons for the existence of Soviet hostility. To overcome this attitude, the West had only to demonstrate its good intentions and prove its friendliness. The question was not *whether* Soviet cooperation could be won for the postwar world, only *how* it could be gained. And if Western efforts did bear fruit and create goodwill, what conflicts of interest could not be settled peacefully in the future? Various Soviet policies and acts during the war—the disbanding of the Comintern (the instrument of international Communism), the ton-ing down of Communist ideology and new emphasis placed on Russian nationalism, the relaxation of restrictions upon the Church, the praise of the United States and Britain for also being democratic, and, above all, the statement of Russian war aims in the same language of peace, democracy, and freedom used by the West—all seemed to prove that if the Western powers demonstrated their friendship, they could convert the Russians into friends.

President Roosevelt and his advisers certainly believed that they had firmly established such amicable relations with the Soviet Union at the Yalta Conference in February, 1945. Stalin had made concessions on a number of vital issues and promised goodwill for the future. On United Nations membership, Stalin had reduced his claim from sixteen seats (one for each of the Soviet Republics) to only three (for the Soviet Union, the Ukraine, and Belorussia) and stated he would support an American claim for parity. He had also accepted the American formula that the veto in the Security Council should be applied only to enforcement action, and not to peaceful attempts at the settlement of disputes. On Germany, he had agreed to a zone of occupation and seat on the Control Commission for France, and to a single administration for all the occupation zones. Moreover, in the "Declaration on Liberated Europe" he had promised to support self-government and allow free elections in Eastern Europe. And regarding the Far East, he had responded to the wishes of the American military and promised to enter the war against Japan. Finally, he had repeatedly expressed his hope for fifty years of peace and "big power" cooperation.

It is little wonder that at the end of the conference the American delegation felt a mood of "supreme exaltation." The President's closest adviser, Harry Hopkins, later recounted: "We really believed in our hearts that this was the dawn of the new day we had all been praying for and talking about for so many years. We were absolutely certain that we had won the first great victory of the peace—and, by 'we,' I mean *all* of us, the whole civilized human race. The Russians had proved that they could be reasonable and far-seeing, and there wasn't any doubt in the minds of the President or any of us that we could live with them and get along with them peacefully for as far into the future as any of us could imagine."

This new era of goodwill was to be embodied in the United Nations. Here the peoples of the world could exercise vigilance over the statesmen in their dealings with one another and prevent them from striking any wicked bargains which might erupt into another global war. The United Nations was regarded as an example of democracy on an international scale: just as the people within democratic states could constantly watch their representatives and prevent them from effecting compromises injurious to their interests, so the people of all countries would now be able to keep an eye on their statesmen, making it impossible for them to arrange any secret deals which would betray the people's interests and shatter the peace of the world. Peace-loving world public opinion, expressing itself across national boundaries, would maintain a constant guard over the diplomats and hold them accountable. Covenants were to be open, and openly arrived at, as President Wilson had once expressed it. Power politics would then be banned once and for all. In the words of Secretary of State Cordell Hull: "There will no longer be need for spheres of influence, for alliances, balance of power, or any other of the special arrangements through which, in the unhappy past, the nations strove to safeguard their security or promote their interests." Reliance would instead be placed upon sound principles and good fellowship. Again, in Hull's words: "All these principles and policies [of international cooperation] are so beneficial and appealing to the sense of justice, of right and of the well-being of free peoples everywhere that in the course of a few years the entire international machinery should be working fairly satisfactorily." The Advisory Commission on Postwar Foreign Policy had been even more emphatic in its stress on the subordination of power politics to principles: "International security was regarded as the supreme objective, but at the same time the subcommittee held that the attainment of security must square with principles of justice in order to be actual and enduring . . . the vital interests of the United States lay in following a 'diplomacy of principle'—of moral disinterestedness instead of power politics." No comment could more aptly have summed up the American habit of viewing international politics in terms of abstract moral principles instead of clashes of interest and power.

Soviet Postwar Expansion

The American dream of postwar peace and Big Three cooperation was to be shattered as the Soviet Union expanded into Eastern and Central Europe, imposing its control upon Poland, Hungary, Bulgaria, Romania, and Albania. (Yugoslavia was already under the Communist control of Marshal Tito, and Czechoslovakia was living under the shadow of the Red Army.) In each of these nations of Eastern Europe where the Russians had their troops, they unilaterally established pro-Soviet coalition governments. The key post in these regimes—the ministry of the interior, which usually controlled the police—was in the hands of the Communists. With this decisive lever of power in their grasp, it was an easy matter to extend their domination and subvert the independence of these countries. Thus, as the war drew to a close, it became clear that the words of the Yalta Declaration, in which the Russians had committed themselves to free elections and democratic governments in Eastern Europe, meant quite different things to the Russians than to Americans. To the Russians, "democratic governments" meant Communist governments, and "free elections" meant elections from which parties not favorable to the Communists were barred. The peace treaties with the former German satellite states (Hungary, Bulgaria, Romania), which were painfully negotiated by the victors in a series of Foreign Ministers' conferences during 1945 and 1946, could not reverse the tight Soviet grip on what were by now Russian satellite states. Democratic principles could not be extended beyond Western power. Russian dominance in the Balkans and Poland was, in short, firmly established, and Russian power now lapped the shores of the Aegean, the Straits of Constantinople, and—through its close relationship with Yugoslavia—the Adriatic.

Greece, Turkey, and Iran were the first states beyond the confines of the Red Army to feel the resulting expansionist pressure of the Soviet Union. In the period from the end of the war to early 1947, the Russians attempted to effect a major breakthrough into the Middle East. Every would-be world conqueror—Napoleon, Kaiser Wilhelm II, and Hitler, to mention only a few of the more recent ones—has tried to become master of this area. Napoleon called the Middle East the key to the world, and well he might, for the area links Europe, Africa, and Asia. The power that dominates the Middle East is in an excellent position to expand into North Africa and South Asia, and thereby gain control of the World-Island.

The pressure on Iran began in early 1946 when the Russians refused to withdraw their troops from that country. These troops had been there since late 1941, when Russia and Britain had invaded Iran in order to forestall increased Nazi influence and to use Iran as a corridor for the transportation of military aid shipped by the West to the Persian Gulf for transit to Russia. The Russians had occupied northern Iran, the British the central and southern sections. The Tripartite Treaty of Alliance signed in early 1942 by Iran, Britain, and Russia specified that within six months of the cessation of hostilities all troops would be withdrawn; the Allies also pledged themselves to respect Iran's sovereignty and territorial and political independence.

The final date set for evacuation from Iran was March 2, 1946. British and United States troops—the latter had arrived after America's entry into the war, to help move the lend-lease supplies to Russia—had already left. Only the Soviet troops still remained. Indeed, the Russians were sending in more troops and tanks. Their goal: to reduce Iran to a Soviet satellite. The Russians had, in fact, begun their campaign in late 1944, when they demanded exclusive mineral and oil rights in northern Iran and offered to supply the Iranians with experts to help administer their government. When the Iranian Government rejected these demands, the Russians had organized a revolt by the Communist-controlled Tudeh Party in the north. The revolt began openly in November, 1945, and the Red Army prevented the Iranian Army from quelling it. The Tudeh Party, renamed the Democratic Party, then formed a government in Azerbaijan. The Russian game was clear: to force the Iranian Government to recognize the Soviet puppet regime in Azerbaijan, which would then send "elected representatives" to the legislature in Teheran. These would then exert pressure on the government to grant Russia the economic and political control it wanted in Iran. The result would have been the conversion of Iran into a Soviet satellite. It was imperative, therefore, that Soviet troops be forced to withdraw. Not until then could the national government and troops attempt to cope with the Communist government in the north.

During this period, the Soviet Union also put pressure on Turkey. Indeed, the Russians had begun to do this as early as June, 1945, when they suddenly demanded the cession of several Turkish districts lying on the Turkish-Russian frontier, the revision of the Montreux Convention governing the Dardenelles Straits in favor of a joint Russo-Turkish administration, Turkey's abandonment of her ties with Britain and the conclusion of a treaty with the Soviet Union similar to those which Russia had concluded with its Balkan satellites, and finally, the lease to the Soviet Union of bases for naval and land forces in the Straits for its "joint defense." In August, 1946, the Soviet Union renewed its demand, in a note to the United States and Britain, for a new administration of the Straits. In effect, this would have turned Turkey, like Iran, into a Soviet satellite.

In Greece, too, Communist pressure was exerted on the government through wide-scale guerrilla warfare, which began in the fall of 1946. Civil war in Greece was actually nothing new. During the war, the Communist and anti-Communist guerrillas fighting the Germans had spent much of their energy battling each other. When the British landed in Greece and the Germans withdrew from the country, the Communists had attempted to take over the capital city of Athens. Only after several weeks of bitter street fighting and the landing of British reinforcements was the Communist control of Athens dislodged and a truce signed in January, 1945. Just over a year later—in March, 1946—the Greeks held a general election in which right-wing forces captured the majority of votes.

The Greek situation did not improve, however. The country was exhausted from the Italian and German invasions, the four years of occupation, and the Germans' scorched-earth policy as they retreated. Moreover, Greece had always been dependent upon imports that were paid for by exports; but her traditional market in Central Europe was now closed. While the masses lived at a bare subsistence level, the black market flourished. The inability of any government to deal with this situation aroused a good deal of social discontent. And the large, 100,000-man army which Greece needed to protect her from her Communist neighbors (Albania, Yugoslavia, and Bulgaria) had brought the country to near-bankruptcy. If Britain had not helped finance—as well as train and equip—the army and kept troops in the country to stabilize the situation, Greece would in all probability have collapsed. It was in these circumstances that in August, 1946, the Communists began to squeeze Greece by renewing the guerrilla warfare in the north, where the guerrilla forces could be kept well supplied by Greece's Communist neighbors.

In all these situations, the American Government was suddenly confronted with the need for action to support Britain, the traditional guardian of this area against encroachment. In the case of Iran, the United States and Britain delivered firm statements which strongly implied that the two countries would use force to defend Iran. The Soviet response in late March, 1946, was the announcement that the Red Army would be withdrawn during the next five to six weeks. In the Turkish case, the United States sent a naval task force into the Mediterranean immediately after the receipt of the Soviet note on August 7. Twelve days later, the United States replied to the note by rejecting the Russian demand to share sole responsibility for the defense of the Straits with Turkey. Britain sent a similar reply. The Greek situation had not yet come to a head, and the need for American action could be postponed for a while longer. But it should be pointed out that the Administration's actions in Iran and Turkey were merely swift reactions to immediate crises. They were not the product of an over-all American strategy. Such a coherent strategy could only arise from a new assessment of Soviet foreign policy.

The Strategy of Containment

A period of eighteen months passed before the United States undertook that reassessment—from the surrender of Japan on September 2, 1945, until the announcement of the Truman Doctrine on March 12, 1947. Perhaps such a reevaluation could not have been made any more quickly. Public opinion in a democratic country does not normally shift drastically overnight. It would have been too much to expect the American public to change suddenly from an attitude of friendliness toward the Soviet Union—inspired largely by the picture of Russian wartime bravery and endurance and by hopes for peaceful postwar cooperation—to a hostile mood. The American "reservoir of goodwill" for the Soviet Union could not be emptied that quickly. Moreover, the desire for peace was too strong. The United States wished only to be left alone to preoccupy itself once more with domestic affairs. The end of the war signaled the end of power politics and the restoration of normal peacetime harmony among nations. In response to this expectation, the public demanded a speedy demobilization. The armed forces were thus reduced to completely inadequate levels of strength. In May, 1945, at the end of the war with Germany, the United States had an army of 3.5 million men organized into 68 divisions in Europe, supported by 149 air groups. Our allies supplied another 47 divisions. By March, 1946, only ten months later, the United States had only 400,000 troops left, mainly new recruits; the homeland reserve was six battalions. Further reductions in Army strength followed. Air Force and Navy cuts duplicated this same pattern.

The Eightieth Congress, which convened in Washington in January, 1947, represented this postwar mood of withdrawal well. The Senate was divided into 51 Republicans and 45 Democrats, and the House into 245 Republicans and 118 Democrats. House Speaker Joseph Martin stated Republican intentions in his opening address to his colleagues: a reduction in government expenditures to allow for a 20 per cent income tax reduction. The Congress thereupon cut the President's budget from $41 billion to $31.5 billion. The Secretary of War denounced the cut and warned that the United States might have to withdraw its troops from Germany and Japan; and the Secretary of the Navy announced that the cut would render the Navy impotent. This deliberate and unilateral disarmament could not have failed to encourage Russian intransigence in Europe and increased Soviet pressure in southeast Europe and the Middle East. As this pressure increased in intensity and scope, however, American policy toward the Soviet Union began to be re-evaluated.

Three positions became clear during this period. At one extreme stood that old realist Winston Churchill. At the end of the European war, he had counseled against the withdrawal of American troops. He had insisted that they stay, together with British troops, in order to force the Soviet Union to live up to its Yalta obligations regarding free elections in Eastern Europe and the withdrawal of the Red Army from Eastern Germany. The United States had rejected Churchill's plea. In early 1946, at Fulton, Missouri, Churchill took his case directly to the American public. The Soviet Union, he asserted, was an expansionist state. "From Stettin in the Baltic to Trieste in the Adriatic, an iron curtain has descended across the continent. Behind that line lie all the capitals of the ancient states of Central and Eastern Europe. Warsaw, Berlin, Prague, Vienna, Budapest, Belgrade, Bucharest, and Sofia, all the famous cities and populations around them lie in the Soviet sphere and all are subject in one form or another, not only to Soviet influence but to a very high and increasing measure of control from Moscow." Churchill did not believe that the Russians wanted war: "What they desire is the fruits of war and the indefinite expansion of their power and doctrines." This could be prevented only by the opposing power of the British Commonwealth and the United States. Churchill, in short, said bluntly that the cold war had begun, that Americans must recognize this fact and give up their dreams of Big Three unity in the United Nations. International organization was no substitute for the balance of power. "Our difficulties and dangers will not be removed by closing our eyes to them. They will not be removed by mere waiting to see what happens; nor will they be relieved by a policy of appeasement." An alliance of the English-speaking peoples was the prerequisite for American and British security and world peace.

At the other extreme stood Secretary of Commerce Henry Wallace, who felt it was precisely the kind of aggressive attitude expressed by Churchill that was to blame for Soviet hostility. The United States and Britain had no more business in Eastern Europe than had the Soviet Union in Latin America; to each, the respective area was vital for national security. Western interference in nations bordering on Russia was bound to arouse Soviet suspicion, just as Soviet intervention in countries neighboring on the United States would. "We may not like what Russia does in Eastern Europe," said Wallace. "Her type of land reform, industrial expropriation, and suspension of basic liberties offends the great majority of the people of the United States. But whether we like it or not, the Russians will try to socialize their sphere of influence just as we try to democratize our sphere of influence (including Japan and Western Germany)." The tough attitude that Churchill and other "reactionaries" at home and abroad demanded was precisely the wrong policy; it would only increase international tension. "We must not let British balance-of-power manipulations determine whether and when the United States gets into a war . . . 'getting tough' never bought anything real and lasting—whether for schoolyard bullies or world powers. The tougher we get, the tougher the Russians will get." Only mutual trust would allow the United States and Russia to live together peacefully, and such trust could not be created by an unfriendly American attitude and policy.

The American Government and public wavered between these two positions. The Administration recognized that Big Three cooperation had ended, and it realized that the time when the United States needed to demonstrate goodwill toward the Soviet Union in order to overcome the latter's suspicions had passed. No further concessions would be made to preserve the surface friendship with the Soviet Union. We had tried to gain Russia's amity by being a friend; it was now up to her leaders to demonstrate a similarly friendly attitude toward us as well. Paper agreements, written in such general terms that they actually hid divergent purposes, were no longer regarded as demonstrating such friendship. Something more than paper agreements was needed: Russian words would have to be matched by Russian deeds.

The American Secretary of State, James Byrnes, called this new line the "policy of firmness and patience." This phrase meant that the United States would take a firm position whenever the Soviet Union became intransigent, and that we would not compromise simply in order to reach a quick agreement. This change in official American attitude toward the Soviet Union was not, however, a fundamental one. A firm line was to be followed only on concrete issues. The assumption was that if the United States took a tougher bargaining position and no longer seemed in a hurry to resolve particular points of tension, the Soviet rulers would see the pointlessness of their obduracy and agree to fair compromise solutions of their differences with the United States and the West. In short, American firmness would make the Russians "reasonable." For they were regarded as "unreasonable" merely on particular issues; that this "unreasonableness" might stem from the very nature of the Communist regime had not yet occurred to American policy-makers. They did not yet agree with Churchill's position that the Soviet government was ideologically hostile to the West and that it would continue to expand until capitalism had been destroyed. The new American position, as one political analyst has aptly summed it up, "meant to most of its exponents that the Soviet Union had to be induced by firmness to play the game in the American way. There was no consistent official suggestion that the United States should begin to play a different game." The prerequisite for such a suggestion was that American policy-makers recognize the revolutionary nature of the Soviet regime.

This recognition came with increasing speed as the Greek crisis reached a peak. By early 1947, it was obvious that the United States would have to play a different game. It was George Kennan, the Foreign Service's foremost expert on the Soviet Union, who first presented the basis of what was to be a new American policy. Kennan's analysis began with a detailed presentation of the Communist outlook on world affairs. In the Soviet leaders' pattern of thought, he said, Russia had no community of interest with the capitalist states; indeed, they saw their relationship with the Western powers in terms of an innate antagonism. Communist ideology had taught them "that the outside world was hostile and that it was their duty eventually to overthrow the political forces beyond their borders. The powerful hands of Russian history and tradition reached up to sustain them in this feeling. Finally, their own aggressive intransigence with respect to the outside world began to find its own reaction . . . It is an undeniable privilege for every man to prove himself right in the thesis that the world is his enemy; for if he reiterates it frequently enough and makes it the background for his conduct, he is bound to be right." According to Kennan, this Soviet hostility was a constant factor; it would continue until the capitalist world had been destroyed: "Basically, the antagonism remains. It is postulated. And from it flow many of the phenomena which we find disturbing in the Kremlin's conduct of foreign policy: the secretiveness, the lack of frankness, the duplicity, the war suspiciousness, and the basic unfriendliness of purpose." Kennan did suggest, however, that

Soviet tactics might change, depending upon circumstances: "And when that happens, there will always be Americans who will leap forward with gleeful announcements 'that the Russians have changed,' and some who will even take credit for having brought about such 'changes.' But we should not be misled by tactical maneuvers. These characteristics of Soviet policy, like the postulates from which they flow, are basic to the *internal* nature of Soviet power, and will be with us . . . until the nature of Soviet power is changed. [Italics added.]" Until that moment, he said, Soviet strategy and objectives would remain the same.

The struggle would thus be a long one. Kennan stressed that Soviet hostility did not mean that the Russians would embark upon a do-or-die program to overthrow capitalism by a fixed date. They had no timetable for conquest. In a brilliant passage, Kennan outlined the Soviet concept of the struggle:

The Kremlin is under no ideological compulsion to accomplish its purposes in a hurry. Like the Church, it is dealing in ideological concepts which are of a long-term validity, and it can afford to be patient. It has no right to risk the existing achievements of the revolution for the sake of vain baubles of the future. The very teachings of Lenin himself require great caution and flexibility in the pursuit of Communist purposes. Again, these precepts are fortified by the lessons of Russian history: of centuries of obscure battles between nomadic forces over the stretches of a vast unfortified plain. Here caution, circumspection, flexibility, and deception are the valuable qualities; and their value finds natural appreciation in the Russian or the Oriental mind. Thus the Kremlin has no compunction about retreating in the face of superior force. And being under the compulsion of no timetable, it does not get panicky under the necessity of such a retreat. Its political action is a fluid stream which moves constantly, wherever it is permitted to move, toward a given goal. Its main concern is to make sure that it has filled every nook and cranny available to it in the basin of world power. But if it finds unassailable barriers in its path, it accepts these philosophically and accommodates itself to them. The main thing is that there should always be pressure, increasing constant pressure, toward the desired goal. There is no trace of any feeling in Soviet psychology that the goal must be reached at any given time.

How could the United States counter such a policy—a policy that was always pushing, seeking weak spots, attempting to fill power vacuums? Kennan's answer was that American policy would have to be one of "long-term, patient, but firm and vigilant containment." The United States would find Soviet diplomacy both easier and more difficult to deal with than that of dictators such as Napoleon or Hitler. "On the one hand, it [Soviet policy] is more sensitive to contrary force, more ready to yield on individual sectors of the diplomatic front when that force is felt to be too strong, and thus more rational in the logic and rhetoric of power. On the other hand, it cannot be easily defeated or discouraged by a single victory on the part of its opponents. And the patient persistence by which it is animated means that *it can be effectively countered not by sporadic acts which represent the momentary whims of democratic opinion, but only by intelligent long-range policies on the part of Russia's adversaries—policies no less steady in their purpose, and no less variegated and resourceful in their application, than those of the Soviet Union itself.* [Italics added.]" Kennan thus evisaged containment as *the* test of American democracy, with our very survival as the stake. If the United States failed to meet the strict requirements of this test, it would suffer the same fate as previous civilizations, becoming no more than a name in history books.

On the other hand, if American society rose to the challenge, it could ensure its future. For containment could contribute to changes within the Soviet Union which might bring about a moderation of its revolutionary aims. The United States, Kennan emphasized, "has it in its power to increase enormously the strains under which Soviet policy must operate, to force upon the Kremlin a far greater degree of moderation and circumspection than it has had to observe in recent years, and in this way to promote tendencies which must eventually find their outlet in either the breakup or the gradual mellowing of Soviet power. For no mystical, messianic movement—and particularly not that of the Kremlin—can face frustration indefinitely without eventually adjusting itself in one way or another to the logic of that state of affairs." Kennan's theory was thus not so new. He was, in effect, asserting the old thesis that within an authoritarian or totalitarian society there are certain strains and stresses, and that these give rise to frustrations which can only be relieved by being channeled into an aggressive and expansionist foreign policy. Kennan's remedy was to prevent this expansion, thereby aggravating the internal tensions in such a way that they would either destroy the Soviet system or force the Soviet leaders to placate the domestic dissatisfaction. Assuming that the Soviet leaders preferred to remain in power and that they would therefore be compelled to adopt the second course, they would have no alternative but to moderate their foreign policy. For a relaxation of international tensions was the prerequisite for coping with their domestic problems. Thus, the Kremlin would have no choice but to surrender its revolutionary aims and arrange a *modus vivendi* with the Western powers—above all, with the United States.

The Truman Doctrine

Whether the United States could meet this Soviet challenge became a pressing question when, on the afternoon of February 21, 1947, the First Secretary of the British Embassy in Washington visited the State Department and handed American officials two notes from His Majesty's Government. One concerned Greece, the other Turkey. In effect, they both stated the same thing: that Britain could no longer meet its traditional responsibilities in those two countries. Since both were on the verge of collapse, the import of the British notes was clear: that a Russian breakthrough could be prevented only by an all-out American commitment.

February 21 was thus a historic day. On that day, Great Britain, the only remaining power in Europe, acknowledged her exhaustion. She had fought Philip II of Spain, Louis XIV of France, Kaiser Wilhelm II and Adolf Hitler of Germany. She had preserved the balance of power which protected the United States for so long that it seemed almost natural for her to continue to do so. But her ability to protect that balance had steadily declined in the twentieth century. Twice she had needed American help. Each time, however, she had fought the longer battle; on neither occasion had the United States entered the war until it became clear that Germany and its allies were too strong for her and that we would have to help her in safeguarding our own security. Now, all of a sudden, there was no power to protect the United States but the United States itself; no one stood between this country and the present threat to its security. All the other major powers of the world had collapsed—except the Soviet Union, which was the second most powerful nation in the world and was wedded to an expansionist ideology. The cold fact of a bipolar world suddenly faced the United States. The country could no longer shirk the responsibilities of its tremendous power.

The immediate crisis suddenly confronting the United States had its locale in the eastern Mediterranean. Direct Soviet pressure on Iran and Turkey had temporarily been successfully resisted. The Russians had now turned to outflanking these two nations by concentrating their attention on Greece. If Greece collapsed—and all reports from that hapless country indicated that it would fall within a few weeks—it would only be a question of time until Turkey and Iran would crumble before Soviet power. But the fall of Greece would not only affect its neighbors to the east; it would also lead to an increase of Communist pressure on Italy. Italy would then be faced with two Communist states to its east—Yugoslavia and Greece—and with the largest Communist party in Western Europe in its own midst. And to the northwest of Italy lay France, with the second largest Communist party in the West. Thus, the security of all of Western Europe would be endangered as well. The immediate danger, however, remained in the eastern Mediterranean; and the Soviet desire for control over this area was underlined by its demands that the city of Trieste at the head of the Adriatic be yielded to Yugoslavia and that Italy's former colonies of Tripolitania and Eritrea in North Africa be placed under Soviet trusteeship.

The United States had no choice but to act in this situation. The results of inaction were only too clear: the collapse of Europe's flank in the eastern Mediterranean, the establishment of Communist dominance in the Middle East, and a Soviet breakthrough into South Asia and North Africa. The psychological impact upon Europe of such a tremendous

Soviet victory over the West would have been disastrous. For Europeans already psychologically demoralized by their sufferings and fall from power and prestige, this would have been the final blow. In short, what was at stake in Greece was America's survival itself.

President Truman was quick to recognize this stark fact. On March 12, 1947, he went before a joint session of Congress and delivered a speech which must rank as one of the most important in American history. The President first outlined the situation in Greece: her lack of natural resources; the cruel German occupation, resulting in widespread destruction; her inability to import the goods she needed for bare subsistence, let alone reconstruction; the Communist efforts to exploit these conditions by spreading political chaos and hindering any economic recovery; and the guerrilla warfare in northern Greece, where the Communist forces were receiving aid from Yugoslavia, Albania, and Bulgaria.

Then Truman came to the heart of his speech. Here he spelled out what was to become known as the Truman Doctrine. The United States, he emphasized, could survive only in a world in which freedom flourished. And we would not realize this objective:

> ... unless we are willing to help free peoples to maintain their institutions and their national integrity against aggressive movements that seek to impose upon them totalitarian regimes. *This is no more than a frank recognition that totalitarian regimes imposed on free peoples, by direct or indirect aggression, undermine the foundations of international peace and hence the security of the United States.* [Italics added.]
>
> The peoples of a number of countries of the world have recently had totalitarian regimes forced upon them against their will. The Government of the United States has made frequent protests against coercion and intimidation, in violation of the Yalta agreement, in Poland, Romania, and Bulgaria. I must also state that in a number of other countries there have been similar developments.
>
> At the present moment in world history nearly every nation must choose between alternative ways of life. The choice is often not a free one.

One way of life is based upon the will of the majority, and is distinguished by free institutions, representative government, free elections, guarantees of individual liberty, freedom of speech and religion, and freedom from political oppression.

The second way of life is based upon the will of a minority forcibly imposed upon the majority. It relies upon terror and oppression, a controlled press and radio, fixed elections, and the suppression of personal freedoms.

I believe it must be the policy of the United States to support free peoples who are resisting attempted subjugations by armed minorities or by outside pressure.

I believe that we must assist free peoples to work out their own destinies in their own way.

I believe that our help should be primarily through economic and financial aid which is essential to economic stability and orderly political processes.

Stressing the impact of Greece's collapse upon Turkey and the Middle East, as well as upon Europe, the President then brought the Congress and the American people face to face with their responsibility. "Should we fail to aid Greece and Turkey in this fateful hour," he said, "the effect will be far-reaching to the West as well as to the East. We must take immediate and resolute action."

Truman asked Congress to appropriate $400 million for economic aid and military supplies for both countries, and to authorize the dispatch of American civilian and military personnel in order to help the two nations in their tasks of reconstruction and provide their armies with appropriate instruction and training. Truman ended on a grave note:

This is a serious course upon which we embark.

I would not recommend it except that the alternative is much more serious . . .

The seeds of totalitarian regimes are nurtured by misery and want. They spread and grow in the evil soil of poverty and strife. They reach their full growth when the hope of a people for a better life has died.

We must keep that hope alive.

The free peoples of the world look to us for support in maintaining their freedoms.

If we falter in our leadership, we may endanger the peace of the world—and we shall surely endanger the welfare of our nation.

Great responsibilities have been placed upon us by the swift movement of events.

I am confident that the Congress will face these responsibilities squarely.

The Congress and the American people did. History had once more shown that when a great and democratic people is given decisive and courageous leadership, the people will respond quickly and wisely. Under Truman's leadership, the American public had made a decisive commitment. The United States was now a full participant in the international arena. There could no longer be any retreat. The survival of freedom was dependent solely upon the United States. The only question was how responsibly and honorably this country would bear its new burden of world leadership.

III. CONTAINMENT IN EUROPE

The Marshall Plan

The commitment to Greece and Turkey was only the first act under the new American policy of containing Soviet expansion. The real crisis was in Europe. Britain's state of near-collapse, which had left the United States no alternative but to become involved in the eastern Mediterranean, was symptomatic of all of Europe's collapse. Basically, Britain's crisis was an economic one. As an island-nation, she was dependent for her livelihood—indeed, her survival—upon international trade. She had to export or die, for the Industrial Revolution she had undergone during the nineteenth century had almost completely urbanized her. Less than 5 per cent of Britain's population was engaged in agriculture. This meant that she had to import much of her food. Before World War II, for instance, she bought 55 per cent of her meat, 75 per cent of her wheat, 85 per cent of her butter, all her tea, cocoa, and coffee, and 75 per cent of her sugar. Except for coal, Britain also had to import most of the raw materials needed by her industries: cotton, rubber, wool, iron ore, timber, and the oil which she was becoming increasingly dependent upon for the fueling of her factories.

Before 1939, Britain had paid for these foods and raw materials by one of three means: services such as shipping, income from foreign investments, and her manufactured exports. But the war had crippled her merchant marine, liquidated most of her investments, and destroyed many of her factories. With the first two means of financing her imports all but gone, she had to increase her export drive. Just to maintain her 1939 standard of living, she had to raise her exports by 75 per cent. By December, 1946, despite an American loan and a severe austerity program which included the rationing of bread, Britain had only reached her prewar level of production. It was in these circumstances that nature delivered what almost proved to be a knockout blow. In the winter of 1946-47, Europe suffered one of its severest cold periods in history; temperatures went below zero. In Britain, the transportation system came to a virtual standstill; trucks and trains could not move, barges were frozen in rivers, and ships could not leave their moorings. Industries could not be supplied with the fuel to keep them running, and factories were closed. By February, 1947, more than half of Britain's factories lay idle. Coal was not even mined any longer, and gas and electricity were in short supply. Electricity to industrial consumers was cut off for several days; and domestic consumers had to do without electricity for three hours every day. When the thaw finally arrived, Britain was beset by floods. It was to take her months to recover.

In the meantime, the export drive had completely collapsed, and Britain had come to the end of her rope. The financial editor of Reuter's saw the true measure of the winter disaster: "The biggest crash since the fall of Constantinople—the collapse of the heart of an Empire—impends. This is not the story of a couple of snowstorms. It is the story of the awful debility in which a couple of snowstorms could have such effects." The future looked bleak and ominous: millions of Britons were unemployed, cold and hungry, worn out by the long years of war and the determined postwar efforts to recover. Despite all the personal and uncomplaining sacrifices they had made, their efforts had come to nothing. Britain's fate could have been worse only if she had lost the war.

For Germany's postwar condition was truly horrible. The war had been carried into the heart of Germany. Few German cities or towns had escaped Allied bombing, street fighting, or willful destruction by the Nazis themselves as they retreated. Old cities like Cologne, Essen, Mannheim, and Nuremberg lay in ruins; others like Berlin, Frankfort, Hamburg, and Munich were almost as badly damaged. Much of Germany was just a mass of broken stones, and people found shelter among this rubble as best they could. To aggravate this situation, 10 million additional Germans came into these ruins from former German territory annexed by Poland; they settled mostly in West Germany, adding further discomfort to the inhabitants already hard-pressed for survival. There was only one word to describe Germany in 1945—

chaos. Millions upon millions of people were faced with the basic necessity of finding food, shelter, and work.

The measure of Germany's collapse was indicated by the fact that the cigarette had replaced money as the prevailing unit of exchange. Cigarettes could buy almost anything. The black market flourished. Even as late as 1947, a package of cigarettes was equivalent to a working man's entire wages for a month; one cigarette had twice the purchasing power of the salary a man could earn in Berlin after a hard day's work clearing away rubble. The Allied target ration of 1,550 calories per day, which was hardly sufficient to sustain a healthy human being, was rarely reached. In March, 1946, the British were forced to cut their rations to 1,040 daily calories, and in April the Americans cut theirs to 1,275 calories. Everywhere people were hungry; the few who found a job to earn a little money often fainted from sheer exhaustion. It was a desperate situation. Respectable girls sold their bodies for one or two cigarettes, a pair of nylons, or an army ration; dishonor was preferable to death. Illegitimate births rose sharply, and so did divorce petitions. Juvenile delinquency increased 400 per cent over the prewar level; stealing became as respectable a way of earning a living for boys, as did prostitution for girls. Along with this economic, social, political, and moral breakdown came the cold weather. There was no fuel for heating. During the severe winter of 1946-47, 200 people froze to death in Berlin alone. Three-quarters of the factories still standing in the American and British zones of occupation were closed. In January, 1947, production fell to 31 per cent of the 1936 level, Germany's best year; by February, it had declined to 29 per cent. Even before this industrial shutdown, German steel production during 1946 had reached only 2 million tons; and this was in part due to the small amount of coal mined by the Germans.

There could not have been a more striking demonstration of the specialization and interdependence of modern industry. The shortage of metallurgical coking coal made it impossible for the steel industry to recover; and the engineering industries which were needed for reconstruction depended upon the production of steel. The shortage of one key material thus set back the entire industry. And one reason for this lack of coal was the absence of incentives for the workers, who could not buy consumer goods with their pay. Yet these commodities could not be turned out until industry had recovered. It was a vicious and seemingly unbreakable circle.

Allied policy was certainly not designed to break it. The Allies were still primarily engaged with Germany's disarmament and demilitarization, and with the elimination of all industries whose output could be used for military production. America and Britain were not particularly anxious to rebuild Germany's industrial power. They recalled only too vividly that it had taken the combined efforts of three world powers to bring the Nazi war machine to a halt and defeat it. And they believed that many of Germany's industrialists had been ardent supporters of the Nazi regime. Nor were the Allies especially concerned with the lot of the German people during the immediate postwar days. After six years of war, such concern could hardly have been expected. The memories of Nazi atrocities and crimes, of wanton destruction, and of millions of innocent people slaughtered in concentration camps were still very much alive. These could not soon be forgotten. The hatred the Nazis had engendered in their opponents could not be erased overnight. After six years of brutal warfare, the Allies were unlikely to display much forgiveness and chivalry toward the Germans.

The French, above all others, were not likely to forget the Nazis. Though their economy had been badly damaged during the war, by late 1946 the French had made a remarkable recovery. But iron and steel production had reached only half the prewar total. Here, too, coal was the key factor, since the iron and steel industry was dependent upon imported coal. But European coal production was still well below the pre-1939 annual average. German production was low, and Britain needed for herself all the coal she mined. Therefore, scarce dollars had to be spent for the purchase of high-cost American coal. The result was another vivid demonstration of the division of labor in the modern economy. Industry was unable to produce sufficient goods to exchange for food. The farmer thereupon withdrew fields from crop cultivation and used them for grazing. He kept more food for himself and his family, and also fed his livestock more grain. Meanwhile, the urban population was short of food, and the Government had to spend its few remaining dollars—which it needed for reconstruction—to buy food from abroad. The winter of 1946-47 aggravated this situation even further by destroying an estimated 3 to 4 million acres of wheat.

This situation was made to order for the large and well-organized French Communist Party. One-quarter of France's electorate—practically the entire working class—voted for the Party. (In Italy, the figure was one-third of the electorate.) The reason for this was simple: capitalism had alienated these people. The workers were, in effect, internal emigrees who voted Communist in protest against a system which they felt had long mistreated them; for they had suffered all the hardships of capitalism, while enjoying few of its benefits like good wages and social opportunities. Workers in Britain and in the United States, especially, had of course gained these benefits, and they therefore had a vested interest in the social and economic order. But in France, deeply divided between the "haves" and the "have-nots," workers felt no such stake in the system; in fact, they believed that its destruction was the prerequisite for an improvement in their standard of living.

As a result, the Communist Party in France was placed in a powerful position in political and trade-union life. The Party was the largest in France and in a key position to prevent any improvement in the workers' conditions. It represented the workers; there was therefore no democratic left-wing alternative. This benefited the conservative forces. Since these would not be challenged by a strong left-center opposition at the polls, they felt no need to pass any reform legislation. This further strengthened the Communist claim that democracy and capitalism would not and could not help the worker, and that his lot would not be bettered while the bourgeoisie remained in power. France was thus caught not only in a vicious economic circle, but also in a political one: the social and economic conditions gave rise to the Communist Party, and the Party in turn could prevent any reforms from being adopted, thereby preserving its *raison d'être*. The Party also controlled the Confédération Générale du Travail, the largest French trade union, which had a membership of 80 per cent of the workers in the immediate postwar years. In 1947, as United States-Soviet tensions increased, the Party used this control to initiate or exploit strikes in order to paralyze the entire economy and bring the Republic to its knees.

With Europe on the verge of collapse, everything seemed to force her into dependence upon America. Most of the items needed for her reconstruction—wheat, cotton, sulphur, sugar, machinery, trucks, and coal—could be obtained in sufficient quantities only from the United States. Yet, Europe, with a stagnating economy, was in no position to earn the dollars needed to pay for these goods. Moreover, the United States was so well supplied with everything that she did not have to buy much from abroad. Thus, the European countries were unable to obtain enough dollars for the purchase of the commodities required for their recovery. The result was the ominous "dollar gap"—a term that frightened the Europeans as much as the "cold war."

In former times, the closing of this gap would have been left to the mechanism of the international market. The European states, unable to pay for the machinery or the raw materials they needed, would simply not have bought them. Their peoples would have had to do without them. If this meant the closing down of factories, large-scale unemployment, millions of hungry and cold citizens, and widespread social discontentment, it was unfortunate. And in the longrun, perhaps it was not really so unfortunate: for the unemployed would have no money with which to buy the goods manufactured with the imported resources or machinery. Thus, the demand would be driven down to the point at which trade would once more be balanced.

This "remedy" could hardly be attempted in the midtwentieth century. The Europeans had not fought the war and suffered so much to face this kind of a future. The war had been fought for a better tomorrow in which men would live decently. In addition, the old-fashioned way of closing the dollar gap was simply incompatible with the humanitarian Judaeo-Christian basis of Western civilization. Nor was it politically possible. In nations where people elect their representatives, governments can hardly allow their constituents to starve, to remain unemployed, to live in cold homes, and to suffer the deprivation of such basic necessities of life as food.

Europe's collapse thus posed a fundamental question to the United States: Is Europe vital to American security? The answer was never in doubt: American independence and security required that we establish a balance of power in the interior of Europe. This was necessary to check any nation with designs on the sea-bordering states as a prerequisite to the elimination of England and eventual world conquest. During most of the nineteenth century, this balance had been maintained by the English Navy. Now that Britain's power had declined drastically, the United States would have to carry out the task alone—particularly because in these post–World War II days, with the advent of long-range bombers, Schnorkel submarines, and guided missiles, our stake in Europe had become even greater. Western Europe controlled the sea gateways vital to American security—the Skagerrak, the English Channel, and the Straits of Gibraltar. It possessed the largest aggregation of skilled workers, technicians, and managers outside the United States. It maintained the second greatest concentration of industrial power in the world. And it exercised control over many of the strategic raw materials (such as rubber, tin, copper, zinc, mercury, cobalt, tungsten, chrome, graphite, and uranium) which the United States needed to maintain its military strength and its capacity to wage war. American security, therefore, demanded a healthy and strong Europe which could help tip the balance of power.

The role of the United States toward Europe, therefore, had to be that of a doctor toward an ill patient—and the prescribed cure was a massive injection of dollars. A large-scale program of economic aid was to be administered in the form of grants, rather than loans, which would only intensify Europe's dollar problems. Only such a program could restore and surpass Europe's prewar agricultural and industrial production, close the dollar gap, and lead Europe to the recovery of its *élan vital,* political stability, and economic prosperity, thereby possibly allowing France and Italy to reintegrate their working classes into their bodies politic.

American aid was made conditional, however, upon economic cooperation among the European states. In this respect, the United States clearly held itself up as a model for the Europeans. The Economic Cooperation Act of 1948 called specifically for European economic integration. America, it stated, was "mindful of the advantage which the United States has enjoyed through the existence of a large-scale domestic market with no internal trade barriers and [believed] that similar advantages can accrue to the countries of Europe." Thus, in official American opinion, European integration became both the prerequisite for Europe's recovery and the necessary basis for Europe's long-range economic prosperity. It is not difficult to see why American policy-makers, with their belief in low-cost mass production, should have felt that Europe's economic recovery and health were dependent upon the creation of a mass market. For decades, the European nations living together on a continent one-fourth the size of the United States had divided their markets off from one another with tariff walls, quota systems, and import and export licenses. By this means, national manufacturers assured themselves of the lion's share of their national markets. Sheltered from external competition, they had little incentive to modernize their equipment or techniques, for they minimized domestic competition by dividing their relatively small domestic markets among themselves. Unlike the United States, Europe, with its tradition of guilds and trade associations, sanctioned monopolistic practices. The different sectors of a nation's economy tended to be controlled by monopolies; there was usually a single producer of a particular item, or if there was more than one producer in a sector, the various firms would divide the market among themselves. In either case, the results were similar: limited production, high prices, and low wages. Moreover, many firms, especially in France, were not large-scale corporations but family businesses whose production was economically inefficient. Their costs and therefore their prices were even higher than those of the larger firms, and they could afford even less to pay their workers a living wage. One result of these market divisions and small productive units was the obsolescence of much of Europe's machinery. In France, for instance, the average age of machine tools in 1938 was twenty-five years, as compared to seven to nine years in Britain and five to seven years in the United States. Indeed, the French economy seemed dedicated above all others to the "survival of the unfit." By the end of the war, this situation was even worse: much of France's and Britain's machinery was by then obsolete. The American aim was to modernize this machinery, to overcome the cartelization of industry, and to destroy the artificial national divisions. Europe's industries were to be compelled to become large-scale and competitive by the creation of a "united states" of Europe.

The economic cooperation required by the United States was first stressed by Secretary of State Marshall's call upon the European states to present this country with a plan for their *common* needs and *common* recovery. The result was the Organization of European Economic Cooperation, whose seventeen members (plus the free state of Trieste) pledged themselves to "cooperate with one another and with other like-minded countries in reducing tariffs and other barriers to trade" and "to promote with vigor the development of productivity through [the] efficient use of the resources at their command." The OEEC's estimate of the cost of Europe's recovery over a four-year period was $22 billion. Congress was to cut this figure down to $17 billion, and the amount actually used by the Economic Cooperation Administration between 1948 and 1952 was just over $12 billion. Britain, France, and Germany received more than half of this amount.

The original invitation by the United States to the nations of Europe to plan their joint recovery was deliberately extended to *all* European countries, including the Soviet Union and the nations of Eastern Europe. If the United States had invited only the nations of Western Europe, it would have placed itself in a politically disadvantageous position in which it would have been blamed for the division of Europe and the intensification of the cold war. Actually, if the Russians had participated, it seems unlikely that Congress would have supported the Marshall Plan: first, because the costs of the Plan would have risen astronomically as a result of the very heavy and extensive damage suffered by Russia during the war; and second, because of the growing anti-Soviet feeling which the Soviet Union had engendered. The risk had to be accepted, however; it had to be the Russians who, by their rejection of Marshall Plan aid, would be responsible for the division of Europe. And the chances that the Russians would do precisely that were very good. For European cooperation would mean that Russia would have to disclose full information about her economy and allow the United States to have some control in her economic planning, as well as in that of her satellites. This was unthinkable to a totalitarian state; a Communist state could hardly permit capitalists to have a voice in its economic development. Soviet participation would also require the Soviet Union and its satellites to contribute toward Europe's recovery with food and raw materials, in return for the help they were receiving from the United States. Thus, the Russians would actually be helping to stabilize European capitalism. But if they did not participate—preferring to exploit Europe's misery—they would be blamed for continuing and aggravating the cold war. In either case, the United States could not lose. Actually, Soviet Foreign Minister Molotov did arrive in Paris with a large delegation of experts, and he gave American policy-makers a momentary scare. But only for a moment. Molotov soon denounced the Plan as an attempt to interfere with Soviet sovereignty and withdrew. Western Europe could now plan the use of America's dollars for its recovery.

Was the Marshall Plan a success? The results tell their own story. By 1950—when the Korean War broke out—Europe was already exceeding its prewar production by 25 per cent; two years later, this figure was 200 per cent higher. English exports were doing well, the French inflation was being slowed down, and German production had reached Germany's 1936 level. The dollar gap had been reduced from $12 billion to $2 billion. The Marshall Plan had indeed been a massive success, and at a cost that represented only a tiny fraction of our national income over the same four-year period and was smaller than America's liquor bill for these same years! Far from bankrupting the economy, as some of the Marshall Plan's critics claimed it would do, the Plan helped the country enjoy an economic boom.

This is not to suggest that there were not grave shortcomings, for there were. The first of these was that the growing economic prosperity was not equitably distributed. One of the purposes of the Marshall Plan had been to gain the political allegiance of the Continent's working classes, and to render them immune to the blandishments of Communism. In France and Italy, however, the workers continued to vote Communist. The reason was simple: they continued to live in relative poverty. In France, for instance, real wages throughout this period were lower than in the prewar days. From December, 1946, to February, 1950, the Government forbade workers to strike for increased wages.

Price controls had been lifted more than a year before, and prices had risen steadily. France suffered from a severe inflation. The economic lot of the working class thus declined even further. As expressed by Theodore White: "It was pointless to explain to the workers that without the Marshall Plan they would have been entirely unemployed, that they might have starved or died, that the Plan had saved them. The workers could see only that what had been saved was the status quo, that the recovery had preserved their discomfort and given its fruits to the privileged. In the slums the Communists held on to their votes even through the happiest days of the Plan." The working classes remained "a nation within a nation," alienated from the national society and hostile to the social and economic system that they felt had mistreated them for so long. Still, the Marshall Plan had laid an economic basis from which future progress and social reform could spring.

The second handicap was that the rate of integration was far slower than the Americans had expected. The belief that one could wipe out the national divisions of a century overnight and reform the business habits formed by decades of experience in a few years proved false. American businessmen in ECA soon discovered that their European counterparts did not like competition and much preferred their monopolistic practices. The result was that in October, 1949, Paul Hoffman, the ECA administrator, reiterated the American desire to have Europe move more quickly toward an integrated European market and liberalization of intra-European trade. Hoffman aptly summed up the American case. Americans, he said, wanted:

> ... to move ahead on a far-reaching program to build in Western Europe a more dynamic, expanding economy which will promise steady improvement in the conditions of life for its people. This ... means nothing less than an integration of the Western European economy ...
>
> The substance of such integration would be the formation of a single large market within which quantitative restrictions on the movements of goods, monetary barriers to the flow of payments and, eventually, all tariffs are permanently swept away. The fact that we have in the United States a single market of 150 million consumers

has been indispensable to the strength and efficiency of our economy. The creation of a permanent, freely trading area, comprising 270 million consumers in Western Europe, would have a multitude of helpful consequences. It would accelerate the development of large-scale, low-cost production industries. It would make the effective use of all resources easier, the stifling of healthy competition more difficult.

Strangely enough, the new impetus toward European integration came from quite a different direction—the military situation.

The North Atlantic Treaty Organization

Soon after the Marshall Plan was launched, it became clear that the Plan by itself would not suffice. For in February, 1948, the Russians engineered a *coup d'état* in Prague, and Czechoslovakia disappeared behind the iron curtain. A few months later, in June, the Russians imposed their blockade on Berlin in an effort to dislodge the Western powers from that city. It is hardly surprising that the Europeans, who lived closer to these events than Americans, felt extremely jittery at these overt signs of Russian hostility and aggressive intent. In this atmosphere of tension and insecurity, it became obvious that Europe's economic recovery was impossible; people do not make the necessary sacrifices and work hard to recuperate today if they feel that tomorrow they will be conquered and that their efforts will all have been in vain. In short, it suddenly became crystal-clear that a prerequisite for Europe's recovery was military security.

The Europeans had already made some moves in this direction. In March, 1947, France and England had signed the Treaty of Dunkirk to provide for their mutual defense against a threat to their security "arising from the adoption by Germany of a policy of aggression, or from action by Germany designed to facilitate such a policy." The latter clause was specifically inserted to counter the aggression of a Russian attack from a Communist Germany. Exactly a year later, in March, 1948, Great Britain, France, the Netherlands, Belgium, and Luxembourg signed the Brussels Pact of collective self-defense. The contracting powers stated that if any of the parties to the treaty were attacked in Europe, the other parties would come to its aid with "all military and other aid and assistance in their power." The Brussels Pact, in fact, was established as a military counterpart to OEEC. Just as OEEC represented an organization dedicated to economic cooperation, the Brussels Pact represented one dedicated to military cooperation. And just as the vitality of OEEC had depended upon American capital for its success, the Brussels Pact members expected their alliance to attract American military support.

They were not to be disappointed. Shortly after the signing of the Pact, President Truman informed Congress that the importance of the Pact "goes far beyond the actual terms of the agreement itself. It is a notable step in the direction of unity in Europe. . . . This development deserves our full support. I am confident that the United States will, by appropriate means, extend to the free nations the support which the situation requires." In June, the Senate supported the President's recommendation and passed the famous Vandenberg resolution, which laid the basis for American participation in an alliance with the European powers. The resolution called for the progressive development of regional and other collective arrangements for individual and collective self-defense under Article 51 of the United Nations Charter, and for the association of the United States with such arrangements if they were based on "continuous and effective self-help and mutual aid." The United States then opened negotiations with the various European nations to build an alliance on an Atlantic-wide basis.

In April, 1949, Belgium, Canada, Denmark, France, Great Britain, Iceland, Italy, Luxembourg, the Netherlands, Norway, Portugal, and the United States signed the North Atlantic Treaty. The Senate ratified the Treaty in July after extended hearings and debates, and the other ratifications were completed by August, 1949. For the United States, this NATO commitment set a precedent: for the first time in its history, this country had committed itself to an alliance in peacetime. The heart of the Treaty was Article 5, and it stated: "The Parties agree that an armed attack against one or more of them in Europe or North America shall be considered an attack against them all; and consequently they agree that, if such an armed attack occurs, each of them, in exercise of the right of individual or collective self-defense recognized by Article 51 of the Charter of the United Nations, will assist the Party or Parties so attacked by taking forthwith, individually and in concert with the other Parties, such action as it deems necessary, including the use of armed force, to restore and maintain the security of the North Atlantic area." This area was defined by Article 6 as "the territory of any of the Parties in Europe or North America, ... the Algerian departments of France, ... the occupation forces of any Party in Europe, ... the islands under the jurisdiction of any Party in the North Atlantic area north of the Tropic of Cancer, or ... any vessels or aircraft in this area of any of the Parties." The inclusion of Greece and Turkey in the alliance in 1951, and the formation of the Balkan alliance between these two nations and Yugoslavia in 1954, meant that the NATO line in Europe had been drawn from Norway to Turkey. To make Article 5 a meaningful deterrent to the Soviet Union, the signatories agreed in Article 3: "In order more effectively to achieve the objectives of this Treaty, the Parties, separately and jointly, by means of continuous and effective self-help and mutual aid, will maintain and develop their individual and collective capacity to resist armed attack."

The pledge that each party concerned would respond to an attack by "such action as it deems necessary, including the use of armed force" was incorporated to obtain support in the Senate for ratification of the NATO Treaty. Constitutionally, only the Congress can declare war; thus, the United States could not legally commit itself to war if one of the signatory powers were attacked. In actual practice, it is difficult to see how the United States could abstain from war once any ally were invaded. Surely if the Treaty meant anything, it meant that Europe had become "our first line of defense" and that we would fight if Russian troops crossed the Elbe River. For it was precisely this knowledge that the United States would fight to preserve Europe's freedom that was supposed to prevent a Soviet attack. Two world wars had proved Europe's vital importance to American security. Instead of again allowing the balance of power first to be upset, and thereby once more becoming drawn into war, the United States now expected to eliminate this contingency by committing itself to the preservation of the European balance in peacetime—that is, *before* the enemy attack took place. The presumption was that the fear of meeting American resistance and fighting an all-out war with the United States would deter the potential aggressor from launching his attack.

This strategy of deterrence relied almost exclusively upon American strategic air power—that is, upon the ability of the Strategic Air Command (SAC) to destroy completely the Soviet Union with atomic bombs. This strategy was based upon four assumptions: first, that the only form of future war would be a total war, which would be precipitated by a direct Soviet attack upon the United States or Western Europe; second, that deterrence or victory could be achieved by air power and its ability to inflict such heavy damage upon an enemy that he would, in effect, be committing suicide if he launched an aggressive attack; third, that the Russians would not dare to risk the use of force until they possessed a sizable atomic stockpile, sufficient means to deliver it, and an adequate defense against American bombers; and fourth, that this reliance upon one branch of one service was considerably less expensive than maintaining a large army and navy.

Two events were to change this reliance upon only one weapon to deter or destroy the enemy. The first was the explosion of the first Soviet atomic bomb in late 1949. This foreshadowed a time when the Soviet Union, too, would possess an atomic stockpile; in short, it portended a significant increase in Soviet capability. The second event was the North Korean attack upon South Korea in June, 1950. Since it was presumed that this attack could not have occurred without Soviet permission, the North Korean aggression suggested a change in Soviet intentions. And this possibility received further support from Communist China's intervention in North Korea in late November; perhaps the Soviet Union was ready, or would soon be ready, for an all-out war. The Western response to these events—especially to the latter —was large-scale rearmament.

This involved three tasks for NATO: the establishment of a command structure, the formulation of a strategy by which to defend Europe on the ground, and the rebuilding of its ground forces. These efforts received their initial impetus when, in the dark days after Communist China's entry into the Korean War, President Truman appointed General

Eisenhower to serve as Supreme Allied Commander in Europe. Eisenhower, in turn, strove to make his command operational. His first move was to establish three commands under him: a Central Europe Command, a Northern Europe Command, and a Southern Europe Command. The reason for this triple division is clear: Western Europe, from the North Cape to Sicily, is a peninsula of the Eurasian continent. With the exception of the British Isles and the Iberian peninsula, this Rimland has two flanks. One is Denmark, which almost touches the Scandinavian countries, and the other is Italy, protected by the Alps and projecting into the Mediterranean. Western Europe was the central and most important front—militarily because here was the plain upon which the Red Army could apply its full force and be met with full counterforce, and politically because Germany, France, and Great Britain lay on this axis.

The strategy NATO adopted was known as the "forward strategy"—that is, a defense at the Elbe. In the early stages of planning, Western strategy had called for an Allied withdrawal to more defensible positions behind the Rhine; but in September, 1950, as NATO rearmament began in response to the Korean War, this plan was revised, and the forward strategy was adopted. Politically, the Europeans wanted no part of a strategy which called for a withdrawal and would bring the Red Army to their borders and most probably into their countries. They had no desire to provide battlefields again; they wanted the Red Army to be kept far from their frontiers. A Communist invasion and occupation was unthinkable, for the Russians would probably be even more ruthless than the Nazis. And liberation in a war in which atomic bombs would be dropped was no liberation at all: one could not liberate a corpse. Indeed, if the first Soviet onslaught were to drive the Allies completely out of Europe, the continent would fall permanently under Soviet control. The atomic bomb forbade another Normandy landing. Thus, from a political standpoint, Allied forces could not retreat. Europe would have to be defended as far east in Western Germany as possible.

Such a defense required troops and proper logistical support. When Eisenhower arrived in Europe, he found only twelve divisions—including the American ones—none of which were at full strength, properly trained, or fully equipped with the latest weapons. Nor were there any effective reserves to back them up. Neither of these facts was perhaps surprising: the European powers had greater needs and more important things to do in the immediate postwar days than to maintain or rebuild sizable military forces. In addition, because of America's atomic monopoly, it had seemed quite safe to rely solely upon SAC for deterrence and to use the troops in Germany solely for occupation duties. In his first annual report, the Supreme Commander described the situation of the forces and the logistical support he had found upon his arrival in Europe as follows:

> Their deployment had no relationship to what would be suitable in resisting attack. Airfields were crowded up in the forward areas, in some cases east of the ground troops that must cover them. Supply lines for British and American forces, almost parallel to the front, ran to the north German ports of Hamburg and Bremerhaven, instead of rearward through France and the Low Countries. We knew that before any division would be engaged more than forty-eight hours, it would require supply shipments of upward to 500 tons a day. For air units, the supply load was comparatively heavy: the jet airplane burns more than a ton of fuel per hour. Obviously, a tremendous amount of depot and airfield construction would be required before forces in this vital area were astride adequate communication and routes.

The immediate task was therefore to shift the supply lines to harbors behind army lines, such as the French ports, and to build supply depots and new airfields in similarly protected areas. At the same time, the ground forces had to be increased so that they could serve two functions.

The first would be to act as a "tripwire." In case the Russians had any delusion that the United States would not go to war to defend Europe, the tripwire troops were to remove this belief. An attack by the Red Army would be bound to run into American troops, some of whom would obviously be killed. This would ensure American retaliation against the Soviet Union. "The dictators of recent times," Secretary Acheson said, "have become involved in war when in their belief, their intended victims would fall an easy prey without substantial risk to themselves. The strengthening of the defenses of Western Europe is designed to prevent a repetition of the tragic consequences of such dangerous self-deception." The second function of the NATO army was to hold the Red Army at the point of attack, the Elbe River, while SAC laid waste to the Soviet Union. Military planners believed that such shield forces would have to be large because of the huge size of the Red Army and the absence of Western tactical atomic weapons to counter this numerical superiority. The estimate of NATO forces needed was placed at ninety-six divisions. The forces expected to be ready on D-day were thirty-five to forty divisions. It was assumed that an army of this size would be able to prevent any surprise attack by the twenty-two Soviet divisions in East Germany. If the Russians should decide to launch an attack, however, they would first have to reinforce their divisions. Such a vast forward movement of Russian troops, armor, and artillery could not go undetected. The Allies would learn of it, and thus have the time to mobilize and call up the rest of their forces. The ninety-six Allied divisions were the goal for D-day plus 30.

This number of divisions faced the European states with a dreadful dilemma. For under the division of labor implicit in NATO, Britain, France, and the other continental countries were to supply the bulk of the ground and tactical air forces, while America supplied the strategic air power. But the European nations were unable and unwilling to mobilize the necessary troops. They were still in the midst of economic recovery and unprepared to make the necessary sacrifices to raise large national armies. Unlike the United States, which was rich enough to produce both guns *and* butter, the Europeans had to choose guns *or* butter. While the Soviet threat made it necessary to have a minimal military protection, the task of economic reconstruction made it undesirable to devote too large a share of national budgets to rearmament. The American answer was the rearmament of Germany. If France and Britain could not supply the necessary troops, Germany would have to supply them. Moreover, this decision seemed an eminently correct one. For the forward strategy meant that NATO would try to hold Western Germany. It was only fitting that the Germans should contribute to their own defense. In turn, of course, German rearmament reinforced the need for a forward strategy. For the West Germans could hardly be persuaded to rearm if they could not be assured that the Red Army could be held on the Elbe, that Western Germany would not be turned into a battlefield, and that German troops would not be used merely for the defense of France and England. Thus, the German question once more raised its head. It was not a new question—but this time it received new answers.

German Recovery and Rearmament

Ever since the middle of the nineteenth century—if not since the Congress of Vienna in 1815—Germany has held the key to the European balance of power. This was true of Germany even in defeat in 1945. Almost from the cessation of hostilities, the Soviet Union and the United States began their contest over Germany. East Germany had fallen into Russian hands; West Germany was occupied by the Western powers. Actually, the Allies were lucky, for Western Germany contained the great majority of Germany's population and held the heart of its industrial power. West Germany, in short, was—and still remains—the chief prize in Europe.

During the war, Stalin, Churchill, and Roosevelt had decided to govern Germany through a four-power Allied Control Commission (with France as the fourth power), which would administer the entire country as a single economic unit. In practice, this task proved impossible. The Russians, the British, and the French, as well as the smaller European nations, had been promised reparations payments in compensation for the widespread destruction the Germans had caused in their countries. The Russian sum was to consist of all the industrial equipment in the Soviet zone, plus one-quarter of the far greater industrial complex in Western Germany (it was assumed during the war that Germany's industrial power would be intact at the end of the war). But —and these were to be the decisive points—the United States and Great Britain had insisted upon two restrictions on these reparations payments. First, Germany was to be left enough of her nonmilitary industries to maintain her standard of living at the same level as the rest of Europe (but definitely not higher); and second, no reparations were to be paid out of current production until Germany had earned enough money with her exports to pay for the imports she needed.

Germany was to support herself. The Allies had no desire—to put it mildly—to spend their money supporting their former enemy.

The Russians quickly began demolishing the industry in their zone with great gusto—never, of course, informing the Western powers how much they were taking. The Russians also cut off the regular food supply from Eastern Germany, which had traditionally been Germany's breadbasket; under the original agreement, they were to furnish this food in return for the three-fifths of capital equipment they were allowed to remove from the Western zones. These Soviet actions were bound to lead to trouble, and they did. Almost exactly a year after V-E Day, the United States announced that it was suspending all further reparations payments to the Soviet Union. They were not to be resumed until the Soviet Union operated its zone as part of Germany under the original terms of agreement. The reason for this American action was clear: if East Germany no longer furnished the necessary supplies of food which West Germany needed, West Germany would have to increase her exports to buy food from abroad; and if she had to increase her exports, she had to increase her production. The British agreed; they were unwilling to spend their few remaining dollars buying food for the Germans. Thus, the wartime agreement to hold German industrial production down for fear that Germany would again use her heavy industry in a secret rearmament program—as she had during the years between the two World Wars—collapsed. The American and British purpose was to make Germany pay for her own needs.

But the two powers also had another and more important aim in mind: as Europe's economic collapse became clearer and the cold war intensified, it became necessary to lift Germany out of her economic stagnation and make her industry contribute to the general economic recovery of Europe. In July, 1946, the United States offered to merge its zone with those of Britain and France; Germany was to be decompartmentalized in order to speed up her industrial recovery. The French, fearing Germany's reviving strength, refused to participate. The result was that in January, 1947, an embryonic German state known as Bizonia (France was to join later) formally emerged. But this fusion would not by itself suffice to achieve Germany's economic recovery. The willing cooperation of the Germans themselves was needed. America and Britain therefore decided to let the Germans begin to take a more active part in running their own country; this, in effect, foreshadowed the eventual establishment of a West German government. Lastly, Germany needed a sound currency; without it, her economy could not recover. The subsequent currency reform carried out by the United States Army became the basis of West Germany's amazing economic recovery.

West Germany's new position in the world, and America's new policy toward Germany, was announced by Secretary of State Byrnes in his speech at Stuttgart in September, 1946. Byrnes came quickly to the point: "It is not in the interest of the German people or in the interest of world peace that Germany should become a pawn or partner in a military struggle for power between the East and the West." It was in this negative way that Byrnes called for Germany's positive participation in the cold war. He opposed any further reduction of Germany's standard of living; and he stated that there were to be no further reparations out of Germany's production as long as Germany was not self-sufficient. Equally important was Byrnes's explicit emphasis that the United States did not accept the Oder-Neisse line dividing Germany from Poland as a permanent frontier. Byrnes thus gave American support to the German desire for the return of at least some, if not all, of the territory absorbed by Poland at the end of the war—territory which Poland had received in compensation for Eastern territory she had lost to Russia during the war. At the same time, the Secretary of State asserted that "the German people, under proper safeguards, should now be given primary responsibility for the running of their own affairs." The United States did not believe "that large armies of alien soldiers and alien bureaucrats, however well motivated and disciplined, are in the long run the most reliable guardians of another country's democracy." The occupying powers should only lay down the general rules "under which German democracy can govern itself" so that Allied troops could be limited "to a number sufficient to see [that] these rules are obeyed." But—and here Byrnes's warning to the Soviet Union was emphatic—"Security forces will probably have to remain in Germany for a long period. I want no misunderstanding. We will not shirk our duty. We are not withdrawing. We are staying here and will furnish our proportionate share of the security forces."

The Russians were quick to recognize the change that Byrnes's Stuttgart speech foreshadowed for American foreign policy, and when, in the spring of 1948, the United States pushed through the currency reform and turned its attention to the creation of a constitution and a new government for Germany, the Russians struck by blockading Berlin. The issue at stake was, of course, more than just Berlin. The issue was Germany itself. Berlin, as the old capital of Germany, was the symbol of the conflict: *quo vadis Germania?* The Russians certainly did not want to see West Germany become a partner of the West. Germany and Russia had fought two wars in forty years. Germany had beaten Russia the first time and almost defeated her again on the second occasion. Moreover, Germany was not a *status quo* power but a revisionist state eying territory now controlled by the Soviet Union and Poland. Whether these defensive reasons, springing from Russia's fear of Germany, were primary in precipitating the Berlin crisis, however, is rather doubtful. For if Russia's fear of Germany was so deep, it is difficult to understand why the Russians did not accept the American proposal, offered them by Secretary Byrnes, of an alliance of twenty-five or even forty years to neutralize Germany. In any case, whereas Russia had been much weaker than Germany before World War II, she emerged from that conflict far stronger—a superpower, in fact—while Germany, in spite of her potential strength, was now only a second-class power. The Russo-German balance of power had decisively changed in Russia's favor, and an independent German attack upon Russia was unlikely in these circumstances. For in any war, whether she acted unilaterally or as an ally of the United States, Germany would be the battlefield and therefore the first country to be destroyed. Fear of this consequence was a sufficient deterrent. The real danger to the Soviet Union of a revived Germany came from the fact that once Germany's power had been added to that of the United States and her allies, the American position in Europe would obviously be greatly consolidated. This, in turn, stood in the way of two Russian objectives: one, the immediate withdrawal of American forces and the liquidation of American bases on the Continent; and two, the long-term aim of winning Germany's participation in a subservient partnership. Germany's recovery, in short, blocked Russia's expansionist purposes in Europe.

In order to forestall Germany's revival, therefore, the Russians resorted to a test of strength. If the Allies could be forced out of Berlin, German confidence in American strength would be undermined. The Germans would hardly attach themselves to a friend too weak to protect them. Indeed, if American will power would crumble under Soviet pressure, France and Britain also might reconsider their adherence to NATO. The Berlin crisis, then, if it were not met, would disintegrate the entire American position in Europe and nullify America's postwar efforts to rebuild Europe as a partner in the struggle against the Soviet Union. The American Commander in Germany, General Clay, certainly saw the Russian challenge in these terms. In a cable to Washington on April 10, 1948, Clay succinctly stated the importance of Berlin to American security: "When Berlin falls, Western Germany will be next. If we mean . . . to hold Europe against Communism, we must not budge . . . if we withdraw, our position in Europe is threatened. If America does not understand this now, does not know the issue is cast, then it never will, and Communism will run rampant. I believe the future of democracy requires us to stay." The American Government believed so, too.

The method of conflict was decided at the outset by the unwillingness of either the United States or the Soviet Union to risk a total war. Thus, the Western powers ruled out almost at the start an attempt to reopen the corridor to Berlin by sending troops and tanks to challenge the Red Army. Instead, they limited themselves to an airlift to supply the city with all its needs. The Russians did not challenge this effort, for they were aware that in doing so they would leave the West no alternative but to fight a total war. Instead, they decided to wait and see whether the Western powers could take care of the needs of Berlin's 2.5 million citizens. It would take a minimum of 4,000 tons of food and fuel daily—an enormous amount of tonnage to fly in by air. After 324 days of waiting, the Russians were convinced that the Americans and the British were more than equal to the task. While the total tonnage did not immediately attain the 4,000-ton target, Allied planes were eventually to fly in as much as

13,000 tons daily. Planes landing at three-minute intervals flew in 60 per cent more than the 8,000 tons that had previously been sent each day by ground transport. By the spring of 1949, West Berliners were eating more than at the beginning of the blockade—and considerably more than the East Berliners! Faced with this colossal Allied achievement, the Russians called off the blockade in May.

America's determination to hold Europe and not to allow further Soviet expansion was demonstrated. The West Germans clearly saw that they could count on America to protect them. Just as NATO had been the prerequisite for Europe's economic recovery, the Berlin airlift was the final American act which led to Germany's resurgence. America had laid the basis for Germany's economic recovery through Marshall Plan funds and the currency reforms; and now, it had given Germany the sense of military security without which her economic reconstruction could not have been completed.

European Integration

Ironically, it was the fear of Germany's rising strength that was now, in turn, to stimulate further efforts toward European integration. The specter of a fully revived Germany struck fear into most of Germany's neighbors. The French, with their memories of 1870, 1914, and 1940, were particularly alarmed. Germany's recovery—stimulated by America's response to the cold war—thus posed a serious problem for Germany's partners: how could they hold Germany, potentially the strongest nation in Europe outside of Russia, in check? Ever since Germany's unification in the late nineteenth century, France had attempted to deal with the inherently greater strength of her aggressive and militaristic neighbor by forming alliances which could balance Germany's power. Since Britain had usually preferred to retain a free hand, and since her interests were also at times opposed to those of France, the French had relied primarily upon Continental allies. Before World War I, they discovered such an ally in Russia, and between the two wars they found partners in Poland, Czechoslovakia, Romania, and Yugoslavia. None of these alliances had saved France, however; in both wars, British power and especially American power had been the decisive factors in defeating Germany (aided by Russian power, of course, in World War II). But once saved, the French again responded in terms of their traditional reflex—despite the extension of Soviet power into the heart of Europe. For France, Germany was still *the* enemy, and in December, 1944, the French signed a Treaty of Mutual Assistance with the Russians, thus making an alliance which they considered as a prerequisite for their security. Soviet hostility soon disillusioned the French and deprived the treaty of any meaning, however, and in fact made it necessary to add Germany's power to that of the West.

The failure of the traditional balance-of-power technique, by which an inferior power had always sought to balance a stronger nation, led France to seek a new way of exerting some control over Germany's growing power. French statesmen found a revolutionary means in European integration. It was through the creation of a supranational community, to which Germany could transfer certain sovereign rights, that German power could be controlled. Only in this manner could German strength be prevented from again causing harm to all of Europe, and at the same time be employed instead for Europe's welfare and security.

France made her first move in this direction of a united Europe in May, 1950, when Foreign Minister Robert Schuman proposed the plan that has since borne his name: a European Coal and Steel Community (ECSC) composed of "Little Europe" (France, Germany, Italy, and the Benelux countries of Belgium, the Netherlands, and Luxembourg). The Schuman Plan was to interweave German and French heavy industry to such an extent that it would become impossible ever to separate them again. Germany would never again be able to use her coal and steel industries for nationalistic and militaristic purposes. The political and military power of the Ruhr, for purely German purposes, was to be destroyed for all time. War between Germany and France would become not only unthinkable but impossible under these circumstances.

But the new French technique of restraining Germany did not consist merely of fusing Germany's superior strength with France's own lesser strength and thereby subjecting Germany's power to a certain degree of French control. "Europeanization" was also a means for France to achieve a balance with Germany. The combination of the French and

German coal and steel industries would strengthen French heavy industry and create a Franco-German equilibrium within ECSC. Economic integration would thus allow France to overcome her inferior industrial strength, which had been imposed upon her in large part by the division of Europe into separate national markets. One of the main reasons for France's industrial lag has been her lack of energy sources. She possessed Europe's largest iron ore deposits, in Lorraine—resources which during Germany's annexation of Alsace-Lorraine from 1871 to 1918 had added in considerable measure to making Germany the second greatest industrial power in the world before 1914. But even when she had regained Alsace-Lorraine after World War I, France still lacked the coal with which to heat the furnaces. Europe's largest coal deposits lay in the Ruhr, and to a lesser extent in the Saar—that is, in Germany. The Schuman Plan now, in effect, held out a bargain to West Germany. France was to receive coal from Germany at the same price paid by German manufacturers—and not at the previously much higher prices that made French products more expensive than German ones. In return, France was to abandon her opposition to raising German production, and prevail upon Britain and the United States to lift *all* controls from Germany's heavy industry—which would mean that Germany could once more compete on the international market. Even more important for Germany, entry into ECSC would be the first step toward regaining equal status with her former Western enemies, recovering her sovereignty, and strengthening her ties with the Western powers so that they would eventually include her in NATO. Thus, the Schuman Plan had both an economic and political appeal for the Germans as well as the French.

The French Plan was not, however, devised only to control Germany's resurgent power or to give France a strength equal to that of Germany. It had a third and more ambitious goal in mind: a united Europe under French leadership. For only by creating Little Europe could France again play a major role in world affairs. France alone was too weak to pursue an active part in a world dominated by two superpowers. Even in the Western coalition, the most influential European nation was Britain, not France; and with Germany's recovery, it was very likely that Bonn's voice and opinions would also outweigh those of Paris in Washington. By herself, France would remain dependent upon her American protector—a "satellite" state, powerless to affect major Western policy decisions. A united Europe, with Franco-German unity at its core, was therefore France's alternative to remaining subservient to the United States and without influence either in NATO or on the world stage. General de Gaulle, with his characteristic foresight, saw this as early as 1950. Recalling in a speech the age-old memory of the battle of the Catalaunian plains, "in which Franks, Gallo-Romans, and Teutons jointly routed the hordes of Attila," De Gaulle stated: "It is time for the Rhine to become a meeting place and not a barrier, for there is no reason why these two nations should not unite. If one did not force oneself to look coolly at things, one would be almost dazzled at the prospect of what German qualities and French qualities, extended to Africa, might jointly yield. That is a field of common development which might transform Europe even beyond the iron curtain." Only through a united Europe could France gain an equal voice with the "Anglo-Saxons" in NATO, and possibly even exert independent pressure upon the Soviet Union.

These, then, were the benefits the French expected to gain from the Schuman Plan, and their approach was a highly realistic one. For they clearly saw that the nucleus of a united Europe would have to be a Franco-German union. The antagonism between these two states, born of their traditional enmity, would first have to be healed. Moreover, the French scheme did more than just invoke the dream of a united Europe, hoping that its vision would so fire people's imagination that they would suddenly discard their narrow nationalistic loyalties for a wider European allegiance. Europe could not be created by sentiment alone. The French rejected "the rosy mists of idealism" and determined to erect the new Europe upon a solid foundation, building from the bottom upward. Europe, they knew, could be forged only by tying together the interests of politically powerful and economically important groups in the various nations *across* national boundaries. For instance, the removal of all trade barriers in the coal and steel sector of the economy would encourage the modernization of mines and plants, as well as the elimination of those mines and plants which continued to operate inefficiently. And once the efficient producers had adjusted to the wider market and witnessed its opportunities, they would want to remove national barriers in other areas. Further, as production increased, Europe's standard of living rose, and French and Italian workers received more of what they believed to be their share, labor would see that its goal of a welfare state could be achieved only at the European level. The French also showed great political astuteness in their selection of heavy industry as the first to be integrated. Coal and steel form the basis of the entire industrial structure—they represent a sector which cannot possibly be separated from the over-all economy. Since the separation created by ECSC was to be an artificial one to begin with, this would create a "spill-over" effect. Or to put it another way: this would exert pressure on the unintegrated sectors of the economy; and as the benefits of the pooling of heavy industry became clearly observable, these sectors would follow suit. The Coal and Steel Community was thus seen as the first stage of an attempt to create a wider market in one particular area of the economy; and it was expected that this approach would be gradually extended to other areas of the economy, such as agriculture, transportation, and electricity, eventually leading to the creation of a "united states" of Europe with a huge market and a mass-production system.

This was a quite different approach to Europe than that of the OEEC and its multilateral clearing house, the European Payments Union. It also differed greatly from the Council of Europe, which despite its official aim "to achieve greater unity between its members for the purpose of safeguarding and realizing the ideals and principles which are their common heritage and facilitating their economic and social progress," has achieved few tangible results and apparently has little or no influence on the individual European governments. These other organizations, which included Britain and therefore represented "Big Europe," depended upon intergovernmental cooperation. But the functional approach stressed supranational cooperation within a limited functional sphere and the creation of common interests within that particular area of activity before extending it to other functional fields. The Schuman Plan took this supranational approach, for it intended to remove national control over the coal and steel industries. This control would be transferred to the ECSC High Authority, a body of nine men nominated by the member governments; however, no individual on the Authority would receive instructions from his government or be responsible to it. The Authority would be responsible only to a Common Assembly chosen by the participating nations; this, too, would be supranational. These institutions would be assisted by: a Court of Justice, which would deal with legal problems; a Consultative Assembly, composed of representatives of management, labor, and consumer interests; and a Council of Ministers, which would coordinate the work of the High Authority with the actions of the different national governments in other areas of their economies. It was the Authority which was the key organ in this organizational complex.

Although the Authority's jurisdiction was carefully confined to its particular sector of the economy, it was quite powerful within this sector. It was empowered to tax, to abolish monopolistic arrangements, to eliminate all quotas and tariffs, and to suppress subsidies and discriminatory pricing practices and transportation rates. The Authority's directives were binding on both states and private enterprises; it could fine business firms for violations and call upon member states to enforce its orders.

These ECSC institutions, then, were the embryo of a united Europe. They were soon to be applied to an area which their initial planners had not expected to include—the military forces of the different nationalities. The French originated this idea, too. American insistence on German rearmament made it unavoidable. To the French, the rearmament of their old enemy was both distasteful and dangerous. But France was faced with the inevitable, since German rearmament was made necessary primarily by France's own inability to supply more troops herself. Yet, the French remained determined that the world would never see another *German* army, *German* general staff, *German* war ministry, or *German* ministry of armaments. The solution they proposed was the formation of a European army. Just as the French had conceived of ECSC as a means for controlling Germany's growing economic strength and harnessing it to Europe's welfare, so they now proposed a European army as an instrument for checking Germany's rising military power and using it for Europe's defense. Control was to be exercised in several ways: small units of approximately 3,000 men would be integrated into multinational divisions (France later said she would agree to 5,000-6,000 men units, with three such units to a division, only two of which could be composed of the same nationality); the new army would wear the same uniforms, use the same weapons, and receive common training; and military production and defense budgets would be coordinated. The Commissariat of this European Defense Community—the equivalent of the High Authority in the ECSC—would be responsible to the same Assembly to which the Authority was responsible; and the same Court would interpret the EDC Treaty.

The first American and German reactions to this Pleven Plan (named for the French Premier who announced it) were negative. But if the United States insisted upon rearming Germany, she had little choice but to accept the essence of the French plan. For France simply refused to accept a German army, and France's geographical position made her cooperation absolutely necessary. If Europe could not be defended well without German power, it could not be defended at all without France. France was NATO's strategic rear; without its harbors, arms and munitions depots, and supply lines, NATO was defenseless. France's determination to create a European army was therefore decisive.

The EDC Treaty was signed in May, 1952. In essence, it incorporated the Pleven Plan. The major modification was that the basic national units would be divisions of 13,000 to 15,000 men, and that these divisions would then be formed into international army corps; no more than two divisions of the same nationality could be included in a corps. Because of language barriers and other difficulties, multinational groups smaller than divisions were not considered battleworthy. The EDC command was to be organized along multinational lines. NATO, of course, remained the supreme command. EDC and NATO were, in fact, formally linked. All EDC members except Germany were members of NATO, and an attack upon one of them would naturally mean an attack upon the organization itself. To take care of the German problem, two protocols were attached to the EDC Treaty by which NATO and EDC promised each other military aid in case of attack; thus Germany was obligated to come to NATO's defense, and vice versa. Britain and the United States further stated that they would keep their forces in Europe indefinitely, and that they would contribute their fair share of the forces needed for the defense of the North Atlantic area. These declarations were meant to soothe French apprehensions that a future withdrawal of Anglo-American forces would leave them to face German forces alone.

For Germany, entry into EDC was another step toward regaining full equality with the other Western powers and asserting her political prestige. Most important, in return for providing EDC with 500,000 men organized into twelve divisions, Germany would recover her sovereignty, with certain limitations. The Allies would reserve their authority to take the necessary measures to protect the security of their forces in Germany (not only against external aggression, but also against possible attempts by the extreme left or right to subvert West Germany from within), to continue governing Berlin, and—in order to prevent any Russo-German deal—to preserve their exclusive right to negotiate with the Soviet Union on the question of German reunification. The kind of Germany they would seek—the United States, Britain, and France declared—would be "a unified Germany enjoying a liberal-democratic constitution, like that of the Federal Republic, and integrated within the European community."

The likelihood of attaining this objective was very small indeed. Western proposals to unite Germany have constantly included terms which the Soviet Union could not possibly accept. These terms have been: reunification via free elections in both halves of Germany, and insistence upon allowing the government of this reunified Germany freedom to conduct its own foreign policy. The former would have meant the end of the Soviet-imposed Communist regime in East Germany; and the latter condition would have allied a unified Germany, probably headed by the pro-Western government of Konrad Adenauer, with the West. NATO would thus be extended to the Polish frontier and the Eastern satellite belt. The Russians were hardly likely to accept such a restriction of their sphere of influence or permit willingly such an advance of Western power. If the Soviet Union would tolerate any kind of united Germany at all, it could only be a neutralized Germany, politically, economically, and militarily disassociated from the Western powers. Allied terms thus ensured a continuation of a divided Germany—which was precisely what they wanted. France did not wish to integrate with a united Germany—only with a split Germany. A re-united Germany would tend to dominate Europe, for it would certainly be more powerful than France and the other nations of Little Europe, as well as Britain. These nations were therefore opposed to Germany's reunification; and they, together with the United States, paid verbal allegiance to this goal only to keep the West German Government of Chancellor Adenauer in power. The latter's claim was that through the alliance with America, Britain, and France, West Germany and the Western powers would be placed in such a strong position that one day they could negotiate Russia's exit from East Germany.

In a sense, this Allied distinction between official and real aims with regard to Germany is rather amusing because it is unnecessary. By and large, the German public has become increasingly indifferent to the question of reunification. To be sure, German politicians and journalists continue to proclaim unification as Germany's supreme goal. Speeches and editorials on German unification are a ritual—but largely a meaningless ritual. In the first place, despite Germany's split, foreign policy is a strictly secondary consideration with the German electorate. Ever since the destruction of their cities and the loss of their homes in World War II, the Germans have been almost completely preoccupied with rebuilding their country, restoring the economy, and, above all else, with individual material gain and the enjoyment of ordinary comforts. In short, in reaction against the Nazi years and the sheer deprivation and want of the immediate postwar years, the Germans have rejected deep involvement in public affairs and concerned themselves almost exclusively with their private affairs—especially with earning a sufficiently good living to buy a home, a car, and all the other amenities of a pleasant life. So successful has Germany's economic recovery and progress been—it is usually referred to as Germany's "economic miracle"—that even most of the 11 million refugees from the East have been integrated into West Germany's political community and have no desire to return to their old homes. For most of Germany's population, the unified Reich is just an old and fading memory.

Quite apart from the general populace, certain powerful groups in Germany either oppose unification or at least do not favor it enough to push fervently for it. Big business, the strongest interest group within Chancellor Adenauer's ruling Christian Democratic Union, is little concerned with the question. It is faced with a long backlog of foreign orders in Europe, Latin-America, the Middle East, and Southeast Asia, and it must also satisfy a rising domestic demand for consumer items. Just as for most Germans reunification would mean a probable loss of consumer goods—which would be sent to the East Germans—so for business it would mean a diversion of much-needed capital funds to raise East Germany's economic level to that of West Germany. Business, like the public, is reluctant to make the necessary sacrifices.

The Christian Democratic Union has another reason for opposing unification. The party is predominantly Catholic, reflecting West Germany's large Catholic population. East Germany is almost completely Protestant. Reunification would thus threaten the CDU's grip on the government. On the other hand, the Social Democratic Party favors reunification as its only means of ever gaining a majority vote and capturing political power. The party has therefore been strongly nationalistic, has opposed Germany's integration into Western Europe, and has called for negotiations with Russia on Germany's reunification on the basis of German neutrality between East and West. The public's constant rejection of this nationalistic program and its continued support of Adenauer's policy of alignment with the West and integration into Little Europe provide clear evidence of the electorate's preference for security within the Western Alliance over reunification purchased at the price of neutrality (sentiments that were intensified by Russia's brutal repression of the Hungarian revolt in 1956), and of the decline of Germany's former intensely nationalistic feeling. The almost complete public indifference to reunification may also be an indication of awareness that the Federal Republic between the Elbe and the Rhine is a Germany without Prussia. South Germany has long been hostile to Protestant Prussia, and the Rhineland has been much influenced by Western (especially French) democratic thought. A reunified Germany, which would undoubtedly stimulate a movement to resurrect Prussia, could hardly be a welcome thought to most West Germans. It might well be said that if Germany had to be divided, the present division which cuts Prussia off from the Western part of Germany could not have been more aptly drawn. It is this latter half which is integrating with the West in defense against the Soviet pressure from the East.

The Soviet Shift to Asia

It seems a cruel twist of fate that this very success of American foreign policy in Europe should have brought about a shift of Communist pressure from Europe to Asia—a shift which in June, 1950, led to the outbreak of the Korean War. The Truman Doctrine had prevented a Russian breakthrough into southeast Europe and the Middle East, and established Western Europe's flank in the eastern Mediterranean. The Marshall Plan had set Europe on the path to economic recovery and health. NATO had guaranteed Europe its security. The lessons of two world wars had been absorbed, and the NATO commitment was the proof of this.

The United States had transformed a position of great weakness and vulnerability into one of relative strength. It had drawn a clear line between the American and Russian spheres of influence, and had demonstrated, in both Greece and Berlin, that it was in Europe to stay. (The Greek crisis had passed when Yugoslavia was ejected from the Soviet bloc in 1948; the Yugoslavs no longer provided aid to the Greek guerrillas.) What all this meant was that Europe was no longer a profitable field for guerrilla warfare, *coups d'état,* or subversive attempts.

Opportunities for immediate expansion had disappeared. To cross the line drawn by the United States was to risk total war, and this risk was hardly one the Soviet Union was willing to assume during a period in which the United States held atomic superiority. The Russian leaders, as George Kennan had said, did not believe in pursuing an "adventuristic" policy which gambled with the very existence of the Soviet state.

So they turned their attention to the Far East. Here was a much more attractive field for political and military exploitation. Most countries in this area had only recently emerged from Western colonialism, and their nationalistic and anti-Western feelings were very strong. Nationalist China's collapse and the establishment of a Communist government on the mainland in late 1949 had even further weakened the Western position in Asia, for it had gravely shifted the balance of power in the Far East against the United States. The United States no longer confronted only Russia; she was now faced with the challenge of the combined power of the Sino-Soviet bloc. Moreover, whereas pressure in Europe united the Western powers, pressure in Asia divided them because they were fundamentally split over the character and nature of the new Chinese regime. And finally, no expansionist move in the Far East would entail the risk of total war. In the American pattern of defense, Europe held strategic priority; Asia was of secondary interest. Europe was so vital to American defense that any Soviet move in Western Europe entailed the risk of an all-out clash with the United States; no single area in Asia was so immediately vital to American security that it was worth the cost of total war. The recovery of Europe and China's collapse, then, created a vacuum in the East and turned Russian pressure toward Asia. It was here that the dramatic clashes of the cold war were to occur during the next four years. And it was these clashes which were to lead to a reaction within the United States itself against American foreign policy.

IV. CONTAINMENT IN THE
FAR EAST

The Fall of China

During World War II, the United States had a twofold purpose in the Pacific: to defeat Japan and to create a powerful and friendly China in her place. It was hoped that a strong and democratic China would play a leading role in protecting the postwar peace in the Far East. The United States took several actions to confer upon China the status of a great power. She renounced her extraterritorial rights in China, repealed the Chinese exclusion laws, established an annual Chinese immigration quota, and made it possible for legally admitted Chinese to become American citizens. At Cairo in 1943, together with Great Britain, she promised to return "all the territories Japan had stolen from the Chinese, such as Manchuria, Formosa, and the Pescadores." The United States also awarded China one of the five permanent seats on the United Nations Security Council; China was thus granted equal status with the Soviet Union, Great Britain, France, and the United States.

The belief of American statesmen that the mere pronouncement of China as a great power could actually convert her into one was typically American: one need only believe strongly enough in the desirability of an event for it to happen. Perhaps American policy-makers also hoped that if China were admitted into the great-power club, she would behave like one. But American faith without Chinese works was insufficient to accomplish the task. It would have taken a miracle to do that; and while statesmen at times delude themselves into thinking that they can perform miracles, such things happen only in storybooks.

The first obstacle to creating a strong China was the sharp

division within the country. Quite apart from the Japanese occupation of large areas of the country during the war, the Chinese were deeply split among themselves. There was not one China; there were two Chinas—a Communist China and a Nationalist China. The Communists were not scattered throughout the whole population, as in Europe; already in control of large segments of northwest China, they extended their sphere during the war by infiltrating into north-central China. In this area, the Japanese held the cities and the major lines of communication, while the Communists organized the countryside. By 1945, they controlled 116 million people, one-fourth of China's entire population, within an area that constituted 15 per cent of China's territory, exclusive of Manchuria. Communist China was, in short, a nation within a nation.

Thus, if the United States wanted to create a united China, it would have to end this internal split. The American aim was to achieve this objective by establishing a coalition government in which all parties would be represented. The desirability of such a government was not questioned. What possible harm could there be in uniting the Nationalists and the Communists? The United States and the Soviet Union were cooperating against the common enemy, and most leaders and officials of the American Government looked forward to friendly postwar relations. If these two nations, each representing a totally different way of life, could overcome past differences and get along together, why should the two Chinese parties not be able to settle their conflict? There was also another and more immediate reason why the United States wished to end China's division as quickly as possible. A China torn apart by internal strife could not make an effective contribution to the winning of the war. Both the Nationalists and the Communists were concerned more with fighting each other than with fighting the Japanese. The Nationalists, for instance, concentrated about twenty divisions, including some of their best troops, against the Communists in an effort to contain them. After Pearl Harbor, Chiang Kai-shek, the Nationalist leader, was assured of victory over Japan. He was quite willing to allow the main burden of this struggle to fall upon the United States, while he—wisely, from his own point of view—concentrated on the internal Communist threat. But the American attitude is that once war breaks out, the total effort must be directed toward the single goal of military victory; any diversion of strength—particularly for "extraneous" political purposes—is considered unjustifiable. The war had to be won in the quickest possible time and with the minimum number of casualties. This attitude, then, reinforced the American desire to establish a coalition government in China.

All our efforts aimed at achieving this goal, both during the war and afterward, were in vain. Neither the Nationalists nor the Communists trusted one another; both sought a monopoly of power. Chiang was quite willing to hand the Communists a few seats in a Nationalist-controlled government, but he insisted that the Communists, in return, would have to place their army under Nationalist command. The Communists considered this offer tantamount to a demand for surrender, and they rejected Chiang's terms. Both sides were constantly aware of the important role which their armies played in the struggle for power: the Nationalists recognized that they would have to deprive their enemy of his army in order to ensure their own survival; and the Communists were realists enough to know that they needed their army to defeat Chiang. At the end of the war, both parties—and particularly the Nationalists—believed that they had the capabilities to defeat their opponent; compromise was therefore unnecessary.

China was not, however, divided only between two irreconcilable parties. Its pro-American Nationalist Government was losing popular support and disintegrating. Perhaps the Nationalists were merely the victims of fate. Except for the two years from 1929 to 1931, the Government was constantly engaged in fighting for its very survival—against the Japanese (who attacked Manchuria in 1931, Shanghai in 1932, and China itself in 1937), as well as the Communists. Faced with both external and internal danger, Chiang Kai-shek had neither the time nor the resources to concern himself with formulating and implementing the political, social, and economic reforms China needed. His principal concern was military: to stem the Japanese advance and maintain himself in power. The problem of modernizing China—above all, of meeting peasant aspirations—was strictly a subsidiary problem. Moreover, Japanese successes during the war changed the basis of Chiang's support and thereby rendered any agrarian reform impossible. By 1939, the Japanese had occupied the entire coastal area of China and had driven the Nationalists inland. This meant that Chiang's Kuomintang Party, which controlled the government, had lost the main pillar of its support, the progressive commercial and financial interests in the coastal cities. Instead, it was forced to rely upon the conservative landlord class.

No government in history likes to commit suicide, and the Nationalist Government proved no exception. A government whose principal social and economic support came from the landlords was unlikely to carry out any land reforms. Probably a majority of peasants were independent landowners; but many of China's peasants were tenants. Both groups were, however, profoundly dissatisfied. Those who rented their land had to pay excessive sums; after the war, these sometimes amounted to 50 to 90 per cent of the peasant's crops. Those who owned their own land were handicapped by the small size of their holding and the lack of capital. The government's taxation policies further impoverished the peasant, who bore the main burden of the taxes. Since the peasant's crops were visible and easily appraisable, corrupt officials usually took more of the crops than the peasant could afford to spare. The result was that the peasant lived in a constant state of impoverishment and indebtedness. In order to survive, he had to seek funds from a moneylender, usually the local landlord, who charged him an extremely high rate of interest, often from 20 to 30 per cent. Consequently, the peasant got himself deeper and deeper into debt.

The fact that the peasants constituted four-fifths of China's population also meant that they had to provide most of the conscripts for the Nationalist Army. But the able-bodied and eligible sons of the rich avoided military service; there were always enough corrupt officials who could be bribed. In the same way, the rich tended to avoid paying taxes. Chiang, in short, seemed to be doing his best to earn the peasants' hatred.

After the war, the Nationalists even managed to alienate the business circles which had formerly supported them. As the Nationalists returned to the coastal cities, they took over all Japanese-owned industries and ran them as state enterprises. This incensed the business community. Some of the Japanese property had formerly belonged to the Chinese, but the government simply neglected to return such property to its owners. Even worse was the fact that private enterprise now found itself faced with the powerful competition of state industries, which were controlled by relatives and close friends of Chiang. Naturally, the American aid funds with which the government supported its enterprises provided great profits for these people. As the American commander in China during the war, General Wedemeyer, observed in 1947 upon his return on a fact-finding mission for the American Government: "Certain rich families, some of whom have relatives in high positions of the Government, have been greatly increasing their fortunes. Nepotism is rife ... sons, nephews, and brothers of government officials have been put into positions within the government, sponsored firms, or in private firms to enable them to make huge profits at the expense of their government and their people."

The Nationalist position deteriorated even further because of China's unchecked inflation. The government had no fixed budget, and its accounting system did not function! When the government needed money, it simply printed it, thereby further inflating the currency. Prices doubled sixty-seven times in the two and a half years from early 1946 to late 1948. No one seemed willing or able to control this spiral. The most devastating impact of this hyper-inflation was upon government officials at the lower level; it provided them with a massive incentive for corruption. Their salaries were wholly inadequate, and they had to find means of supplementing their meager incomes. Honesty in these circumstances simply did not pay. Corruption became rife throughout the government.

As Chiang's government lost popularity, it began to resort increasingly to force to hold its position. The resulting police and military measures only further alienated the people. Wedemeyer found this situation: "Secret police operate widely, very much as they do in Russia and as they did in Germany. People disappear ... No trials and no sentences ... Everyone lives with a feeling of fear and loses confidence in the government." This was particularly true of the intellectuals, who together with the peasantry have been the traditional supporters of China's governments. Professors were dismissed, even arrested, when they began to criticize the government for its policies. Students similarly inclined were also thrown into jail.

The behavior of the army also spread hatred of the government. The Manchurian episode was typical. In Manchuria, according to Wedemeyer, "the Central Government armies were [at the end of the war with Japan] welcomed enthusiastically by the people as deliverers from Japanese oppression. Today, after several months of experience with the Central Government armies, the people experience a feeling of hatred and distrust because the officers and enlisted men were arrogant and rude. Also, they stole and looted freely; their general attitude was that of conquerors instead of liberators."

To sum up the position of the Nationalists: the government had alienated important segments of the politically articulate minority, especially the businessmen and intellectuals. The more inarticulate and passive peasants were tired of the constant fighting, the high rents and taxes. All three groups had either lost confidence in the ability of the government to take care of the problems of postwar China, or felt that the government was not interested in their welfare. But only minorities in each group turned to the Communists. The majority simply disengaged themselves from the Nationalists and became indifferent to the outcome of the civil war. They did not rise up against the government in a "popular revolution." Postwar China did not experience the kind of spontaneous uprising that France, for instance, underwent in 1789. The Chinese peasants did not suddenly lay down their hoes, join together and march toward the landlord's house, haul him out, and hang him from the nearest tree. Later on, it was to take the Communists several months to organize the peasants and arouse them enough to establish people's courts in which the landlords would be tried and condemned to execution. Similarly, Chinese businessmen might have become disenchanted with the government, but this did not mean that either all or a majority of them joined the Communists. But if the Communists won the civil war—and the military conflict would play the decisive role in determining this issue—they, like the peasants and the intellectuals, were willing to give them the benefit of the doubt and allow them to demonstrate that they could give China a more effective government.

One reason for this lack of popular hostility and suspicion toward the Communists was, of course, the reverse side of the widespread anti-Nationalist sentiment. But another was the favorable picture the Communists presented of themselves to the Chinese population. The policies they pursued in the areas under their control were responsible for this. They did not destroy the traditional tenure system and expropriate or eliminate the landlords and moneylenders. They only reduced the rents to a fixed maximum and lowered the interest rates which could be charged on borrowed money. They permitted private enterprise and allowed all factions to participate in local government. Though they did assure Communist control by retaining the power to approve all candidates, their activities nevertheless seemed to support their claim that they stood for democracy, freedom, and individual liberty. Certainly, their economic and political practices demonstrated little Marxist bias. They appeared, instead, in the guise of genuine democrats; and their pose as agrarian reformers was widely accepted—precisely because, as an agrarian-based party, they actually did act as agrarian reformers!

If the Communists acted as if their only wish was to reform China along democratic and capitalistic lines, this was, of course, a tactical device. But the point remains that it was effective and achieved its purposes: it attracted minority support among the various strata of China's population disaffected by Nationalist policies, and it gained extensive acquiescence among the rest of the population. Chiang had alienated most of his popular support; in their bitterness and disillusionment, most of the people had become indifferent to his fate. The Communists, by cleverly hiding their real intentions, exploited this feeling of neutrality. For their purposes, a large neutral public was almost as beneficial as positive majority support; the only thing that really mattered was that this support had been withdrawn from Chiang.

The Communist position for the final military struggle was further strengthened when, near the end of the Pacific war, the Russian Army marched into Manchuria. Once established, the Russians did two things which badly hurt China. First, they dismantled Manchuria's industry and transported the machinery back to Russia to help restore their own badly destroyed industry; as a result, Manchuria, China's industrial heartland, was unable to contribute to the country's economic recovery. Second, the Russians allowed the Chinese Communists to infiltrate into the countryside, and handed them large stocks of Japanese arms and ammunition. Conversely, the Russians delayed the return of Nationalist troops, who had to launch a major offensive to establish their control over Manchuria. The government forces did capture the cities, but the Communists remained in control of the countryside. The Soviet invasion of Manchuria thus was a serious blow to the Nationalists.

The blame for these events has often been attributed to President Roosevelt and the Yalta "betrayal," which granted Russia, among other things, a restoration of the rights Russia had held in Manchuria before her defeat by Japan in 1904-05: the lease of Port Arthur as a Soviet naval base; the internationalization of the commercial port Dairen, which, unlike Russia's own Siberian port of Vladivostok, was not ice-bound part of the year; and the joint Sino-Soviet operation of the Chinese-Eastern and South-Manchurian Railroads, which served these three cities. To take this charge seriously, though, one has to deny certain clear facts of wartime military strategy: namely, that American military men were unsure that the atomic bomb would be a success; that they believed an invasion of Japan would be necessary to bring about Japan's surrender; that they expected to suffer at least 1 million casualties, and feared even more if the Japanese reinforced the home-island garrison with troops from Manchuria and northern China; and that they therefore wanted the Red Army to tackle these mainland forces before our invasion. The American Government was willing to pay the Russians the price they demanded if this would help save the lives of American soldiers, and this willingness was further increased by its suspicion that the Russians planned to restore their Czarist position in Manchuria by declaring war on Japan at the moment when the United States seemed on the verge of victory. The Russian take-over would then be a practically bloodless operation, with a minimal contribution to Japan's defeat. American officials wanted Russia to pay some kind of price, at least, for what she could actually take for nothing. Finally, they wanted to secure a promise from the Russians that they would sign a treaty of alliance and friendship with the Nationalist Government. The purpose of this treaty was to secure the Soviet Union's support for Chiang Kai-shek and to isolate his Communist opponents; this would enable Chiang to consolidate his grip on China and perhaps allow him to defeat his domestic enemy. The Russians did, in fact, sign such a treaty, but then proceeded to violate it by aiding their Chinese comrades. However, Stalin apparently did not believe that this help strengthened the Chinese Communists sufficiently to defeat the Nationalists. He is reported to have counseled Mao Tse-tung to join Chiang in a coalition government and accept Chiang's supremacy; in this respect, Stalin's policy seemed to have been the same as Truman's. Mao is said to have nodded his assent to Stalin's advice and then disregarded it; he was more confident than Stalin in a final victory.

So was Chiang, as the decisive stage of the civil war began in 1947. The Nationalist Army had a strength of approximately 2.7 million troops, while the Communists had 1.1 million men, including 400,000 guerrillas; the Nationalists held a superiority of rifle firepower of more than three to one. However, the Nationalists should not have been so confident. In the first place, Chiang tended to choose his top generals for their personal loyalty rather than their ability. He constantly interfered in the chain of command. He would send orders to officers in the field countermanding those of the local commanders, or change generals in the middle of a battle or campaign. This lack of continuity in the field command and Chiang's own interventions caused uncertainty, confusion, and resentment. In the second place, Nationalist strategy was unsound and could not have been better selected to ensure defeat. Chiang and his commanders were imbued with the "wall" psychology: their military strategy was to employ their forces only to capture cities and then to hold these cities. Instead of conducting a war of maneuver in order to find the Communist armies and destroy them in battle, the Nationalist forces immobilized their strength by walling themselves up in the cities. Consequently, they failed either to hurt the Communists' strength or to weaken their hold on the countryside. At the same time, however, their armies in the cities degenerated from the status of field armies capable of offensive operations to that of garrison troops; this sapped them of any aggressive spirit.

At the end of the war, Chiang did have armies capable of offensive operations—primarily the forces trained and equipped by the United States during the last years of the hostilities. After Japan's surrender, Chiang sent these troops into Manchuria, despite the warnings of his American military advisers. They believed—correctly, as it turned out—that Chiang would be overextending himself. They counseled the Nationalist leader, first, to concentrate his efforts on stabilizing south China by instituting a large-scale political, economic, and social reform program; and second, to recover north China and consolidate his political and military position there through similar reforms before attempting to recover Manchuria. By disregarding their advice, Chiang himself turned Manchuria into the crucial theater of war. But poor generalship, including that of Chiang plus the static defense, meant that it was only a question of time until the Nationalist armies would be defeated. These forces were almost completely dependent for their supplies upon the railroad. But the Nationalists did not possess sufficient forces to hold both the cities and the railroad. This allowed the Communists to cut the supply line where it was either unguarded or weakly defended. As a result, beginning in the summer of 1948, the Nationalists were forced to employ an airlift to drop military supplies to their troops. Moreover, since these forces remained bottled up in the cities and were never used to counter Communist control of the countryside, the garrison troops and civilian populace found themselves without food. However, the airlift was incapable of parachuting in the required military equipment and ammunition as well as the necessary food stocks. This was an intolerable military situation, but the Nationalists refused to withdraw their troops until it was too late.

Throughout 1946 and 1947, the Communists limited their operations largely to raiding supply depots and communication lines, ambushing Nationalist forces, engaging in skirmishes, and attacking isolated garrisons. These local tactical successes heightened the Communist forces' confidence and morale, just as it added to their opponent's demoralization. By 1948, the Communists had so increased the strength of their forces and firepower that they no longer had to rely solely upon hit-and-run tactics; they now sought out the Nationalist forces in order to completely annihilate them by concentrating superior masses of troops against them and attacking without respite. Throughout the whole campaign, the Communists kept the initiative; it was they who constantly chose the time and place of attack. By February 1, 1949, they controlled Manchuria. Nationalist strength had by then declined to 1.5 million men, including 500,000 service troops. Up until mid-September, 1948, the Nationalists had been able to replace their combat losses and thereby maintain their army at a strength of 2.7 million men. In other words, in only four and a half months, the Nationalists had lost 45 per cent of their troops. Meanwhile, Communist strength had risen to 1.6 million regular troops—partly as the result of defections from the Nationalist armies. Eighty per cent of the American equipment furnished to the government forces during and after the war had been lost, with an estimated 75 per cent of it falling into the Communists' hands. General Barr, the head of the American military mission in China, summed up the situation succinctly: "No battle has been lost since my arrival due to lack of ammunition or equipment. Their [the Nationalists'] military debacle, in my opinion, can all be attributed to the world's worst leadership and many other morale-destroying factors that led to a complete loss of the will to fight." Nowhere was this more clearly demonstrated than in Chiang's failure, after his loss of northern China, even to attempt a defense of south China by making a stand along the Yangtze River. Chiang thereby forfeited the mainland, and he withdrew to Formosa, an island lying 100 miles off the mainland coast. In the fall of 1949, Mao Tse-tung proclaimed the People's Republic of China.

One question about Nationalist China's defeat remains: Could the United States have prevented it? The answer is "Probably"—if American officers had taken over the command of the Nationalist armies; if the United States had been willing to commit large-scale land, air, and sea forces to fight in China; and if the United States had been willing to commit even greater financial aid than the approximate $2 billion it had already given in grants and credits since V-J Day. But these conditions could not have been met. Our helter-skelter demobilization left us with insufficient forces either for supplying the officers for the direction of the Nationalist forces or for intervention in China. The United States had only one and one-third divisions at home. Nor did the American people seem to be in any mood to rearm in 1947-48, particularly to fight a war in China.

The problem of extending further economic aid to Chiang was equally vexing. His corrupt, inefficient, and reactionary government did not provide a politically effective instrument through which to carry out the social and economic reforms China needed. Aiding Chiang seemed to be "pouring money down the drain." In contrast, our economic aid to Europe, which the Administration considered the area most vital to American security, had a good chance of achieving its objective—political and economic recovery for Britain and the Continent. It would probably have been unwise in these circumstances to divert a very large slice of the government's not unlimited dollar funds to attempt to restore a government which had lost the confidence of its own people. It is therefore difficult to disagree with Secretary Acheson's conclusion: "The unfortunate but inescapable fact is that the ominous result of the civil war in China was beyond the control of the Government of the United States. Nothing that this country did or could have done within the reasonable limits of its capabilities could have changed that result; nothing that was left undone by this country has contributed to it. It was the product of internal Chinese forces, forces which this country tried to influence but could not. A decision was arrived at within China, if only a decision by default."

Re-evaluation of American Far Eastern Policy

Despite Chiang's debacle and the disintegration of the Far Eastern balance of power, the United States Government took an optimistic view of developments. Shortly after the Nationalist collapse, Secretary Acheson expressed his belief that despite the common ideological points of view of the Chinese and Russian regimes, they would eventually clash with one another. He pointed out that the Kremlin was already "detaching the northern provinces of China from China and . . . attaching them to the Soviet Union. This process is complete in Outer Mongolia. It is nearly complete in Manchuria, and I am sure that in Inner Mongolia and Sinkiang, there are happy reports from Soviet agents to Moscow." The Secretary emphasized that "this fact that the Soviet Union is taking the northern provinces of China is the single most significant, most important fact, in the relation of any foreign power with Asia."

Acheson predicted that Russia's appetite for a sphere of influence in Manchuria and northern China would alienate Chinese nationalism. The implications of this point of view are clear. The first is that if the Chinese Communists were genuinely concerned with the preservation of China's national interest, they would resist Soviet penetration. Mao Tse-tung might, therefore, be a potential Tito. On the other hand, if Mao proved himself to be subservient to Russia, he would lose the support of the Chinese people. Since he would have shown that he served not the interests of China but those of another power, his regime would be identified with foreign rule. Given time, Acheson declared, the Chinese people would throw off this "foreign yoke." Thus, whichever of these two developments occurred, the United States could only gain from the antithesis between Communism and Chinese nationalism.

This analysis of Sino-Soviet relations indicated that the United States must first disentangle itself from Chiang Kai-shek. Until this disassociation had been completed, the United States would remain identified with the government rejected by the Chinese people. This could only foster the growth of anti-American sentiment in China. It was precisely this which had to be avoided, for the attention of the Chinese people should not be diverted from the Soviet Union's detachment of the northern provinces. Russia's actions would unmask her real purposes. Under no circumstances, Acheson emphasized, must we "seize the unenviable position which the Russians have carved out for themselves. We must not undertake to deflect from the Russians to ourselves the righteous anger, and the wrath, and the hatred of the Chinese people which must develop." Only by disengaging ourselves from Chiang Kai-shek could the United States exploit the alleged clash of interests between China and Russia.

The first step taken by the Administration to implement this policy was the release of a White Paper which argued that the Nationalists had lost control of the mainland despite adequate American economic and military aid. The clear implication was that Chiang was no longer worthy of American support; hence, American recognition of Chiang's government as the official government of China should be withdrawn. Conversely, it was suggested that the Communists should be recognized as the official government of China, both as a matter of fact and as a gesture of friendship. A second act was an announcement that American forces would not be used to defend Formosa, and that the Administration would no longer provide the Nationalists with military aid or advice: "The United States Government will not pursue a course which will lead to involvement in the civil conflict in China." This opened the way for the Chinese Communists to take Formosa—an event which was expected before the end of 1950. The Communist Government would then be the only claimant to represent China, and the United States could extend it recognition. Chiang, through whom containment had been impossible because he had been not a container but a sieve, would have been eliminated; containment of Russia could then be implemented through "Mao Tse-tito." But before this could happen, war had broken out in another area in the Far East—Korea.

The Korean War and the Truman-MacArthur Controversy

Korea had been a divided nation since 1945. Soviet forces had entered Korea two days after Japan surrendered. The nearest American troops at the time were in Okinawa, 600 miles away, and in the Philippines, 1,500 to 2,000 miles away. Consequently, the two powers decided to divide the country temporarily at the 38th Parallel; the Russians would disarm the Japanese above the Parallel, the United States below. With the beginning of the cold war, this division became permanent. All American attempts to negotiate an end to the division and establish a democratic and united Korea failed.

As a result, the United States took the problem to the United Nations in late 1947 and called upon that organization to sponsor a free election throughout all of Korea. The General Assembly thereupon established a Temporary Commission in Korea and charged it with the responsibility of holding and supervising such an election. The Russians, however, refused to grant the Commission access to North Korea, and the election was thus limited to South Korea. Afterward, the United States recognized South Korea as the official Republic and the government of Syngman Rhee as its legitimate representative. The American Government also extended to Rhee economic, technical, and military aid to bolster his non-

Communist government and help Korea establish a democratic society. Thus, while South Korea was not an ally of the United States, there could be little doubt that the young Republic was America's protégé.

It was this country which the North Korean Communists attacked in late June of 1950. The Communist aggression took the American Government by complete surprise. American policy-makers had believed that the Soviet leaders, like themselves, thought only in terms of all-out war. It was precisely this single-minded American preoccupation with total war which had accounted for Korea's being left outside the American Pacific defense perimeter, which ran from the Aleutians to Japan, through the Ryukyus (Okinawa) to the Philippines. This made Korea militarily dispensable within the pattern of American security, for in a global war its fate would be decided in other theaters of war. A Soviet occupation of Korea would not raise Korea's strategic significance, since the peninsula could be neutralized by American air and sea power. American troops had therefore been withdrawn from Korea, because in a major war they would be vulnerable to Russian land power and would probably be trapped. The resulting absence of pledged American military support to resist North Korean aggression rendered South Korea highly vulnerable; indeed, it left South Korea as an attractive vacuum inviting Communist expansion. On June 25, the North Korean Army struck.

Overnight, the survival of South Korea became identified with the survival of the United States itself. For North Korea's aggression, which could hardly have been launched without Soviet encouragement and support, altered the basis upon which Korea's stategic significance had been calculated. Korea's value could no longer be assessed in terms of its relative importance during a total war. The cold war focused attention upon the wider political and military implications of a Communist occupation of South Korea and upon the threat such an occupation would pose for the entire containment policy. If the principal purpose of containment was to prevent further Soviet expansion, American inaction in the face of Soviet aggression could only encourage further aggressive acts in the future. The appetites of dictators—as both Hitler and Stalin amply demonstrated—are insatiable. And if containment was possible only through an alignment of

United States power with that of its allies, then failure to respond to South Korea's pleas for help must result in the disintegration of the alliance system and the isolation of the United States. If the United States merely stood by while South Korea fell, this country would demonstrate to the world that it was either afraid of Russian power or unconcerned with the safety of its allies. American guarantees to help preserve their national integrity and political independence would thereafter be regarded as valueless; and this would leave nations whose security depended upon our willingness to live up to our commitments with no alternative but to turn to neutralism for protection—a state in which they would be subject to increasing Soviet pressure and possibly eventual domination.

This reasoning applied particularly to Japan. With the demise of Nationalist China and the disintegration of the Far Eastern balance of power, the United States was about to turn Japan into an ally and rearm it in an effort to recreate some semblance of strength in the Pacific. This reasoning applied equally to the NATO countries in Europe. If NATO collapsed, the balance of power would shift drastically in favor of Russia. In these circumstances, the consequences of American inaction were extremely grave. In fact, the United States had no choice but to oppose force with force—if it wished to prevent the disintegration of the global balance of power and its own strategic isolation.

Nevertheless, the limited Soviet aggression did not fit our strategic doctrine, based on a one-sided concentration upon air-atomic striking power. The Russians had cleverly faced the United States with the dilemma of either risking a total war for a limited objective or taking no action at all and thus surrendering South Korea. American policy was prepared to deal only with an all-out Soviet surprise attack upon the United States or Western Europe; such an attack would be met by the power of SAC. But American strategy was completely unprepared to deal with the kind of less than total challenge which the Russians had now posed in Asia. The North Korean aggression, in effect, meant that massive retaliation outside of Europe was not an effective policy. For the deterrent effect of our retaliatory power depends upon whether an enemy believes that this country will actually "unleash" this power if he commits an aggression. The limited attack in

Korea clearly demonstrated that the Soviet leaders were not deterred by the policy of massive retaliation, despite America's far greater atomic stockpile and ability to deliver it. They did not believe that the United States would risk all-out war to save Korea. For the Korean type of challenge could only be met by local response and primarily through the commitment of American ground forces. Containment depended not just upon the capacity to deter total war with strategic air power; it required, in addition, an army to meet precisely this kind of limited incursion.

But it was the Army forces that the Administration had been cutting since the end of World War II. General Marshall recalled in 1951 that the Army had been so small in the years preceding the Korean War that there had been only one and one-third divisions in the United States. The Chiefs of Staff had had so few troops at their command that they had even been worried about obtaining enough men to guard airstrips at Fairbanks, Alaska. According to Marshall, "We had literally almost no military forces outside of our Navy and outside of an effective but not too large Air Force, except the occupation garrisons, and . . . even in Japan they were only at about 60 per cent strength."

Yet, if the United States was to escape the dilemma of total war or surrender, the Japanese occupation divisions— undermanned and undertrained, but luckily near the scene of battle—had to be committed. For two days, on June 27 and 28, the United States tried to stem the North Korean advance with air and sea forces alone. But on June 29, General MacArthur, the American Commander-in-Chief in the Far East, reported that Korea would be lost unless ground forces were employed to halt the enemy army. These forces were then sent in under the aegis of the United Nations. This was done for two reasons. First, because by virtue of the free election it had sponsored in South Korea, the United Nations had been intimately concerned with the birth of the young state. Secondly, one of the aims of American foreign policy was to associate its cold-war policies with the symbolic, humanitarian values of the United Nations. Though it is traditional for nations to attempt to justify their policies in such a manner, the United States has shown a marked propensity for doing so. American depreciation of power and reluctance to recognize it as a factor in human affairs makes it psychologically necessary to rationalize actions in the international arena in terms of ideological objectives and universal moral principles. American power must be "righteous" power used not for purposes of power politics and selfish national advantage but for the peace and welfare of all mankind. Inherent in this public image of the United States as a noble and unselfish crusader on behalf of moral principles was an extreme danger, however—namely, that if the enemy were not properly punished through total defeat, the reaction to the war would be one of frustration and disillusionment, which could only jeopardize the containment policy itself.

This was precisely what was to happen, although, after initial setbacks, the war went well for a while. In a daring operation on September 15, General MacArthur, now United Nations Supreme Commander, landed an army at the west-coast port of Inchon, 150 miles behind the North Korean lines. The landing quickly achieved its aims: Korea's second largest port was captured; the North Koreans were confronted with a two-front war; and supplies were cut off from their army at the Pusan beachhead, where the rest of the U.N. forces had been bottled up for over two months. These forces now launched their own offensive and drove northward, thereby trapping more than half the enemy army. The rest of the shattered Communist army was in flight. On September 30, the U.N. forces reached the 38th Parallel.

The question now confronting the United States was whether to cross the Parallel. The war had been fought to restore South Korea; this implied a negotiated settlement on the Parallel. This goal was now abandoned. The military situation favored the fulfillment of an American goal of several years' standing: the unification of the whole of Korea. The Administration therefore shifted its emphasis from containing the expansion of Soviet power to the forceful liberation of a Soviet satellite. Inchon, in short, transformed the whole character of the war—from a defensive action seeking only to re-establish the *status quo,* to an offensive one designed to effect a permanent change in the *status quo.*

The United States Government believed that it was politically safe to attempt this. The Administration did not believe that the Chinese Communist leaders would consider the United Nations advance as a threat to their security, because they were Chinese first and Communists second. Mao and his colleagues were already thought to be so involved in their struggle with the Soviet Union over the detachment of northern China, Manchuria, and Sinkiang that their eyes were fixed on their own northern provinces rather than on North Korea. "I should think it would be sheer madness on the part of the Chinese Communists to do that [interfere]," Secretary Acheson had said a few days before Inchon. He repeated that in northern China "a great cloud from the north, Russian penetration, is operating." And he continued: "Now I give the people in Peiping [Communist China's capital] credit for being intelligent enough to see what is happening to them. Why should they want to further their own dismemberment and destruction by getting at cross purposes with all the free nations of the world who are inherently their friends and have always been friends of the Chinese against this imperialism coming down from the Soviet Union I cannot see." In short, there was nothing to fear. The new objective of a militarily unified Korea was sanctioned by a United Nations resolution on October 7.

But American policy-makers miscalculated, for the Chinese sent their armies into North Korea under the guise of "volunteers," and in late November they launched a major offensive which drove the U.N. forces back below the 38th Parallel. Throughout December, 1950, and early January, 1951, there was no certainty that U.N. troops could hold the peninsula; but the tired, defeated, and outnumbered troops managed to rally and stem the Chinese offensives. By March, they had once more advanced to the 38th Parallel. The Administration was again faced with a decision: whether to seek a militarily unified Korea or to accept a divided Korea.

There was no doubt about what our field commander wanted to do. MacArthur insisted that the political aim of the war was the establishment of a unified Korea. He maintained that failure to prosecute the military campaign with the vigor necessary to achieve this objective would constitute rank appeasement: it would be a betrayal of our pledge to the Koreans; it would provoke further acts of aggression by the Chinese, who would regard our abandonment of our October 7 objective as a sign of weakness; and it would alienate the free nations of Asia. Above all, MacArthur felt that the United States should take advantage of China's intervention to counter the latter's growing strength. China was, in his opinion, "a new and dominant power which for its own purposes has allied with Soviet Russia, but which in its own concepts and methods has become aggressively imperialistic with a lust for expansion and increased power normal to this type of imperialism. . . . The aggressiveness now displayed not only in Korea, but in Indo-China, Tibet, and pointing toward the south, reflects predominantly the same lust for power which has animated every would-be conqueror· since the beginning of time." He wished, therefore, to "severely cripple and largely neutralize China's capability to wage aggressive war and thus save Asia from the engulfment otherwise facing it." This purpose, MacArthur felt, could be achieved with minimum risk, since the Soviet Union would not dare to resort to war until its atomic and industrial power more nearly matched our own. MacArthur's aim, in short, was not only to unify Korea but to change the entire strategic picture in the Far East while we still held the global balance of power.

The strategy with which MacArthur expected to accomplish these objectives consisted of: a naval blockade of the Chinese coast; air bombardment of China's industrial complex, communication network, supply depots, and troop assembly points; reinforcement of his forces with Chinese Nationalist troops; and "diversionary action possibly leading to counter-invasion" by Chiang against the mainland.

The Administration, however, rejected MacArthur's proposals because they were considered too risky. It was feared that bombing China and inflicting a defeat upon Russia's principal ally would probably precipitate World War III. The Sino-Soviet Treaty of February, 1950, bound the Soviet Union to come to the aid of China if the latter were attacked by Japan "or any other state which should unite with Japan" (an obvious reference to the United States). But even without this treaty, China was the Soviet Union's largest and most important ally. Russian self-interest in the Far East and the necessity of maintaining Russian prestige in the Communist sphere would make it difficult for the Soviet Union to ignore a direct attack upon the Chinese mainland. There were, Secretary Acheson explained, a number of courses which the Russians could follow. "They could turn over to the Chinese large numbers of planes and 'volunteer' crews for retaliatory action in Korea and outside. They might participate with the

Soviet Air Force and the submarine fleet." Or, the "Kremlin could elect to parallel the action taken by Peiping and intervene with half a million or more ground-force 'volunteers'; or it could go the whole way and launch an all-out war. Singly, or in combination, these reactions contain explosive possibilities, not only for the Far East, but for the rest of the world as well."

But even if the Soviet Union remained a spectator, the United States could not extend the war. A "war of attrition" waged by Chinese manpower in Korea would "bleed us dry" and make it impossible to build a strong military defense in Europe. A large-scale diversion of American power to Asia would expose Europe to Soviet armies and might very well incite an attack at a moment of maximum American weakness on the Continent. The United States had to conserve its strength to check its principal enemy, the Soviet Union; this country could not afford to dissipate its power in a peripheral area against a secondary enemy. Said General Bradley, Chairman of the Joint Chiefs of Staff: Nothing would delight the Kremlin more than the "enlargement of the war in Korea to include Red China. . . . It would necessarily tie down additional forces, especially our sea power and air power, while the Soviet Union would not be obliged to put a single man into the conflict. . . . A 'limited war' with Red China would increase the risk we are taking by engaging too much of our power in an area that is not the critical strategic prize." In short, MacArthur's strategy would involve us in the wrong war, at the wrong place, at the wrong time, and with the wrong enemy.

This view was shared by Britain and France. America's chief allies were naturally reluctant to see American power diverted to the Far East before Europe was secure against Russian attack; and they had no desire to risk such an early outbreak of World War III for an area that was of minor strategic significance to them. Thus, if the United States decided to carry the war to China, it would have to act unilaterally. But the objective of balancing Soviet might or winning a total war was predicated on NATO's unity and combined strength. As President Truman put it, "If we go it alone in Asia, we may destroy the unity of the free nations against aggression. Our European allies are nearer to Russia than we are. They are in far greater danger. If we act without regard to the danger that faces them, they may act without regard to the dangers that we face. . . . We cannot go it alone in Asia and go it with company in Europe."

Finally, the Joint Chiefs of Staff rejected MacArthur's proposals because they were judged militarily ineffective. A naval blockade would be of very limited use for two reasons: first, because China was so lacking in industrialization and specialization that a blockade would not have sufficient immediate impact; and second, because China's essential supplies came overland from Russia. Air bombardment of China's population and industrial centers would have an equally limited effect, for Communist China's arsenal lay in the Soviet Union. Even with the complete destruction of China's industrial heartland in Manchuria, Russia would still be in a position to supply China with the military equipment and ammunition she required. It was therefore decided to concentrate our airpower upon the 200 miles of supply line in North Korea in order to interdict the Chinese logistical system. The employment of Nationalist troops was rejected because they had already demonstrated their ineffectiveness in China. Moreover, the Chinese people were hardly likely to welcome Chiang back as, for example, the French people had welcomed Napoleon upon his return to the mainland; unlike Napoleon, Chiang had forfeited his popularity. It was precisely this lack of popular confidence that had ensured his defeat; a year's absence had not further endeared him to the Chinese people.

Inherent in the Administration's rejection of MacArthur's strategic recommendations was the reversal of its position of October 7, that its objective was a militarily unified Korea, and a reassertion of its original attitude that the aim of the war was to restore the *status quo*. The Communists had attempted to erase the 38th Parallel and incorporate South Korea into the Communist bloc; neither the North Koreans nor the Chinese Communists had succeeded in achieving this objective. The Communists had also hoped to destroy the Western Alliance and isolate the United States; in this, too, they had failed. NATO had been preserved and greatly strengthened by its rearmament program and the stationing of four new American divisions in Europe. And the primary purpose of U.N. action in Korea, to put the Communists on notice that the Western powers would not tolerate Communist expansion by force, had been achieved. Thus, the wisest course seemed to be to attempt to end the war where it had begun.

However, MacArthur refused to accept this dismissal of his strategy and limitation of the war to the Korean peninsula. He continued to assert that his strategy was both feasible and without great risk. If the United States really possessed the superior atomic force—as he believed, and the Administration claimed—the Soviet Union would hardly precipitate a global war simply because American bombers had attacked Chinese cities. MacArthur, in fact, charged that the Administration had no faith in the validity of the very instrument that it proclaimed as the basis of its foreign policy. Thus, it divorced theory from practice: theoretically, it maintained that SAC had the power to deter the Soviet Union from launching an all-out war; but practically, it acted upon the assumption that the Russians had so little respect for our strategic striking forces that they would rather risk suicide than tolerate a limited extension of the war. The Far Eastern Commander-in-Chief maintained that if the United States held the atomic balance, SAC would continue to deter Russia and ensure that the limited hostilities, although somewhat extended, would remain confined to the Chinese-Korean theater of war. MacArthur pointed to the paradox that the side with the inferior strategic striking strength had paralyzed the will to act of the side which possessed the more effective atomic retaliatory power.

General MacArthur therefore continued to urge the President and the Joint Chiefs of Staff to lift the restrictions they had imposed upon him; and when they refused, he attempted to force their hand by taking his case into the public arena and appealing over their heads to the opposition party in Congress and to the American people themselves. This produced an intolerable situation. It is the President who is responsible for the formulation of foreign policy; he is the nation's chief diplomat and Commander-in-Chief. No government can allow a field commander to challenge its policies, to appeal to the public and the opposition for a change in these policies, thus undermining its control over the military. The soldier must obey his orders. He is judged not by the nature of the policy he executes—only by how well he executes it. If he cannot accept this policy, he must resign; otherwise, he must be dismissed. In early April, President Truman did precisely that. The resulting furor brought to the surface the public's disillusionment with containment.

The Reaction to Containment

MacArthur's dismissal was met with a storm of disapproval throughout the United States. The President received a flood of vituperous telegrams and letters informing him in no un-certain terms that his decision had been a mistaken one. In his first public appearance after MacArthur's dismissal, when President Truman attended the first baseball game of the season to throw out the opening ball, he was booed. Several state legislatures condemned him for his "irresponsible and capricious action." Republicans in Congress announced their intention of initiating impeachment proceedings against him and Secretary Acheson. Both Truman and Acheson were burned in effigy in many communities throughout the land. In contrast, MacArthur was received everywhere, not as a man who had openly attempted to undermine the cherished American principle of civilian supremacy over the military, but as a great returning hero. In each of the cities he visited—San Francisco, Washington, Chicago, Boston—millions turned out to cheer him. In New York City alone, an estimated 7.5 million people lined the streets to see him—twice the number that had witnessed General Eisenhower's triumphal return from Europe in 1945; 2,850 tons of ticker tape, confetti, and streamers were showered upon MacArthur; New York looked as if it had been hit by a snowstorm in April.

This almost hysterical reception was primarily the result of the nation's frustration with the containment policy, which was psychologically and emotionally in contradiction with American values and experience in foreign affairs. Tradition-ally, the United States had abstained from involvement in foreign affairs. Attention had, instead, been focused on do-mestic development. The business of America had been America—not foreign countries. When foreign affairs had oc-casionally interrupted this preoccupation with domestic con-cerns, such matters had been quickly settled: if a Latin American state "misbehaved," a few thousand marines soon "corrected" the misdeeds of the offender; or if—as did hap-pen twice in this century—Germany set out to conquer continental Europe, our nation harnessed all its resources, maximized its military strength, and crushed the enemy in the shortest possible time. Whatever the technique employed, the main point was that the conflict was settled quickly and completely. Only if the external crisis were solved immediately and totally could the American people return to their more important tasks: the internal development of their country and earning their living. In this context, foreign affairs were merely an annoying but temporary diversion.

Containment ran directly contrary to this experience. The cold war did not draw a clear-cut line between peace and war. It allowed the United States neither to abstain from foreign entanglement nor to harness its giant strength for one quick and all-out military effort to "punish" the enemy who had forced it to divert its attention from more pressing domestic matters. The Administration's aim was not the destruction of Russia and its satellites, but only the creation of a balance of power to effect the "containment" of further Soviet attempts to expand. The objective of the government was not to erase the Soviet Union with a swift blow, but to accept the basic fact of coexistence. Truman and Acheson sought only to strengthen the United States and its allies in order to improve the terms of coexistence and the possibility of survival, not to end the Soviet threat once and for all.

To be sure, the short-term aim of containment was to deter the Russian leaders from attempting to achieve world domination by resort to total war and to lead them instead to the negotiating table to settle all outstanding East-West differences; and the long-term objective was to increase the stresses and strains within Soviet society to such a degree that its leaders would have to moderate their aims or witness the disintegration of their political system. But these two aims were actually coincidental. The Administration did not expect to achieve the first objective before the realization of the second objective. To negotiate with the Russians, Secretary Acheson had once said, was like dealing with a force of nature: "You can't argue with a river, it is going to flow. You can dam it up, you can put it to useful purposes, you can deflect it, but you can't argue with it. . . . So far as agreement is concerned, I think we have discovered that even the simplest thing growing out of the war, which is to make peace . . . has become impossible." In short, only negotiations could end the cold war; and the cold war could not be ended until the Communists had, in effect, ceased being Communists. The Soviet threat thus promised to be a lasting one, and so would America's involvement in a "neither war nor peace" situation.

The frustrations of such a continued defensive and negative policy, which left the initiative to the Soviet Union, were bad enough; failures made it intolerable. This was especially the case with China. Americans had long regarded China as their special ward. Whereas American foreign policy toward Europe during the last fifty years had been limited to two short but decisive military interventions occasioned by Germany's threats to the European balance of power, American involvement in the Far East, and particularly in China, had been active since the turn of the century. The original interest in China had not been political but commercial: China was potentially a huge market for American products. But our policy toward China had contained some elements of altruistic intent as well: a genuine interest in the welfare and Christian salvation of the Chinese people. In fact, the United States had long regarded itself as the protector of China from foreign exploitation and invasion. Through the Open-Door policy—aimed at preventing Great Britain, France, Russia, Germany, and Japan from shutting American commerce out of China and at obtaining an equal opportunity to sell on the Chinese market—the United States had become politically committed to preserve the territorial integrity and political independence of China. Since the American people had never been prepared to fight for this objective, however, the United States had failed to protect China from external pressures and invasions: the Russians had established a sphere of influence in Manchuria about 1900, and the Japanese had replaced the Russians as the actual rulers of this strategic area after the Russo-Japanese War. During and after World War I, Japan had expanded its influence and control over China, and in 1931 Japan had initiated the Sino-Japanese War to consummate its ambition to turn China into a Japanese vassal or colony. The Open-Door policy, then, had been largely a verbal policy; indeed, since the United States had never been prepared to support this policy with force, it had usually disregarded its commitment whenever Russia or Japan had challenged it. But Americans, even in those days, believed that words were a substitute for an effective policy; out of this arose the illusion that the United States had long been China's protector and friend, extending to the Chinese people the bountiful benefits of Western Christianity, political ideals, science, and medicine.

Americans were, therefore, shocked by Chiang Kai-shek's collapse in 1949 and the establishment of Communist control of the Chinese mainland. Certainly, they were totally unprepared for, and deeply resentful of, the propaganda emanating from Peiping accusing the United States of being "the Chinese people's implacable enemy . . . a corrupt imperialistic nation, the world center of reaction and decadence . . . a paper tiger and entirely vulnerable to defeat." They had expected that a "loyal" and fundamentally democratic China, grateful to America for past protection and help, would emerge from World War II as a strong friend of this country and as a powerful and reliable ally in the Far East. The failure of these expectations in late 1949 came as a blow to the American public. Suddenly, the relative security founded on the successful application of containment policies in Europe—the Truman Doctrine, the Marshall Plan, the Berlin airlift, and NATO—seemed to have disintegrated. It appeared that the United States had stemmed the Communist menace in Europe, only to allow it to achieve a breakthrough in Asia. The resulting insecurity and anxiety were further heightened by two other events at about the same time: the news that Russia had exploded her first atomic bomb and thereby shattered the American monopoly of the weapon widely regarded as the principal deterrent to a Soviet attack; and the conviction in early 1950 of Alger Hiss—followed shortly by the trial of Judith Coplon and the confession of Klaus Fuchs—suggested continued Soviet espionage in high places. The outbreak of the Korean War and Communist China's subsequent intervention added more fuel to the fires of discontent.

The public did not understand the causes of its frustration; it could not comprehend the reasons for these alleged failures of American foreign policy. Whenever the United States had been drawn into the international arena in the past, its actions had met with quick success. We had beaten the British, the Mexicans, the Spaniards, the Germans, and the Japanese. America had never been invaded, defeated, or occupied as most other nations had been; it had, to be sure, committed mistakes, but with its great power, it had always been able to rectify these. To a nation in which one popular slogan expressed confidence in doing "the difficult today, the impossible tomorrow," failure was a new experience. America's history had been a witness to victories only; her unbroken string of successes seemed evidence of national omnipotence.

It was this unquestioned assumption that the United States was omnipotent that suggested the reason for America's political and military failures: treason within our own government! For if America was all-powerful, it could not be our lack of strength that accounted for our defeats. It could not be that there was a limit to our ability to influence events abroad far away from our shores. Our setbacks must have been the result of our own policies. Ostensibly, the reason that China fell was that the "pro-Communist" administrations of Franklin Roosevelt and Harry Truman had either deliberately or unwittingly "sold China down the river." This charge—made primarily by the Republican Party, and particularly by Senators Taft, McCarthy, and Nixon—was simplicity itself: America's China policy had ended in Communist control of the mainland; the Administration leaders and the State Department were responsible for the formulation and execution of foreign policy; thus, the government must be filled with Communists and Communist sympathizers who "tailored" American policy to advance the global aims of the Soviet Union. In short, disloyal or grossly incompetent American statesmen were responsible for the "loss" of China; it was to them, not to China, that the collapse of Nationalist China was due. Low Nationalist morale, administrative and military ineptness, and repressive policies which had alienated mass support had nothing to do with it; nor did the superior Communist organization, direction, morale, and ability to identify itself with popular aspirations.

This conspiratorial interpretation thus bridged the gap between the public's illusion of American omnipotence and the limits of America's power. The belief that Communist victories were caused by the treachery or stupidity of American policy-makers made it unnecessary both to recognize this fact or to re-evaluate our traditional approach to foreign policy. It was also highly flattering to our chauvinistic sense of pride, for it permitted the public to continue to believe in America's omnipotence—and in our opponent's inferiority.

Secretary Acheson had once said: "Our name for problems is significant. We call them headaches. You can take a powder, and they are gone. These pains [brought on by the world situation] are not like that. They . . . will stay with us until death. We have got to understand that all our lives danger, the uncertainty, the need for alertness, for efforts, for discipline will be upon us. This is new to us. It will be hard for us." MacArthur's return demonstrated that it was still very hard for us. The American people were still looking for the aspirin which would dissolve all our foreign-policy problems.

It was precisely because MacArthur identified himself with this illusion of omnipotence that he received such a tumultuous welcome upon his return to the United States. He understood the public's frustration, and he gave voice to it in familiar—one might even say, in "American"—words, words of victory holding forth a view of a quick and successful end to the bloodshed on the battlefield, words of confidence and praise for an America strong enough to accomplish anything she had the mind to do in this world, and words of condemnation for those who, driven by fear of Russia and troublesome allies, chained the proud and invincible American giant to the rock of "weakness" and "appeasement." War, he said, indicated that "you have exhausted all other potentialities of bringing the disagreements to an end," and once engaged, "there is no alternative than to apply every available means to bring it to a swift end. War's very objective is victory—not prolonged indecision. In war there is no substitute for victory." The very term "resisting aggression" indicated "that you can destroy the potentialities of the aggressor to continually hit you" and not "go on indefinitely, neither to win or lose." One cannot fight a "half war." The Administration's policy was based upon the assumption that "when you use force, you can limit that force." This introduced "a new concept into military operations—the concept of appeasement."

Here was the kind of words the public could understand. Once the diplomats had failed to keep the peace and war had erupted, the military expert took over and fought a technically efficient war. As a nonpolitical figure, he should not be burdened with extraneous political considerations. His sole aim was the complete destruction of the enemy's forces— in short, military victory. The enemy needed to be punished for provoking us. Only his total defeat would achieve this aim. Only in this way could the nation's principles be safe-guarded; America's full power, if necessary, had to be applied to destroy the aggressor who threatened these principles. De-liberate self-restraint was, in these circumstances, a betrayal of America's national honor. Evil must we wiped out; to allow its continued existence was intolerable. Such compro-mise implied weakness or softness. To accept it was "un-American."

The reaction to the Korean War was thus twofold. On the one hand, the public demanded a return to an "Ameri-can" policy, a "dynamic" or "positive" policy which would brook no compromises with the enemy and would withstand Allied pressure to "appease." Such a "tougher" policy, it was hoped, would restore America's dignity, prestige, and initia-tive on the world scene. On the other hand, the public wanted relief from the almost constant foreign-policy involvements and costs of the past few years. This indicated a lowering of international tension: ending the Korean War, reducing our commitments, and cutting expenditures. The contradictory nature of these aims was symptomatic of the intense desire to return to the traditional way of conducting foreign policy: either to concentrate on domestic affairs and to abstain from all foreign policy, or to assert America's power without fear or compromise. It was this double and paradoxical legacy which the Eisenhower Administration inherited from the Truman Administration.

V. THE STRATEGY OF BRINKMANSHIP

Eisenhower Liberation

During the Presidential election campaign of 1952, the Republicans cleverly exploited the public's frustration with containment—a frustration grounded in the popular illusion of national omnipotence. America's great insecurity and her present involvement in the Korean War, they asserted, was the result of the "tragic blunders" that Roosevelt and Truman had committed at the Teheran, Yalta, and Potsdam Conferences with the Russians. It was there that the Democratic leaders had deliberately and stealthily paved the way for Communism's postwar expansion by selling out Eastern Europe and betraying Chiang Kai-shek. The two Presidents had, according to the Republican Party platform, "flouted our peace-assuring pledges such as the Atlantic Charter, and [they] did so in favor of despots, who, it was well known, consider that murder, terror, slavery, concentration camps, and the ruthless and brutal denial of human rights are legitimate means to their desired ends. Teheran, Yalta, and Potsdam were the scenes of those tragic blunders with others to follow. The leaders of the Administration acted without the knowledge or consent of Congress or the American people. They traded our overwhelming victory for a new enemy and for new oppressions and new wars which were quick to come." In other words, America's wounds were self-inflicted.

Similarly, the Republicans charged that Truman's postwar foreign policy was self-defeating. It underwrote the false premise that American power was limited and committed the United States to continued coexistence and constant involvement in foreign policy. As John Foster Dulles, the chief Republican spokesman on foreign policy, put it: "We are not working, sacrificing, and spending in order to be able to live *without* this peril—but to be able to live *with* it, presumably forever." The Administration's policies were "treadmill policies, which, at best, might perhaps keep us in the same place until we drop exhausted." The failures of containment were many: it was a negative policy; it surrendered the initiative to the enemy; it merely reacted to counter the Communist danger wherever and whenever the latter chose to attack; it was so costly that it would bankrupt the country; and it aimed only at preserving the *status quo*. In short, Dulles condemned the policy of containment as "negative, futile, and immoral."

The aim of American foreign policy, Dulles stressed, should not be to coexist indefinitely with the Communist menace; it should be to eliminate that menace. And the United States could do this if it adopted the "psychological and political offensive." The Communists were winning the cold war because they were waging it with social ideas which were "stirring humanity everywhere"; and conversely, the United States was losing the cold war because its policies were static and materialistic. To reverse the trend, this nation had to reassert its traditional moral mission and identify itself with the universal longing for freedom. Dulles called for an American policy based on spiritual values—primarily on the Declaration of Independence and the philosophy of Abraham Lincoln. Such a policy would again make the United States the hope of the oppressed and the despair of aggressors. Dulles said: "We should let truths work in and through us. We should be *dynamic,* we should use ideas as weapons; and these *ideas* should conform to [our] moral principles."

The result of such a change in policy, based on universal principles, would be a rollback of Soviet power. The United States had only to proclaim its stand for freedom and announce that it would never be a party to any "deal" which confirmed Soviet despotism over alien peoples. Such a declaration would preserve the courage and hope of the satellite peoples and prevent them from accepting the Soviet regime. In Dulles' words, the United States "should make it publicly known that it wants and expects liberation to occur. The mere statement of that wish and expectation would change, in an electrifying way, the mood of the captive peoples. It would probably put heavy new burdens on the jailers and create new opportunities for liberation."

Never had the illusion of American omnipotence received a greater tribute. America's cause was righteous, and in order to be victorious she need only publicize this cause by launching a moral crusade. Right would then again prevail over might. The Republican program of action apparently envisaged the future Secretary of State, John "Joshua" Dulles, marching around the walls of the Kremlin empire, sounding the call of freedom upon his trumpet. The walls would then come tumbling down, the enslaved peoples would be liberated, and Soviet power would be forced to retreat. The world would once more be safe for democracy.

The Republicans thus appeared not only to promise an eventual end to the cold war—they also pledged themselves to do it at less cost. For they claimed that the Democrats' foreign policy of indefinite coexistence, with its vast outlay for armaments and economic aid, would undermine the nation's economy. The Republicans asserted that it was Russia's aim to destroy America by forcing this country to spend itself into bankruptcy—an aim furthered by Democratic policy. America's defense had to be provided with a healthy economic foundation. This would require a sharp cut in the present huge foreign aid and military expenditures. The Republicans, in brief, promised the nation at one and the same time an offensive strategy, a balanced budget, and reduction of taxes. They pledged a rollback of Soviet power on the one hand, and on the other, a cut in the appropriations for America's defense.

Such goals were not only incompatible; they were unattainable. The mere enunciation of the doctrine of liberation would not free any Soviet satellite; good intentions, unsupported by concrete political and military policies, possess a notorious impotence on the international scene. But perhaps this did not really matter, since the policy of liberation seems to have been devised primarily to roll back the Democrats in the United States, not the Red Army in Eastern Europe. And for this domestic purpose, liberation was a highly effective strategy.

For the country desperately wanted a more vigorous and forthright anti-Communist policy that promised an end to the cold war. At the same time, it was unprepared to take the risks involved: that is, a policy which actively sought the liberation of the satellite states would have to accept the very definite risk of all-out war with the Soviet Union. In these circumstances, the only kind of dynamism the country could afford was a verbal dynamism. And this was all the people seemed to want: it allowed them to delude themselves that the United States once again pursued a vigorous and forthright policy which would defeat our opponent. Liberation was the Republican Party's therapy for a public that refused to accept the facts of America's limited power in the world and rejected any changes in its traditional approach to foreign policy. That this policy of liberation was probably never meant to be more than a verbal appeal to the American people was clearly demonstrated at the time of the anti-Communist revolt in East Berlin and other East German cities in June, 1953, and during the national uprising in Hungary in late 1956. In neither case did the Eisenhower Administration act—except to condemn the Soviet Union for its suppression of Germans and Hungarians and to express its sympathy for the victims of Soviet despotism. In Berlin, it substituted food packages to the East Berliners for liberation; and in Hungary, it even reassured the Soviet Union that it had no intention of intervening. The *status quo* was thereby reaffirmed. Liberation had returned to the "womb" of containment.

The Administration did, however, carry out its promises of military and economic retrenchment. This involved three measures. The first of these was to end the Korean War, which would allow the Administration to cut the size of the army and avoid the cost of maintaining large standing ground forces. The second was to draw a clear line around the entire Sino-Soviet bloc. The Democrats had already drawn such a line from Norway to Turkey; the Republicans expected to strengthen this line and extend it to the Middle and Far East. The third measure was to preserve this global line around the Communist world with the deterrent power of the Strategic Air Command. The Russians and Chinese could cross the line only at the risk of total war with the United States; the fear of total destruction was expected to deter them.

This reliance upon strategic air power was also expected to appeal to the American public. In the first place, "massive retaliation" simply sounded more dynamic than containment; at the same time, it made possible a reduction of over-all military expenditures. It was obviously considerably cheaper to concentrate military spending upon a one-weapon system than to build up and maintain large balanced forces to meet any contingency. This was made very explicit by Secretary Dulles when he said:

> So long as our basic policy concepts were unclear, our military leaders could not be selective in building our military power. If an enemy could pick his time and place and method of warfare—and if our policy was to remain the traditional one of meeting aggression by direct and local opposition—then we needed to be ready to fight in the Arctic and in the Tropics; and in Asia, the Near East, and in Europe, by sea, by land, and by air; with old weapons and with new weapons.... This could not be continued for long without grave budgetary, economic, and social consequences.... [The "new look" that we will rely on will] depend primarily upon a great capacity to retaliate, instantly, by means and at places of our choosing. That permits a selection of military means instead of a multiplication of means.

The second appealing feature of massive retaliation was that it, in fact, rejected the concept of limited war, or "half war," and reasserted the old American doctrine of either abstaining or fighting an all-out war. This return to the more traditional American approach to war was natural in 1952. The Republicans had been elected largely because of the deep popular revulsion against the Korean War; it was clear that the people wanted no more Koreas. In these circumstances, the Administration felt that it had little choice but to rely almost exclusively on massive retaliation.

Basically, then, Eisenhower's policy was not to be very different from his predecessor's: containment of Communism by building a wall around the Sino-Soviet periphery and supporting that wall with nuclear air power. But in one essential aspect the new Administration's policy was different—and this difference was crucial. Truman and Acheson had also relied upon air-atomic striking power to deter a total attack upon either the United States or America's "first line of defense" in Europe. But in Asia, once the Communists had faced them with a limited aggression, they had met this challenge with local ground resistance. The Eisenhower Administration also expected to deter an all-out war with the threat of massive retaliation. But, unlike the Truman Administration, it would not fight local ground wars. It proposed to prevent any future limited attacks by threatening to retaliate against the Soviet Union or Communist China. This basic policy decision reflected Secretary Dulles' own strong conviction that the only effective means of stopping a prospective aggressor was to give him an advance warning that if he committed aggression, he would be subjected to such overwhelming retaliatory blows that his possible gains would be far outweighed by the punishment he would suffer. Dulles believed strongly that Korea would never have been invaded if the Communists had known that their attack would have been met with retaliatory air strikes on Moscow. It was the absence of such a warning that had led the Communists to miscalculate. The Eisenhower Administration did not intend to repeat this mistake. It meant to draw the line so clearly that the enemy could be left in no doubt whatsoever of what would happen to him if he crossed it. The expectation was that by going to the "brink of war," the United States would be able to deter future Koreas. This policy, which later became known as "brinkmanship," was to be applied first in an attempt to bring about a cease-fire in Korea.

Ending the Korean War

Truce talks in Korea had begun in the summer of 1951, but the negotiations had dragged on fruitlessly until they reached a final deadlock over the issue of prisoners of war. Traditionally, prisoners are returned to their homelands at the end of a war. But in Korea, 46,000 Chinese and North Korean prisoners refused repatriation. The United States, in turn, refused to compel them: such action would have been inconceivable from a humanitarian point of view; and politically, of course, this issue represented a heavy loss of prestige for the Chinese Communists.

When the Eisenhower Administration took office in January, 1953, it made two decisions in an attempt to end the war. First, it "unleashed" Chiang Kai-shek. At the beginning of the Korean War, President Truman had neutralized Formosa by sending the Seventh Fleet into the Straits of Formosa charged with a dual function: to prevent the Communists from invading the island and to prevent the Nationalists from attacking the mainland. Eisenhower now announced that the Fleet would no longer "shield" the mainland. The intention behind this move was to pose a threat to the Chinese Communists' flank. While Chiang was, of course, incapable of launching an invasion by himself, it was believed that Mao Tse-tung would not be sure whether we might give Chiang our support to make such a landing possible. The resulting uncertainty would force him to redeploy some of his troops from Korea to meet this potential threat.

Second, the Administration decided that if its efforts to gain an armistice failed, it would bomb Chinese bases and supply sources in Manchuria and China, blockade the mainland coast, and possibly use tactical atomic weapons "to provide a tremendous beef-up in the United Nations punch." Dulles conveyed this decision to Prime Minister Nehru of India in late May, 1953, on the assumption that Nehru would pass the message on to the Chinese Communists.

In early June, the deadlocked negotiations were resumed, and in late July the armistice was signed. Whether the Administration's decisions alone were primarily responsible for the Chinese Communists' willingness to conclude the war is difficult to say. Probably other factors did play a significant role. For instance, Stalin had died in 1953, and his successors were proclaiming their belief in "peaceful coexistence" and trying hard to convince the non-Communist world that they wanted to relax international tension. Agreement on an armistice and an end to the war would provide evidence of their earnestness. But in Dulles' own mind, it was his threat to unleash American air power against China that induced the Chinese Communists to agree to end the fighting; in turn, this reinforced his faith in the utility of the advance warning coupled with the threat of heavy punishment.

Under the armistice agreement, the prisoner-of-war issue was settled by a face-saving device. Under the supervision of a Neutral Repatriation Commission, the Communists were to be granted an opportunity to persuade their prisoners to return home. Those who still refused to be repatriated at the end of a certain period would be released as civilians. Syngman Rhee attempted at the last minute to upset this arrangement by releasing 27,000 Chinese prisoners guarded by South Korean troops. Rhee, of course, wanted to renew the war in the hope of reunifying his country; he had bitterly opposed an end to the fighting which again left Korea divided. But his maneuver failed. The Chinese refused to accept his challenge and to use his act as a pretext for renewing hostilities.

Thus, the Korean War concluded just about where it had begun—on the 38th Parallel (actually, South Korea gained 2,350 square miles north of the Parallel and lost 850 miles to the south). It had taken three years of fighting to decide that this line was to become part of the global line dividing the Communist bloc from the non-Communist bloc. In August, the United States signed a mutual security pact with South Korea designed as a deterrent to another attack. This alliance had already been preceded by a declaration, signed by the fifteen nations who had fought in Korea, warning the Chinese Communists that, in the event of renewed aggression, it would probably be impossible to confine hostilities to Korea. And they added this significant warning: the armistice must not "result in jeopardizing the restoration or the safeguarding of peace in any other part of Asia." Events in Indochina were soon to prove the meaninglessness of this statement.

The Indochinese War and SEATO

After World War II, strong nationalist movements in colonies which had long been ruled by European powers demanded independence for their countries. The British met these demands in India, Burma, and Ceylon. The French did not meet them in Indochina—partly because the French concept of colonialism differed from the British. British imperialism always held as its ultimate objective the independence and self-government of the peoples whom it ruled. French policy had an entirely different aim: it sought to assimilate the natives it ruled. These people were part of a "greater France"; once they had matured, they were to be awarded French citizenship. If successful, such a policy would, of course, allow France to remain a great power. A France, not of 40 million, but of 100 million Frenchmen could still play a substantial role in world affairs. This refusal by the French to grant their colonies independence and their need to continue thinking of themselves as the *grande nation* was reinforced by the humiliation of France's defeat in 1940. It was characteristic that in the announcement of the first postwar imperial conference in 1944, which rejected the thought of any autonomy outside the French Empire, the word "self-government" was spelled in English—as though, Herbert Luethy has said, it were "an alien body unassimilable even linguistically."

The result of this policy was that the French, returning to Indochina after years of Japanese occupation, refused to grant any meaningful concessions to the dominant nationalist Vietminh movement. Instead, they tried to suppress the movement. The consequences were twofold: war broke out in December, 1946; and the Communists, under Ho Chi-minh, became the spokesmen for Indochinese nationalism. All subsequent French attempts to identify themselves with this nationalism failed. French concessions, when they were finally offered in response to circumstances, were constantly too little and too late. For instance, in 1949, France established the state of Vietnam under the Emperor Bao Dai, and Cambodia and Laos were declared to be "associated states" within the French Union. Vietnam was to receive autonomy in internal affairs, but France was to remain in charge of Vietnam's foreign policy and defense. In reality, this meant continued French domination. The Indochinese saw through the French scheme, and they regarded Bao Dai, who spent much of his time on the French Riviera, as a French puppet; Bao could not, in fact, have survived one day in office without the presence and support of French arms. The civil war therefore went on unabated. The ensuing military picture was not unlike that in China after World War II. Ho, like Mao Tse-tung, conducted a guerrilla operation; the nature of the terrain and the forests which covered much of Indochina favored this kind of warfare. The French, who generally held the cities, were at a disadvantage from the beginning, for in the absence of genuine independence, the Vietnamese identified themselves with the Vietminh and the French with continued colonial rule. The cost of this war in terms of French manpower, material, and morale was very heavy. The number of French officers who died annually equaled all the new officers graduated each year from Saint-Cyr, France's West Point. And the annual expenditure to prosecute the war was about $600 million, while total French investments in Indochina were approximately only half that figure.

During the first few years of the war, American public

opinion was unsympathetic to France's attempt to re-establish her colonial control over Indochina. But two events were to lead to United States involvement in this conflict. The first one was the defeat of Chiang Kai-shek. This was a blow to France, because it meant that the Chinese Communists could now provide assistance to the Vietminh. The second event was the outbreak of the Korean War, which led to an increased awareness of the strategic importance of Indochina as the gateway to the whole of Southeast Asia. It could not be allowed to fall. The United States and Britain now recognized Bao Dai; Russia and China recognized the Vietminh government.

The Administration began to provide France with economic and military aid. By 1954, the United States was paying about 75 per cent of the costs of the war. The French position continued to deteriorate, however, especially once the Korean armistice was signed. For despite American warnings, Communist China had now shifted her pressure from Korea to Indochina and was rendering increasing assistance to the Vietminh. On March 13, 1954, the entire French position in northern Vietnam suddenly threatened to disintegrate as the Vietminh forces launched an assault upon the French fortress at Dienbienphu. It became painfully clear that the French could not hold the position alone. Only American intervention could save Dienbienphu and the French hold on Vietnam. What was the United States to do?

President Eisenhower had already declared that the fall of Indochina "would be of a most terrible significance to the United States of America," and he had termed Southeast Asia of "transcendent importance" to American security. The Secretary of State had issued several statements which rather strongly suggested that America would not stand idly by while Indochina fell. He had warned the Chinese Communists in the same terms he had used after the armistice in Korea: any aggression—that is, open intervention—would incur "grave consequences which might not be confined to Indochina." This warning also applied to any indirect Chinese intervention—namely, supplying overt assistance in the form of military advisers, equipment, and training for the Vietminh forces. Of prime importance was the strategic significance of Indochina, not whether the Chinese expanded by direct or indirect means. On March 29, Dulles had explicitly stated:

Under the conditions of today, the imposition on Southeast Asia of the political system of Communist Russia and its Chinese ally, by *whatever* means, would be a grave threat to the whole free community. The United States feels that that possibility should not be passively accepted, but should be met by united action. This might have serious risks, but these risks are far less than would face us in a few years from now if we dare not be resolute today.

Dienbienphu was for the Administration, therefore, the moment of decision. Eisenhower and Dulles had declared Indochina to be of strategic importance to American security, and had cautioned China against direct or indirect intervention by threatening her with massive retaliation. The Chinese had ignored these warnings. The United States Government now had to "put up or shut up." It shut up; its threats turned out to have been only bluffs.

The reason for this is fairly clear: because of the nature of American domestic politics, the Eisenhower Administration was—despite its recognition of Indochina's vital location—unwilling to involve the United States in another Korea. Moreover, the Administration was already cutting the size of the army, and apparently there were not sufficient divisions available for fighting in Indochina. The Army Chief of Staff certainly counseled against intervention on this ground. Only two possible courses of action remained. The first was to stop the Communist advance with air power alone. But this was a wholly unfeasible proposition, since air strikes by themselves could not possibly have halted a ground advance. They had failed to do so during the opening days of the Korean War, and it had been this failure which had necessitated the commitment of the army. And even if such air strikes had been tried in an attempt to stop the Vietminh, they would have been ineffective; for quite apart from Indochina's topography, the Vietminh were fighting a guerrilla war. Thus, the use of ground troops would have been as mandatory in Indochina as in Korea.

The alternative strategy was, of course, to attack China itself. Everything indicates that this is what the Administration should have done. Its entire policy of massive retaliation was predicated upon two principles of action: first, issuing a clear warning that would allow no doubt of American intentions and no room for Communist miscalculation; and second, if the Communists deliberately ignored our warnings, punishing the enemy so heavily that he would never again dare challenge us. Yet, in Indochina we had not followed our warning with such punishment. As a result, containment failed, and American power and prestige received a very heavy blow.

Why did this happen? The answer is simple: it is one thing to deliver a threat of massive retaliation to an opponent, and quite another for him to believe it. The Russians had not believed it in Korea; nor did the Chinese in Indochina. Both apparently rejected the notion that the United States would risk a total war for anything less than an all-out attack on either the United States or Europe. Thus, the United States was faced for a second time with the terrible dilemma of either doing nothing or risking all-out war (since the Eisenhower Administration shared the Truman Administration's fear that an attack on China would precipitate Russian intervention).

Truman's experience with Korea had clearly shown that containment could not be successful without the willingness and capability to fight a limited war. Reliance upon strategic air power and an all-or-nothing strategy paralyzed American diplomacy. Our ability to drop atom bombs on Moscow or Peiping was less than useless to defeat limited incursions in areas which we were unwilling to defend at the risk of total war. Ground forces were absolutely necessary if the United States was to escape either defeat or involvement in total war. (Indochina demonstrated that this was all the more true when the Communists expanded, not by outright military attack as in Korea, but by the indirect method of aiding indigenous forces who were conducting large-scale guerrilla warfare.) The Eisenhower Administration had ignored these lessons of the Korean War. It had persuaded itself that Korea had happened only because the enemy had not received a previous warning that an attack upon South Korea would bring retaliatory strikes. While such warnings were certainly desirable to prevent enemy miscalculation, Indochina now proved that warnings alone were not enough. They needed to be backed up by the willingness and ability to commit American ground forces. If these conditions did not exist, the

United States had no choice but to lose one area after another where the Communists faced it with limited challenges; step by step, the enemy could in this manner slowly change the global balance of power without ever once facing the United States with the major challenge that was "worth" a total war —the only kind of war for which we were prepared. The lesson of Indochina, therefore, reaffirmed the one already learned in Korea: American strategy could not escape the necessity of maintaining sufficient ground forces to fight limited engagements. Containment was thus incompatible with heavy budget cutting. As Herbert Luethy caustically remarked after Indochina: "Never did the so-called strategy of 'massive retaliation,' that lame compromise between the crusading spirit and the spirit of budgetary economy, more strikingly demonstrate its incapacity to respond to the limited reversals, the local conflicts, and the pinpricks which constitute the daily fare of international conflict. Reduced to the sole device of threatening apocalyptic war on every occasion, it sowed terror among America's allies and protégés without making much impression on her enemies, and finally ended in resounding inaction."

The result of this demonstration of American impotence was the French Government's decision to make the best of the situation by negotiating with the Communists directly for an end to the war. The French people were as weary of the fighting as the American public had been of Korea. Just as the latter had elected Eisenhower to end the war, the French National Assembly had elected Pierre Mendès-France Premier to end the Indochina hostilities. The new Premier now announced that he was willing to conclude the war, and on July 20, 1954, an armistice agreement was reached which divided the country at the 17th Parallel. The Communists were left in control of northern Indochina (or Vietminh); it seemed only a matter of time until they would take over the rest of the country through subversion.

But the United States did manage to prevent this. The Administration was well aware that perhaps the chief reason for the French defeat was that the people had identified the Vietminh cause with national independence and the French cause with colonialism. The United States therefore deposed Bao Dai and replaced him with a strong anti-Communist nationalist leader, Ngo Dinh Diem, and it extended him economic and military aid to help him stabilize the situation in Vietnam. The danger of Communist subversion gradually receded. The 17th Parallel, like the 38th Parallel in Korea, became part of the international frontier separating the Communist and non-Communist worlds.

The Administration also decided to extend this line to defend the rest of Southeast Asia. Its predecessor had already signed security pacts with the nations lying off the Asian mainland—Japan, the Philippines, Australia, and New Zealand. The collapse of the French position in Indochina and the rising threat of Communist China made it imperative to bring the line inland. In September, 1954, the United States, Britain, France, Australia, New Zealand, the Philippines, Pakistan, and Thailand signed the Southeast Asia Collective Defense Treaty to defend the area of the South Pacific, with the exception of Hong Kong and Formosa. A protocol to the treaty extended SEATO's protection to Vietnam, Laos, and Cambodia. The Manila Pact (as it was also called) provided for joint action to meet aggression; an attack upon any of its members would be considered as a danger to the security of all, and each would then act to meet the common danger in accordance with its constitutional processes. In case of subversion, the parties agreed to consult one another immediately and agree on common measures to meet this threat. The United States attached a specific reservation to the treaty declaring that as far as she was concerned, aggression referred only to Communist aggression; it agreed only to consult in cases of other attacks. The American qualification was meant to reassure India that the United States would not support Pakistan in case of war between those two countries.

SEATO, unlike the NATO alliance which it resembled, did not possess a unified command or joint forces. The principal force behind the alliance was American sea and air power. The crucial element—land power—would have to be supplied by the member nations if the occasion arose. If Indochina was any precedent, this was not a very promising concept of defense. Moreover—and again unlike NATO—SEATO did not contain within it most of the nations located in the area. India, Burma, Ceylon, and Indonesia would not join. They had just emerged from Western colonialism and they were unwilling to be tied again to the West through a military alliance. They preferred to remain neutral in the struggle between the Western powers and the Sino-Soviet bloc. Of the Asian nations that did join the pact, the Philippines did so because of its traditional ties to the United States, and Pakistan because she wished to strengthen herself against India; only Thailand was genuinely concerned with Communist China's expansion, for the French collapse in Indochina had brought Chinese power closer to her borders. But if the Manila Pact was primarily a non-Asian alliance for the defense of an Asian area, its chief purpose was to warn the Communists of America's stake in that portion of the world. And if the United States felt its security in the area threatened by direct or indirect Communist aggression, SEATO provided her with the opportunity for unilateral intervention to hold the line in this area of the world. Secretary Dulles referred to the treaty as the Monroe Doctrine for Southeast Asia; whether it would prove to be so depended upon the extent of American power and American willingness to use this power when it became necessary.

The Formosa Straits and the Offshore Islands

No sooner had the Indochina crisis passed than a critical situation arose in the Formosa Straits. During the summer of 1954, the Chinese Communists openly proclaimed their intention of taking Formosa, and began shelling the Nationalist-held offshore islands (Quemoy is only nine miles outside the harbor of Amoy; Matsu lies almost as close, blocking the harbor of Foochow; and the Tachen islands are 200 miles north of Formosa). In December, the United States and the Nationalists signed a Treaty of Mutual Defense, by which this country guaranteed the security of Formosa and the nearby Pescadore islands. The Nationalists also pledged themselves not to attack the mainland or reinforce their offshore garrisons without United States consent. Chiang was thus "released."

The offshore islands, however, were not included under the terms of the treaty. But President Eisenhower sent Chiang his personal assurances that the United States would defend Quemoy and Matsu. Moreover, as the situation in the Straits grew more tense in January, 1955, the President requested and received from Congress the authority to employ American armed forces to protect Formosa and the Pescadores. This authority extended to the protection of "such related positions and territories" as the President judged necessary. And Secretary Dulles announced that while the United States would not defend Quemoy or Matsu "as such," it would protect them if an attack upon them seemed to be a prelude to an attack upon Formosa itself. "The basic purpose is to assure that Formosa and the Pescadores will not be forcibly taken over by the Chinese Communists. However, [Chinese Communist] Foreign Minister Chou says that they will use all their force to take Formosa, and they treat the coastal islands as means to that end. . . . Thus the Chinese Communists have linked the coastal positions to the defense of Formosa." What Dulles would have done if the Chinese Communists had attempted to invade the islands with the specifically announced purpose of merely clearing the approaches to Amoy and Foochow is difficult to say. But it probably would have made no difference if the Communists had disavowed any intention of taking Formosa. For in Dulles' mind, Quemoy and Matsu had to be defended to maintain the Nationalist Government's morale. Even more important, the islands had to be guarded since the alternative was to cede them; and this would have been interpreted as a sign of weakness by the Chinese Communists, spurring them on to further aggression. It was this test of wills which was really at stake in the situation; and Dulles' determination to demonstrate American resolution to the Chinese Communists may have been reinforced by the Indochina debacle. It would seem, therefore, that in case of attack, the Administration would have committed American armed forces to the defense of the offshore islands. At least the Communists thought so, and they abstained from any invasion attempts on Quemoy and Matsu. (The Nationalists had, meanwhile, evacuated the Tachens.)

Three years later, in August, 1958, the American position became clear when the Communists again began to shell the offshore islands very heavily. The Seventh Fleet—with orders to retaliate if fired upon—escorted Nationalist supply ships to within three miles of the beleaguered island and helped them to break the blockade; and the Nationalist air force, equipped by the United States with air-to-air missiles, defeated the Communist air force's attempt to establish air supremacy in the sky between the mainland and Quemoy. United States marines also moved several eight-inch howitzers, capable of firing nuclear shells, from Okinawa to Quemoy, emplaced them, and turned them over to the Nationalists. The shells themselves, which remained in American hands, if exploded above an invasion fleet would doom any invasion. There was no invasion. "Tactical" atomic weapons had for the first time in history played a role in deterring an attack.

Thus, the line remained where it had been before the two Formosa crises—a few miles off Communist China's coast. Some months later, Dulles reaffirmed this line when he firmly rejected Chiang's calls for the reconquest of the mainland. Chiang's only "way back," Dulles stated, would come if a "Hungarian type" of uprising occurred in China. If—but only if—a "recognized government" then called for help, the United States would permit Chiang to "answer the call." There is no indication that Dulles thought such an internal revolt to be a likely possibility.

American policy in the Straits was therefore clear: preservation of the *status quo*. Each side should keep what it had and refrain from attacking the other. The Administration had finally recognized what neither it nor its predecessor had been willing to admit openly before: that the Nationalist expectation of reconquering the mainland was a myth. At the same time, it tacitly acknowledged the Chinese Communist Government as continental China's *de facto* government. It reconciled itself to the Communist conquest of the mainland. Containment had once more replaced liberation. The Administration was, moreover, resolved to back up its "disengagement" policy with force: in the Straits, it could support its political position with sea and air power; ground forces were not needed.

For the moment, the situation in the Far East had been stabilized—at the 38th Parallel in Korea, in the Formosa Straits, at the 17th Parallel in Indochina, and at the line drawn by SEATO. Communist attention now turned to the Middle East.

The Middle East and Suez

In 1955, the United States completed its line around the Sino-Soviet periphery. Under her sponsorship, Britain, Turkey, Iraq, Iran, and Pakistan established the Middle East

Treaty Organization. Thus, the Baghdad Pact (as this treaty was called) extended the NATO line from Turkey to India. But this "northern tier," drawn along 3,000 miles of Russian frontier, drew a sharp reaction from the Soviet Union. She had been forced to withdraw from Iran in 1946, but she had not surrendered her ambitions in this area. The Middle East linked Europe, Africa, and Asia. For Britain, the area—and especially the Suez Canal—had traditionally been the lifeline of her old empire and of her present Commonwealth. Above all, Europe's economy was becoming increasingly dependent upon the Middle East for oil; without oil, Europe would collapse. The power that could deny her this oil would be able to dictate her future. Soviet dominance of the Middle East would thus allow her to neutralize Europe without firing a shot. In short, for Russia the Middle East was the means to outflank and disintegrate NATO. Her opportunity to attempt to do this came as a result of the bitter Arab-Israeli conflict, the only slightly less bitter Anglo-Egyptian quarrel, and Egypt's own expansionist ambitions.

Arab antagonism toward Israel is understandable. In 1917, Britain had pledged herself in the Balfour Declaration to the establishment of a "national home" for the Jewish people in Palestine; at the same time, she had also promised not to prejudice the civil and religious rights of non-Jews. These promises were contradictory. Certainly, Zionists expected to convert Palestine into a Jewish state; they considered Palestine, a British mandate after the collapse of the Ottoman Empire during World War I, as their ancient and traditional homeland.

Britain's troubles became serious after Hitler's assumption of power in Germany—and impossible after World War II. Hitler had slaughtered 6 million Jews in his concentration camps; few of the survivors wished to remain in Europe, with its unhappy memories. Many emigrated to Palestine. The Jews were now determined to establish a Jewish state, while the Arabs feared that the Jewish immigration would crowd them out of what they also regarded as their rightful homeland. British troops numbering 96,000 were unable to keep the peace between the Arabs and Jews. Under these circumstances, Britain—already gravely weakened by the war, forced to curtail her commitments throughout the world—decided to end her burdensome mandate over Palestine.

In November, 1947, the United Nations decided to partition Palestine into two independent states, one Jewish and the other Arab. The Arabs refused to accept this solution, however; they wanted Palestine to become an Arab state. On May 10, 1948, as Britain ended her mandate, the Jews proclaimed the state of Israel, and the armies of the Arab League (Egypt, Jordan, Syria, Lebanon, and Saudi Arabia) invaded the new state. In the ensuing war, the Israeli Army defeated the larger Arab armies. The Jews had fought for their very survival, and the state of Israel had now become a fact of political life.

The Arabs, however, refused to recognize it as such. Though they did sign an armistice in February, 1949, they refused to conclude a peace treaty. They continued to regard the Jews as infidels who had no right to be in Israel. Moreover, they felt deeply humiliated by their defeat. The Arabs awaited their day of revenge; meanwhile, they continued to proclaim their intention to destroy Israel. They conducted a constant guerrilla warfare against Israel—sabotaging, pillaging, and murdering (so did the Israeli Army when it intermittently took revenge by launching heavy assaults into Arab territory); they refused to allow Israeli shipping through the Suez Canal and blockaded the Gulf of Aqaba; and they tightened the ring around Israel—in April, 1956, Egypt, Syria, Saudi Arabia, and Yemen formed a joint command against Israel under Egyptian command, and in October, 1956, Egypt, Jordan, and Syria announced another joint command "the principal concern of which is the war of destruction against Israel." Earlier (in late September, 1955), Egypt had concluded an arms deal with Czechoslovakia, although the actual agreement was signed with the Soviet Union; under this arrangement, Egypt received a large quantity of arms, including planes and tanks. Egypt now had the tools with which to achieve a decisive military superiority over Israel. This, in turn, raised a very vital question for Israel: should it strike now or wait until Egypt and her allies were ready for the "second round"? As Egypt solidified the encirclement of Israel, grew increasingly aggressive, and began to absorb the Soviet arms, the Israelis decided to strike before it was too late. All that was needed was the right condition for launching their preventive attack.

This condition, which was to occur in October, 1956, was the product of Anglo-Egyptian antagonism. Britain had controlled Egypt since 1881, when she had established a protectorate over Egypt in order to safeguard her communications through Suez to India. The 1936 treaty between the two countries had converted this status into an alliance. By its terms, British troops were confined to the Canal Zone, and their presence was declared to be neither an occupation nor an infringement of Egyptian sovereignty. To the Egyptians, however, British soldiers on their soil continued to represent a violation of Egyptian independence, pride, and dignity.

World War II intensified Egyptian nationalism and heightened the demand for a withdrawal of British forces from Egyptian soil. But negotiations on this question broke down, while other postwar events further increased Egypt's anti-British sentiment. The Egyptians resented the Palestine partition plan, for which they blamed Britain as well as the United States. During the war against Israel, Britain withheld arms from the Arabs because they were opposing a United Nations decision. A Western attempt in 1951 to organize a Middle East defense organization was seen as a means of preserving Western dominance in the area and using the Arab countries as pawns for Western purposes. In late 1951, the Egyptian Parliament abrogated the 1936 Anglo-Egyptian treaty, and a few months later anti-British feeling boiled over into violent mob action in Cairo against British buildings and residents. The new military regime which took over the Egyptian Government from King Farouk in July, 1952, pressed for the removal of British troops with renewed vigor. The Eisenhower Administration supported this Egyptian demand. Faced with this opposition, and aware of her own unpopularity in Egypt, Britain signed a new Anglo-Egyptian treaty in 1954, by which she agreed to withdraw all her troops from Suez over a twenty-month period. Britain was granted the right to return to the base if any member of the Arab League or Turkey were attacked by any nation except Israel. The Egyptians would not even allow the British Army to maintain its own personnel to look after the installations on the base; this was to be done by civilian technicians employed by private English firms. British influence over Egyptian politics had come to an end.

Britain now shifted the focus of her power from Egypt to Iraq, a long-time ally. She therefore joined the Baghdad Pact, of which Iraq was already a member, in order to protect her vital strategic and economic interest in the Middle East. But President Nasser of Egypt did not regard METO merely as a means of containing Russia; he saw it as an instrument to preserve Western domination throughout the area, and since Iraq had always been Egypt's traditional rival for Arab leadership, he considered it a personal challenge as well. Nasser therefore set out to destroy the Baghdad Pact by forming a counteralliance and undermining pro-Western Arab governments. His means of achieving these objectives was to place himself at the head of the Arab struggle against Israel and Britain. Thereby, he would become the foremost exponent of Arab nationalism and win the allegiance of the Arab masses. Once he had gained this loyalty of the people, no Arab government would dare oppose him, for if it did he would call on the people to overthrow that government. "Revolution in the street" was an accepted Arab method of making and unmaking governments. Moreover, by exerting his influence over the Arab world in this manner, he would gain control over the area's oil resources; this would place him in a position in which he could siphon off the oil revenues to help Egypt's economic development. Thus, partly as a reaction to Israel and Britain, and partly as a result of his own strong ambitions, Nasser began to use pan-Arabism as an instrument of expansion.

Nasser's influence grew quickly. He formed close links with Saudi Arabia, Yemen, Syria, and Jordan (whose pro-Western government he first successfully overthrew). But the act which really endeared Nasser to the Arab masses was his dramatic arms deal with the Soviet Union. This agreement made Nasser the great new hero, the modern Saladin—the staunch opponent of the West- and champion of Arab nationalism. At the same time, the Soviet Union became the Arab's greatest friend. Soviet-Egyptian bonds became closer: an estimated 1,000 Soviet military technicians and military officers were stationed in Egypt, and several hundred Egyptian military personnel were sent to Eastern Europe for training. Soviet satellite embassies increased their staffs sizably.

And the Egyptian press and radio began to rely on official Soviet and Chinese agencies for their news. This Moscow-Cairo axis frightened not only Israel, but also Britain; if Russia and Egypt gained control over the Middle East, Britain would be cut off from her oil supplies, which for her were a question not just of profit, but of survival. The situation thus became inflammable.

Only an incendiary incident was needed to start a conflagration. The United States provided this when, on July 19, 1956, it informed the Egyptian Government that this country would not help finance Nasser's Aswan Dam, a high dam on the Upper Nile whose purpose was to raise Egypt's low standard of living by irrigating new land and providing electricity for industrial development. The American retraction of its offer to help build this dam was a heavy blow to Egypt's hopes to raise itself by its own "sandal straps." For the American loan had been a prerequisite for further aid from the World Bank and Britain; these offers, too, were now withdrawn. The Administration's action was occasioned by several considerations: Nasser had attempted to blackmail the Administration into providing more money by hinting that the Russians had offered to finance the entire project; Egypt had moved too close to Russia and had recognized Communist China; Nasser had also probably mortgaged the funds he was supposed to provide for Egypt's share of the cost of the dam to buy Russian arms—which, in effect, meant that the entire cost of the dam would fall upon the United States and Britain.

A withdrawal of the American offer under these circumstances would, Secretary Dulles felt, accomplish two purposes. First, it would call Russia's hand in the economic competition between the two countries for the allegiance of the peoples living in the underdeveloped nations. Dulles was convinced that Russia's various offers of economic aid were primarily propaganda and that she was economically incapable of delivering on her promises. Second, it would teach the neutral nations that they could not count upon American aid for their economic development if their neutrality became a neutrality against America. It was one thing to help a genuinely neutral nation; it was quite another to give dollars to a country that aligned itself closely with Moscow. John Beal, Dulles' biographer, put it this way:

... The spectacle of Nasser, seemingly more and more pro-Communist, apparently about to win U.S. help on one project almost as costly by itself as America's entire world economic expenditures for 1956, began to have an effect on friends as well as neutrals. Stout allies like the Philippines and Pakistan began to ask themselves whether it was worthwhile to take sides in the world struggle if by holding aloof the reward was help from both camps. Nasser was making it look as though the United States could be played for a sucker.... There comes a time when tolerance must give way to firmness.

Nasser regarded this American firmness as a personal and national humiliation. In this he was right, for that is precisely what Dulles intended it to be, according to Beal: "The choice was between letting him down easily, through protracted renegotiations that came to nothing, or letting him have it straight. Since the issue involved more than simply denying Nasser money for a dam, a polite and concealed rebuff would fail to make the really important point. It had to be forthright, carrying its own built-in moral for neutrals.... As a calculated risk, the decision was on a grand scale, comparable in the sphere of diplomacy to the calculated risks of war taken in Korea and Formosa." And so it turned out to be. For a few days later, on July 26, Nasser announced that he would nationalize the Suez Canal and use the revenues collected from it to finance the dam. Arab nationalists were ecstatic, and Nasser's stature, already strong, reached new heights.

Unlike the crises in Korea and Formosa, however, the consequences of Secretary Dulles' act fell not on the United States, but on our allies—above all, on Britain. And her government reacted sharply to Nasser's seizure of the Canal. Prime Minister Eden did not trust the Egyptian dictator; although Nasser guaranteed that all ships, except Israel's, could still pass through the Canal, Eden feared that the Egyptian dictator would use the Canal as an instrument of political blackmail. Moreover, if Nasser could face the West with such a major act of defiance and go unpunished, Western influence would be destroyed throughout the Middle East. Other Arab governments would expropriate Western oil interests, and all opponents of Nasser would be discouraged and come to terms with him. Western prestige—and especially British prestige, since Britain was the leading Western power in the Middle East—had to be upheld. If it were not, the Cairo-Moscow axis would dominate the entire area and be in a position to strangle Europe. The British were therefore determined to stand up to Nasser, and they insisted upon some form of international control for the Canal; Nasser was not to be left in sole control. But the Egyptians rejected all proposals to wrest their newly won control out of their hands and denounced them as "collective colonialism." All attempts to bridge this gap were therefore doomed to fail.

It was in these circumstances that war broke out. The United States was busily engaged in the last days of its Presidential election campaign, and the Soviet Union was concentrating on crushing the Hungarian uprising. On October 29, only four days after Jordan's Chief of Staff announced that the time had come to launch the Arab assault on Israel, the Israeli Army marched into Egypt. The Israelis quickly defeated the Egyptian forces in the Sinai peninsula. The British and the French (who sought Nasser's downfall because of his aid to the Algerian rebels who wanted to free Algeria from French control) intervened twenty-four hours later. At this point, the United States saved Nasser. Although the Administration had pressured Britain to sign the Anglo-Egyptian treaty by which all British troops had been removed from Suez, and had withdrawn the Aswan Dam offer, thus precipitating Nasser's seizure of the Canal and the British attack, it now opposed the use of force to settle this issue. The reason was that despite its disapproval of Nasser's action and the pro-Soviet direction in which he was leading Egypt, it saw his foreign policy in terms of a reaction against Israel and Western colonialism. If Israel had not existed, and if Egypt and the Arab states had not long been subjected and exploited by the Western powers (especially Britain), Arab nationalism would not be anti-Western and pro-Soviet. The Administration therefore saw the invasion of Egypt as a golden opportunity to win Egyptian and Arab friendship. When the Jews had originally proclaimed the state of Israel, the United States had, because of domestic political considerations, recognized the new state within eleven minutes. Here was a chance to show the Arabs that the United States was not as pro-Jewish as they thought it to be, and that this country could even be pro-Arab. Since Egypt's actions were also the product of her anti-British resentment, it would be beneficial to oppose the British attempt to reassert control over the Suez Canal. By saving Nasser, the United States could align itself with Arab nationalism; supporting Britain, France, and Israel would have left the Soviet Union as the sole champion of Arab aspirations. American opposition to the Egyptian invasion would, in short, identify the United States with the anticolonialism of the entire underdeveloped world, and particularly with the anti-Israeli and nationalistic sentiments of the Arab world. Since continued evidence of British power in the Middle East only antagonized the Arabs, the destruction of this power and its replacement by American influence would be in the interest not only of the United States, but of all the Western powers. In this way, the West's strategic and economic interests could be more adequately safeguarded.

America's opposition to the Suez invasion was the decisive factor in stopping the fighting. Egypt had already blockaded the Canal, and the Syrians had cut the pipelines running across their country from Iraq. Britain was therefore dependent upon American oil to replace her losses from the Middle East; and the Administration threatened to use this economic sanction if Britain did not cease the attack. Faced with this dire prospect—plus opposition to the invasion within Britain, the Commonwealth (Canada, India, and Pakistan), and the United Nations—the British Government accepted a cease-fire and later withdrew its forces; France and Israel had little choice but to follow suit.

It is ironic, however, in view of America's leading role in halting the attack on Egypt, that it should have been the Soviet Union—and not the United States—that was to reap the benefits from America's opposition. After it had become clear that the United States would not support the British and French invasion, Russia threatened "to crush the aggressors"; she sent notes to the British and French governments warning of possible rocket attacks on their countries, and she bluntly told Israel that her very existence was at stake. She even asked the United States to join forces with her to stop the war. And after the cease-fire, she and Communist China threatened to send "volunteers." In short, the

Soviet Union risked nothing to deliver these threats, but it was she who received most of the credit from the Arabs for saving Nasser by her threats to exterminate Israel and attack Britain and France. Suez thus resulted in the collapse of British power in the Middle East, the strengthening of Arab nationalism, and the consolidation of Egyptian-Russian links.

Nasser's great political victory—despite a humiliating military defeat at the hands of Israel—increased his self-confidence. Supported by the Soviet Union—whose aim it was to weaken, if not to eliminate all Western power in the Middle East— Nasser continued his expansionist drive. Jordan abrogated the Anglo-Jordan Treaty by which Jordan had received an annual subsidy to maintain its economy; Egypt, Saudi Arabia, and Syria promised to replace the British funds, and Jordan announced that she would seek to establish a federal union with Egypt and Syria. The last two states did, in fact, join together into a union, the United Arab Republic, in early 1958. Attempts to undermine the Iraqi Government continued, and these became so serious that in late November, 1956, the United States announced that a threat to the territorial integrity and political independence of Baghdad Pact members would be viewed with the "utmost gravity." In the spring of 1957, the Egyptians organized riots against the government in Lebanon.

It was in Jordan, surprisingly enough, that Nasser received his first serious setback. Here the young King Hussein, hardly out of school, opposed his government's increasingly pro-Communist and Nasser leanings. In April, 1957, after discovering a plot to depose and, if necessary, assassinate him, Hussein dismissed his government, formed a new one, purged the army of its pro-Nasser elements, and imposed martial law upon his country. Hussein received immediate support from Saudi Arabia, where King Ibn Saud, a feudal monarch who was very dependent for his income upon the Western oil market, had become increasingly worried by Nasser's close links to Russia. Early in 1957, Saud paid a state visit to the United States, and later he visited his fellow monarch in Iraq. Iraq's isolation in the Arab world had ended, and in February, 1958, Jordan and Iraq announced a federation of their two kingdoms.

The first step taken by the Administration after the Suez crisis was the formulation of the Eisenhower Doctrine. This joint resolution of Congress in the spring of 1957 declared that the United States considered the preservation of the independence and integrity of the Middle Eastern nations as vital to American security, and that it was prepared to use armed force to assist any nation or nations *"requesting* assistance against *armed* aggression from any country controlled by international Communism. [Italics added.]" It was difficult to understand what this Doctrine meant. Russia itself bordered on only one Arab state, Iraq, which was already protected by the Baghdad Pact and, through its association with Britain and Turkey, by NATO; so the Doctrine could not be directed against Russia. Moreover, the Soviet Union did not need to attack Iraq, for it had already leap-frogged the "northern tier" by establishing close relations with Egypt and Syria. And Suez had demonstrated that the United States did not regard such association as turning a country into a Communist-controlled vassal; if it had, it would surely have supported the invasion of Egypt.

But the Administration, viewing Nasser's continued attempts to undermine Western power in the Middle East, his vicious attacks upon all the Western nations, including the United States, and his continued flirtation with Russia, soon reconsidered its views of Nasser. At Suez, it had thought that by demonstrating its friendship, the United States could win his trust. Post-Suez events proved this expectation to have been misfounded. A reversal of policy was thus in order, and this required a reinterpretation of the Eisenhower Doctrine. First, the term "armed aggression" was no longer to refer only to the direct attack of one nation upon another, but also to attempts to overthrow pro-Western governments through internal revolt aided from the outside; and second, "any country controlled by international Communism" was now meant to include nations with close bonds to the Soviet Union.

The Doctrine was first applied in Jordan, where King Hussein's dismissal of the pro-Nasser and pro-Communist government led to a general strike, massive street demonstrations, and riots. Jordan's days as an independent state appeared to be numbered. In this crisis, Hussein charged, on April 24, that international Communism was responsible for the efforts to overthrow him. On the same day, the United States announced that it regarded "the independence and integrity of Jordan as vital." And to prove that it meant what it said, the Administration dispatched the United States Sixth Fleet to the eastern Mediterranean, and extended Jordan $10 million for the support of her army and economy. The Hussein Government survived, but in a country whose population included over 60 per cent of pro-Nasser Palestinian Arabs, survival did not mean stability.

In the summer of 1958, an even more serious crisis arose when, on July 14, a group of nationalist officers led by General Kassem overthrew the pro-Western government of Iraq and murdered the King and Prime Minister. Although the new regime did not withdraw from the Baghdad Pact until some months later, this revolt, in effect, eliminated Iraq, the pivot on which the alliance had been centered. The United Arab Republic immediately hailed the revolution and recognized the new government; and the two countries quickly signed an alliance. There was little the United States could do but recognize the Kassem Government. Arab nationalism seemed to be sweeping everything in front of it. Only Lebanon, Jordan, and Saudi Arabia were still outside the Nasser camp, and the first two were teetering on the verge of revolution. The whole Western position in the Middle East seemed to be on the brink of disintegration.

The Eisenhower Administration now resorted to force. Lebanon had been plagued for some time with civil war between Moslems and Christians. The Moslems wanted close relations, if not union, with the United Arab Republic, and the Christians favored a pro-Western policy and the continued independence of Lebanon. With the Iraqi revolution, men and arms for the pro-Nasser elements began to be smuggled in over the Syrian border. In Jordan, too, the situation took a turn for the worse; the Iraqi example was hardly a happy one for King Hussein, who also had his pro-Nasser masses and army officers. Both countries now invoked the Eisenhower Doctrine and asked for military support. The British sent paratroopers into Jordan, and the United States sent 14,000 men into Lebanon. The large size of the American contingent seems to have been deliberate: apparently, it was meant to warn the new Iraqi Government against nationalizing Western oil resources. Kassem quickly gave the assurance that he had no such intention, and possible American intervention in Iraq was thereby forestalled. Loud Soviet hints of intervention also turned out to be hollow when countered by resolute American action. Both Britain and the United States withdrew their troops in late October.

The Anglo-American action had saved, at least temporarily, Lebanon and Jordan. But it also had two other highly important effects. First, it demonstrated to Nasser that he could not go on challenging the West's vital interests with impunity. America had demonstrated at Suez its sympathy for Arab nationalism; it had recognized that some changes in the old *status quo* were desirable, and thus it was willing to go far to accommodate the new national pride and dignity of Egypt. But it was one thing to welcome this new national desire for independence and equality in the tradition of the American revolution; it was quite another to allow it to undermine the entire Western position throughout the Middle East. The 1958 intervention, in effect, warned Nasser that there were definite limits beyond which the United States would not tolerate his demands. This was the lesson that the British had tried to teach him at Suez. The Administration had now accepted the British position that opposition to nationalism *per se* was not bad. It depended upon whether this nationalism had legitimate grievances which should be satisfied or whether it was merely a convenient mask for expansionist aims. The other impact of the intervention—perhaps even more important—was to show Nasser and the Arabs that there were limits to Soviet willingness to come to their aid. Nasser's personal ambitions were, by themselves, relatively unimportant; the decisive factor which had reaped success for Egypt's pan-Arab policy was Soviet power. The Western powers, in thinking of counteraction against Egypt, could never eliminate the possibility of Soviet intervention. Could the Soviet Union afford to leave its new Arab friend to his fate? Would this not gravely weaken Soviet prestige and Soviet ability to use Arab nationalism to eliminate Western influence and power from the Middle East? The Russian threats of intervention during Suez had given the Arabs the impression that in a crisis the Soviet Union would come to their rescue. This, in turn, further encouraged Nasser's expansionist drive. The Anglo-American action in Lebanon and Jordan disabused the Arabs of this notion. Prior to the intervention, the Russians had again threatened to send "volunteers" to oppose the Western "imperialists," and had carried out conspicuous military maneuvers in Turkestan and Trans-caucasia. The firmness of the American position, and the failure of the Soviet Union in the face of Eisenhower's determination to do more than to denounce the intervention and call for a diplomatic settlement, made it very clear that there were limits to Soviet willingness to bail the Arabs out of trouble. This had a dampening effect on Nasser's anti-Western drive.

There was another unexpected turn of events which influenced this situation. The new regime in Iraq, instead of turning out to be pro-Nasser—as almost everyone, including Nasser, had expected—took an anti-Nasser position. It was not long before it began to challenge the Egyptian ruler's leadership of Arab nationalism. Nasser quickly recognized this threat of Egypt's traditional rival and attempted to overthrow the Kassem Government. But the revolt by a group of pro-Nasser officers was quickly squashed. At the same time, the Soviet Union gave economic and military support to the Kassem Government. Iraq's opposition to Egyptian expansion and the shift in Soviet support antagonized Nasser, of course, and he began to attack the Soviet Union openly. But a complete rift did not occur. Nasser was too dependent upon Russia for arms; the Soviet Union had committed itself to construct the Aswan Dam; and, for political reasons, Nasser could hardly swing back to the West overnight, since the very popularity of his regime had been based upon its bitter anti-Western attitude and drive. Slowly, however, he began to rebuild his bridges back to the West. In December, 1959, Britain and Egypt exchanged ambassadors for the first time since Suez. In the meantime, Nasser was becoming increasingly isolated in the Arab world: Jordan, Lebanon, and Saudi Arabia had remained independent; Libya and the Sudan had resisted his attempts to subvert them; Syria was restless in the United Arab Republic; and Iraq had become a rival for Arab leadership. These events forced Nasser to turn increasing attention to domestic affairs. Not only had the United States made foreign adventure increasingly dangerous, but Iraq's rivalry made it necessary to focus more attention on Egypt's economic progress. In a long-term peaceful competition between the two states, Egypt was in a bad position because of its poverty. It lacked resources and unused land, while Iraq was rich in oil. Internal development was, therefore, a necessary prerequisite for the preservation of Egyptian leadership of the Arab world. Nor was this situation materially changed by the events of the early 1960's: Kassem was overthrown; Syria revolted and quit the United Arab Republic; and the countries between Syria on the one hand and Egypt on the other—Jordan and Saudi Arabia—improved their relations with Nasser. Despite the common pan-Arab aspirations of Egypt, Syria, and Iraq, a real Arab union remained as elusive as ever. Syria and Iraq were unwilling to permit Nasser to dominate them; and Nasser was unwilling to form a union he could not control. The Egyptian leader's emphasis on domestic reform—or what he called "Arab socialism"—therefore became crucial to his fight for Arab leadership, even though he continued his attempts to overthrow traditional pro-Western regimes—for example, in Yemen—and he remained generally anti-Western in his policy positions.

Meanwhile, the United States had almost become a full-fledged member of the Baghdad Pact (now renamed the Central Treaty Organization) by joining its economic, military, and countersubversion committees; she was also bound to each of the three Moslem states individually by bilateral defense agreements. But behind these developments remained all the essential problems which had given rise to the turmoil after 1955: the conflicts among the Arab states, the Arab-Israeli quarrel (likely to become even less amenable to settlement as the Arab states continue to compete in terms of nationalism and anti-Israeli sentiments), the overshadowing competition between the United States and the Soviet Union, and, above all, Arab nationalism with its frequent xenophobic overtones, the result of the people's misery. Despite the vast oil wealth, the Arab masses remain very poor, and they suffer from illiteracy, malnutrition, and disease. Social discontent and political instability are the results. Only long-term Western economic aid and Arab sharing of oil profits between the "have" and "have-not" nations can begin to meet these problems. Particularly important in this respect is the development of the principal rivers of the area—the Nile, Euphrates, Jordan, Tigris, and Litari—for the Arab countries are agricultural, and an expansion of cultivated land is therefore urgently required to raise their standards of living. The difficulty is that each of these rivers is shared by two or more states. This means that a political settlement among the Arab states and between them and Israel is the prerequisite for economic development. Such a settlement seems very unlikely. Thus, while the area has simmered down for the time being, all the explosive forces remain below the surface.

Western European Union and the Common Market

In Europe, the defense line had already been drawn by NATO. But the strength of this line on the ground depended upon supplementing NATO forces with West German troops. EDC was the means the Allies had chosen through which to achieve this goal. But in August, 1954, the French National Assembly rejected EDC by a decisive majority. This was a real blow to the efforts toward creating a situation of strength in Europe. The whole basis of NATO strategy and European integration was suddenly imperiled.

France's allies were upset. That they should have been so is surprising. To be sure, France had first suggested EDC as a means of harnessing West German manpower to Europe's defense; and it may have been logical, therefore, to expect France to ratify the treaty. Moreover, the French knew that their opposition could not prevent West Germany's rearmament; the American Government was set on it. EDC would at least have given France a large measure of control over Germany's strength and over the purposes to which it would be used. But the question of Germany was hardly a rational one for Frenchmen. They had too many memories; there is hardly a French village which has not erected a monument commemorating the dead of World War I. Another reason for France's opposition was the fear that a rearmed Germany would be stronger than France—allowing Germany to dominate the Continent and granting her a more potent voice than France in Allied councils. This fear was increased by French apprehensions that despite all assurances to the contrary, America and Britain would one day pull their troops out of Europe and leave France to face Germany alone. It was natural, therefore, that with the ending of the Korean War and the subsequent relaxation of international tensions, the French tended to return to a policy of "NATO without German rearmament," or at least as little German rearmament as possible and as late as possible. Lastly, EDC was the victim of a resurgence of French nationalism. After years of governmental integrationist policies and slogans, nationalist forces on the right wanted to defeat EDC in order to discredit all the federal enterprises undertaken during the last few years. By the same token, they wanted to maintain France's national identity and honor. A France integrated into a European community would be a France separated from her overseas possessions. It was upon a *Union Française* that French nationalists placed their hope of reviving France's strength and preserving her great-power status. These nationalists also resented being pushed by Britain and America into a scheme that neither of them would join: Britain refused to join any European federal organization because, like the French nationalists, she felt her status and power to be more dependent upon close association with the Commonwealth; and the United States, while preaching integration, was perhaps the most sensitive of all the NATO powers to any infringements upon her own sovereignty. That West Germany was willing to join EDC was no answer to French nationalists. The German case was entirely different: for West Germany, entry into EDC was a means of ending her moral and political isolation, of ending the Allied occupation and recovering her sovereign status, and of dominating continental Europe militarily and politically. It was for these reasons that the French preferred to kill EDC at its inception.

The response of the Eisenhower Administration was a self-righteous one. Instead of taking the lead in finding a way out of this impasse, it simply withdrew from the problem and waited for the European powers to resolve it. Secretary Dulles only repeated his previous threat that the United States would make an "agonizing reappraisal" if the deadlock were not broken. This could only mean that the United States would either rearm West Germany without French consent or withdraw its troops from the European continent and rely solely upon air and sea power for America's defense. Both these possibilities would probably disrupt NATO. It was Britain's Prime Minister Eden who took the lead in averting such a collapse and seeking a way of rearming West Germany with French approval. He found it in the forgotten Brussels Treaty.

This organization was now to be revised by the inclusion of Germany and Italy. The new alliance, which pledged all its members to come to one another's aid if attacked, would be known as the Western European Union. Yet WEU was not really an alliance, no forces were assigned to it, and it had no responsibility for formulating a strategy to defend its members. These remained within the functions of NATO. WEU's role was to channel West German troops into NATO, while at the same time maintaining a set of controls over West Germany similar to those included in EDC. It set a ceiling on the size of the armed forces which its members could contribute to NATO; the number of German divisions remained fixed at twelve, and France's at fourteen. Raising the ceiling, moreover, would require the unanimous consent of all WEU members. WEU was also to enforce West Germany's unilateral agreement not to manufacture atomic, chemical, or biological weapons, long-range missiles, certain types of mines and bombers, large warships, and certain other weapons. In order to tighten the grip on West German forces even further, SACEUR's (Supreme Allied Commander in Europe) authority was extended: no forces in Europe could be deployed without his consent; he was to maintain the present level of integration of national forces; he was to assume greater responsibility for the logistical support of the forces placed under his command; and he remained in sole charge of directing the training of these troops and the commanders assigned to SHAPE. Lastly, Britain agreed to keep a minimum number of troops—four divisions and a tactical air force—on the Continent. These forces could not be withdrawn against the wishes of the majority of WEU members, except in case of an acute overseas emergency. Britain's pledge was little more than a formalization of Britain's responsibilities under the Dunkirk, Brussels, and NATO treaties. But to the French it seemed an important new commitment; they now felt assured that they would not someday be left to face German troops alone.

These commitments, embodied in the Paris Pact, came into force in May, 1955. Thus, ten years after Germany's defeat, the occupation came to an end, and the Federal Republic regained her sovereignty and entered NATO via WEU. West Germany's military power could now be added to Western strength. Two important declarations were appended to these Paris agreements. In the first, the West German Government subscribed to the principles of the United Nations, recognized the defensive nature of the Brussels and NATO treaties, undertook "never to have recourse to force to achieve the reunification of Germany or the modification of the present boundaries of the German Federal Republic," and to resolve all disputes between herself and other states by peaceful means. In the second, the United States, Britain, and France declared that they recognized the Federal Republic as the only freely and legitimately constituted government entitled to speak for all of Germany; that they would pursue German unification by peaceful means; and that they would continue to exercise their responsibilities with regard to the security of West Germany and West Berlin.

With Germany safely enrolled as a member of NATO, the WEU members now took a momentous step toward further economic and political integration. The six states which composed this Little Europe had gained increasing benefits from this movement. On June 1, 1958, they established the European Economic Community, usually referred to as the Common Market, whose objective was to join them together into an economic union. Their plan was to achieve this in a twelve- to fifteen-year period. During this time, all six states would completely eliminate the tariffs and quota systems still hampering trade among them (agriculture was to be the exception—the Market expected to develop a common policy of subsidies and price supports, and eliminate discriminations among farmers within the Community); they would also abolish restrictions on the movement of labor, capital, and services among them, although this commitment was a qualified one. But these moves, the "Six" realized, would not suffice. A government might abolish a tariff, but it could compensate its producers through subsidies or impose internal taxes which would discriminate against foreign products. Production costs also reflected national regulations on wages, hours, working conditions, and social welfare programs; producers in nations with lower standards would have an obvious advantage against foreign competition. Thus, to ensure maximum free competition in the Common Market, subsidies were forbidden (except for use in developing backward areas); discriminatory taxes, price fixing, and division of markets by cartel arrangements were not permitted; and the need to equalize hours, wages, and working conditions was recognized as urgent.

At the same time, three funds were established to help realize the Common Market. First, there was the European Investment Bank as a supplement to private capital within each member state to make loans for the development of backward areas, to help inefficient firms modernize to meet competition or convert to a different type of production. Second, there was the European Social Fund, which would be used for such tasks as helping any member's expenses in retraining workers for different kinds of labor, resettling them in new areas, or in certain instances providing them with unemployment benefits. The third was the Development Fund to be used for the economic development of the members' overseas territories, especially France's North African territories, which were also to be linked to the Common Market. Duties on imports to the Common Market from these overseas areas would be abolished, but these territories would be allowed to charge customs duties on imports from the Six in order to collect funds for their development. Lastly, member states agreed that once the Market had been realized, they would establish a common tariff against third parties.

What were the chances for the development of this market? The economic benefits suggested that they were excellent. As trade barriers were lowered and then disappeared, the increasing competition would result in the growth of efficient companies and the elimination of the less efficient ones unless they modernized or converted to new lines of production. All members would also gain from the capital funds. Italy would receive capital for the development of her southern area; France and her overseas territories would also receive development capital. While Germany would contribute a large share of these funds that would benefit her partners, she would in return receive access to their European and African markets—and Germany was in the strongest competitive position of the Six. A final factor was that the Community expected to receive advantages against third parties. It would be in a strong bargaining position to demand reciprocal lowering of tariffs. All these advantages outweighed the burdens each nation would suffer as a result of economic dislocation and hardships, which would, in fact, be minimized by being extended over a twelve- to fifteen-year period (the plan's initial successes have already cut this period down by five years) and by being shared among all members. Moreover, the Common Market was to be supported by EUR-ATOM, a cooperative venture among the Six to develop the peaceful applications of atomic energy. Western Europe's energy needs were rising rapidly, and she was becoming increasingly dependent on oil to supply this demand. Naturally, the European nations wished to decrease their dependence on the politically unstable Middle East. The use of atomic energy could achieve this goal. (Actually, however, the original urgency for construction of atomic power plants has decreased somewhat, and Europe at present suffers from a coal glut.)

Above all, the principal advantage of the Common Market would be political. For a common market needs common policies; only one set of rules—not six—can govern its competitive behavior. One nation cannot be allowed to pay its workers considerably lower wages than its neighbor in order to achieve a competitive advantage. There would therefore have to be some standardization of wages, as well as of such related items as overtime, hours worked per week, and various welfare benefits. In the long run, if the Market developed successfully, it would therefore also undoubtedly lead to the adoption of common fiscal policies to control the ups and downs of the business cycle, a common currency, and a central bank. Thus the economic "spill-over"—from a common market in coal and steel into a common market for all sectors of the economy—could be expected to stimulate political unification as economic integration compelled the Common Market members to harmonize their social and economic policies. Economic union would, in brief, encourage increasing political integration. It was precisely this objective to form a political union that had originally inspired ECSC.

EEC was the culminating act of the movement, initiated by France and strongly supported by Chancellor Adenauer, to tie Germany so closely to a European Community that she would never again be able to use her power for purely national ends. The formation of the Inner Six was nothing less than the last link subjecting Germany to European restraints and responsibilities. Its success would make it impossible thereafter for Germany ever again to pursue a unilateral course. The Common Market was also the end product of France's desire to supplement her own strength with that of a united Europe, so that she would gain an equal voice with

Britain in the Atlantic alliance and not always remain subservient to the United States. France did not want to pursue a NATO policy dictated largely by Anglo-American interests; she wanted the alliance to take her interests into account as well. When Charles de Gaulle assumed the Premiership, and later the Presidency, of the Fifth Republic in 1959, he made France's long resentment of Britain's special status in NATO very clear by demanding that the United States, Britain, and France establish a directorate for the determination of the alliance's global strategy. Since the French attributed America's willingness to listen to Britain's voice largely to her possession of her own atomic deterrent, the French also determined that they would create a nuclear arsenal of their own. For, just as the badge of a great power before World War I was an empire, such status today is signified by the possession of atomic weapons; just as Germany before 1914 strove with great energy to gain her "place in the sun," so France now felt that she had to explode her own bomb in order to make her voice heard once again. In February, 1960, the French succeeded in this enterprise. This underwrote the influence of the rising new European world power, which both De Gaulle and Adenauer sought as a means of safeguarding German and French interests in a world dominated by two superpowers.

It was hardly surprising, therefore, that Russia reacted quickly against the Common Market and attempted to break up this potential united states of Europe. A strong and united Europe, economically prosperous and politically stable, would block Soviet ambitions to dominate the European Rimland. Indeed, such a Europe would not only prove to be a powerful barrier to Soviet expansionist ambitions, but it might well threaten the Soviet *status quo* in Eastern Europe. The existence of a free Germany had already had an unsettling effect upon the whole satellite system.

West Berlin, especially, has had a tremendous impact in this respect. The existence of this city, alongside Communist East Berlin, had impeded Soviet control of East Germany. Through West Berlin escaped many young, skilled, and professional men and women of East Germany; it was an escape hatch that was depopulating East Germany of the very people it needed to run its society. In West Berlin, the United States, Britain, and France had, moreover, established agencies to

gather intelligence about Eastern Europe. There was a constant flow of information about the West from West Berlin into the Russian-controlled satellites; this defeated the very purpose of the iron curtain, which was to stop incoming information that might lead to comparisons of the Communist and free systems. West Berlin, in short, made the complete integration of East Germany into the satellite system impossible, and this, in turn, affected the political stability of all of Eastern Europe. If the existence of West Berlin and West Germany made the Communist *status quo* insecure, how much greater the Soviet apprehensions of a united Europe must have been. For such a Europe threatened to undermine this *status quo*.

Yet, it was essential for the Soviet Union to maintain its position in Eastern and Central Europe. Khrushchev simply could not acquiesce in the collapse of a Communist government. Any de-Communization, whether in East Germany or elsewhere in the satellite belt, would be a major defeat for world Communism and a great blow to the Soviet Union's prestige. Such a retraction of Soviet power would contradict the basic tenet of Communist propaganda: that capitalism is historically doomed and rapidly decaying, and that Communism is the inevitable wave of the future because its superior way of life attracts the masses everywhere. Moreover, the disintegration of any part of the satellite belt would jeopardize the entire Soviet position in Eastern Europe. This explained why the Russians crushed the Hungarian revolt before any of the other Eastern European nations could imitate the Hungarian example and overthrow their own Communist regimes. This was also the reason behind Khrushchev's repeated declarations that the Soviet Union would not allow the capitalists to dismantle socialism in East Germany. In one such declaration, he said: "Our consent to the reunification of Germany on a capitalist basis . . . would dishonor us . . . reunification of Germany at the expense of the G.D.R. [German Democratic Republic] would narrow down the front of socialism. . . . We have not been born and we do not live to yield to capitalism." The Soviet Premier was, however, well aware that the continuation of socialism in the G.D.R. required the continued presence of the Red Army on German soil.

The stability of the Soviet position in Eastern and Central

Europe thus depended upon two factors: one, gaining Western recognition of the East German "Democratic" Republic; and two, destroying the freedom of West Berlin. To achieve these objectives, the Soviet Union announced in November, 1958, that at the end of six months she intended to end the four-power occupation and would hand control of East Berlin and the routes leading into West Berlin over to the East Germans. The clear implication was that in the future free access to Berlin would require that the Western powers deal directly and officially with the East German Government. The Russians also repeated their former proposal for the unification of Germany: that East and West Germany should join in a confederation. This, too, was a tactical device to gain the Federal Republic's recognition of what the West Germans still usually refer to as the Soviet zone of occupation. The Russians obviously wanted to entice the West Germans to start negotiating with the East Germans on the issue of unification; at the same time, it was also clear that the Russians were not in the least interested in any form of unification. Their proposal was, in fact, so constituted that it precluded Western acceptance. A confederation half democratic and half dictatorship was a contradiction in terms and was totally unfeasible. How could a government of such a confederation ever agree on economic policies? Most industry in East Germany was owned by the government; West Germany was a booming private-enterprise state. The government would not even be able to agree on its jurisdiction. The G.D.R. had recognized the Oder-Neisse line as Germany's eastern frontier; West Germany had not yet acknowledged the permanent loss of the territories Poland received from Germany at the end of World War II. As if to ensure the rejection of their terms, the Russians also demanded that East Germany, with a population of a little more than 17 million, and West Germany, with a population of more than 53 million, should be equally represented in the confederated government. The Soviet Union naturally did not want the East Germans to be outvoted constantly—with the possible result that East Germany would be voted out of existence—but Khrushchev could hardly have expected the Western powers or the Adenauer Government to accept such equality. The Soviet leader seemed only to be supporting the statement he had previously made to two German Social Democratic leaders who had come

to him to talk about reunification: "Let's face it," he told
them bluntly, "no one is really interested in Germany's
unification." The Russian Ambassador to West Germany
made this explicit in early 1960 when he stated that the precondition for German reunification was not German neutrality, but the nationalization of West German big industry,
the "breaking up of the power of monopoly capital," and the
"domination of the working class." None of the Western
powers, let alone the Federal Republic, was likely to accept
these conditions.

If the Soviet proposals, then, were meant to elicit Western
recognition of East Germany, this goal still remained subsidiary to the primary aim of strangling West Berlin. What
the Russians were actually calling for when they declared the
end of the four-power occupation was an Allied withdrawal
from West Berlin, turning it into a "free city." This was, in
effect, a demand for the incorporation of West Berlin into
East Germany. Once Western troops had left the city, the
West Berliners would feel isolated and unprotected, abandoned and completely helpless. They would be surrounded
by the Russian Army and the East German Army and police.
In these circumstances, they would be subjected to a variety
of pressures—some crude, some more subtle, but all with only
one purpose in mind, to compel the defenseless West Berliners to come to terms with the East German regime. The
day would then come on which the Russian and East German
governments would jubilantly announce that the "free city"
of Berlin had voluntarily requested incorporation into the
German Democratic Republic.

At this point, the Russians would have eliminated a very
troublesome thorn in their side. They would then be in a far
better position to stabilize the *status quo*. But the destruction
of West Berlin would not only have accomplished the Soviet
Union's defensive aims; it would simultaneously have attained Russia's long-standing offensive purpose of weakening
its opponents, perhaps fatally. If the Russians could drive the
Western powers, especially the United States, out of Berlin,
they would also be able, first, to cut off the development of
the Common Market before it gathered too much momentum, and second, to shatter the NATO alliance. It was, above
all, American power that guaranteed the freedom of the 2
million Germans living in West Berlin. If the United States

were to abandon these people under pressure, faith in America's protective power and willingness to live up to its commitments would collapse in Europe as well as in the rest of the world. The Germans would be the first to read the lesson: that since America could not guarantee their security, they must approach the Russians independently. Whatever the nature of the terms the Russians would offer them, they would certainly include clauses demanding the abandonment of all Germany's political, economic, or military ties to the West. But without Germany, there could be no Common Market, since Germany's partners were dependent upon her for much of the capital required for their economic development. And if Germany pulled out of the Atlantic alliance, American troops would have to be withdrawn back to the United States, since it would be politically and strategically impossible to station them in France. Yet, these troops were a symbol of our commitment to defend Europe; they were psychologically and politically indispensable to the preservation of NATO unity and morale. No written guarantees could be substituted for this living embodiment of America's stake in Europe. Certainly, the withdrawal of our ground forces would indicate to the Europeans that America was no longer willing to defend them now that the United States was herself becoming increasingly vulnerable to a Soviet nuclear attack.

This was, in the final analysis, the fundamental issue posed by the Berlin crisis. The Soviet proposals had included the ultimatum that if West Berlin's status had not been "renegotiated" *à la Russe* within six months, the Russians would place the East Germans in control of the railroads and highways leading into West Berlin. If the East Germans then interfered with Western traffic, the West would have to employ force to break any blockade; and Khrushchev stated that any such Western attempts would meet Soviet resistance. The defense of West Berlin therefore posed the definite possibility of total war. But would the United States be willing to take this risk, when it no longer possessed an atomic monopoly? Threatening the Russians with SAC might, at a time of nuclear parity, be rather ineffective. The Russians, too, had the capability for massive retaliation. Was Berlin worth the devastation of most of America's cities and 100 to 180 million dead and wounded? The Russian challenge was a clever one:

it faced the United States with a limited challenge and offered us the choice of surrendering West Berlin or fighting a total war for its preservation. It was American will power which was thus really at stake in Berlin, and a failure of will would disintegrate the entire American position in the European Rimland.

Berlin was thus *the* test of postwar American policy. Nor was it a repeat of the 1948 situation. At that time, Stalin had acted upon two assumptions: first, that the far larger size of the Red Army would deter an Allied attempt to break through on the ground; and second, that the United States and Britain could not keep West Berlin alive through an airlift. The first assumption proved to be correct, but the second was mistaken. When Stalin realized this, he had either to call off the blockade or shoot down Allied planes and risk a war. America's atomic monopoly favored the first solution. By late 1958, Khrushchev did not have to feel so worried about America's nuclear arsenal; he had a sizable stockpile of his own. American brinkmanship, given this circumstance, would risk suicide. Yet, if the United States would not accept this risk to prevent Russia from slowly strangling West Berlin to death, the question inevitably arose: What objective was worth the cost of total war? If Berlin was not, what was? Berlin was thus a crisis of massive retaliation; for the Soviet action questioned the very feasibility of our basic strategy. Could strategic air power, upon which the Eisenhower Administration depended almost exclusively to preserve the line around the Sino-Soviet periphery, fulfill this task in an age of nuclear plenty, when World War III was merely a pseudonym for suicide? The answer seemed to be that too great a reliance upon SAC was gravely weakening our ability to preserve this line. Nuclear bombs were just *too* powerful; they were *too* enormously destructive to be used in any situation but the ultimate one. Our strategic power was—ironically—*so* great that it tended to paralyze our will to use it; it therefore paralyzed our diplomacy as well. The Berlin crisis was, in brief, the most serious challenge to the American approach to war—indeed, to foreign policy—up to this point in the postwar period.

VI. BERLIN AND THE CRISIS OF
MASSIVE RETALIATION

Mutual Deterrence and Suicide

No policy could have been more typically American than massive retaliation, which was designed to deter an attack by drawing a line around the Sino-Soviet periphery and threatening to destroy Moscow or Peiping if the Russians or the Chinese crossed that line. Under the Truman Administration, American retaliatory power would have been invoked if the Russians had attacked either the United States or Western Europe; but the Eisenhower Administration, because of the public reaction against the Korean War, threatened to invoke SAC even to deter limited aggressions outside of Europe. This strategy was a strictly military one, completely divorced from political considerations. The separation of force and diplomacy was, indeed, twofold.

In the first place, under massive retaliation, purely military considerations were to be dominant during the war. The only cause for war was enemy aggression; our military power was to be unleashed only in reaction to a hostile attack. But once it became clear that the diplomats had failed to keep the peace, the military would take charge and their aim would be total victory. The enemy was to be punished by completely defeating him. A maximum of violence was required to achieve such a military victory, making nuclear weapons ideal for this task. A single ten-megaton bomb—by no means the most powerful the United States possesses—packs five times the total explosive power of all the bombs dropped on Germany during four years of war, and one hundred times the power of those dropped on Japan. Such a bomb could devastate an entire city at one blow; and those not killed or injured by the heat and blast effects of the bomb would, in all probability, fall victim to the radioactive fallout which accompanies the explosion. A combined attack upon the enemy's (or our own) major population and industrial centers would paralyze the entire country and reduce it to a mass of rubble and radioactive dust. Massive retaliation, in brief, carried the American doctrine of war to its logical culmination.

In the second place, even in "peacetime," massive retaliation was to be concerned only with strictly military matters. Our statesmen constantly repeated that we would resort to force only to resist aggression. Since the sole reason for war was to be a purely military one, massive retaliation had no bearing on any political issues. Containment was supposed to create a situation of strength from which the United States could negotiate with the Soviet Union in order to resolve its basic differences with Russia and create a more stable situation. But how could the Russians be forced even to sit down with us to negotiate, much less to compromise their interests, unless pressure was exerted upon them? Yet, it was precisely such pressure which massive retaliation could not apply. Only a Soviet attack could unleash our military power; short of that, it was not to be invoked. American diplomacy was therefore, in fact, unsupported by force, and this renunciation of force eliminated any incentive for the Soviet leaders to grant any concessions. The result was a paradox.

On the one hand, for almost a decade the United States held either an atomic monopoly or a far superior capacity to deliver its atomic, and later its hydrogen, bombs. The Russians did not explode their first atomic bomb until late 1949, and their Long-Range Air Force was not developed until after the Indochina crisis in 1954. On the other hand, the United States could not utilize this superior strategic power for a favorable transformation of the political situation. American power could not, therefore, affect any of the political questions which had precipitated the cold war, such as the division of Germany or the incorporation of Eastern Europe into the Soviet empire. It could not even deter the Soviet Union from constant probing actions. Nor was this surprising, since we had renounced the use of force except in retaliation against a direct attack. Indeed, the irony of the situation was that throughout this whole period the Russians were most aggressive, constantly seeking to expand by means short of total war—by guerrilla warfare, *coups d'état,* internal Communist Parties, anti-Western nationalist movements, "volunteers," and satellite armies. This is not hard to understand, for if we were unwilling to fight a total war unless presented with an unambiguous threat to our security, the Russians had no need to compromise. In fact, they had every reason not only to be obdurate, but to continue their attempts to fill, as George Kennan had said, "every nook and cranny . . . in the basin of world power." The only thing they had to avoid was an attack upon the United States itself or upon those areas the United States had designated as of vital interest to her security.

Thus, in terms of the crises this country has confronted since 1945, strategic air power has proved to be an almost useless instrument. It did not prevent the Soviet Union from trying to turn Iran into a satellite state; it did not deter Communist guerrillas from attempting to undermine Greece's independence or exerting great pressure upon Turkey; it could not protect Czechoslovakia from the Communist *coup d'état;* it did not stay Stalin's blockade of Berlin; it could do nothing to halt the Communist conquest of China; it did not even deter the Russians from openly resorting to force in Korea; nor did it stop the Chinese Communists from sending their troops into Korea or providing maximum aid to the Vietminh in the decisive test at Dienbienphu; it proved totally unable to prevent the establishment of the Moscow-Cairo axis or the Soviet-Egyptian attempts to eliminate all Western influence in the Middle East; nor did it help the brave people of Hungary. In each of these cases, the American Government rejected outright the possibility of fighting a total war. In Iran, it sent the Soviet Union a stern note; Greece and Turkey were saved by the Truman Doctrine, which, like the subsequent Marshall Plan, was essentially an economic measure; Berlin was saved by the airlift; Korea was held by the use of army forces and tactical air power, but we did not dare to use our strategic air power against China itself; and in Indochina, despite all our warnings, the crisis of Dienbienphu was met with a decision *not* to intervene at all.

Never, in a single one of these crises, did the United States invoke massive retaliation; neither the Truman nor the Eisenhower Administration was at any time willing to precipitate a total nuclear war. The response to each of these limited challenges demonstrated the deep reluctance of the American Government, whether Democrat.: or Republican, to invoke SAC; and this was so despite the fact that for the first decade of the postwar era, the United States held an unchallengeable atomic superiority and was practically immune to attack. This restraint was reinforced during the late 1950's by the Soviet buildup of a nuclear stockpile with the capacity to hit targets in the United States. This meant that the two powers had reached a stage of "saturation parity," in which both sides could destroy each other. In this stalemated position, it was believed, neither side would dare attack the other. The "balance of terror," as Churchill called it, would ensure the peace; indeed, in President Eisenhower's words, "there is no alternative to peace." His participation at the 1955 summit conference in Geneva with Soviet Premier Bulganin (front man for Khrushchev, who was at that time not yet Premier but Secretary of the Communist Party of the U.S.S.R.) was generally recognized as testimony to this fact. War was no longer a rational instrument of national power; by simply meeting, the leaders of the two most powerful countries of the world were said to have "signed" a tacit nonaggression pact.

Actually, American policy handed the Soviet Union the opportunity to break this stalemate. For the age of nuclear plenty has increased our strategic dilemma. Our all-or-nothing strategy has meant that each limited Soviet challenge has confronted our government with the question of whether the defense of the objective under attack was worth the destruction of most of America's cities and their inhabitants. Estimates of the dead have ranged from 100 to 180 million. These figures are so high not only because of the destructive impact of H-bombs, but also because few of the injured could be saved. Most hospitals would be destroyed, most doctors and nurses killed or wounded, any remaining blood plasma inadequate, and all sanitary conditions completely eliminated. And of course, the country would be living under radioactive clouds. Faced with this prospect if it responded to the less than total Soviet challenges, the American Government had a strong incentive to do nothing. This meant that the Communists could gradually turn the nuclear balance of power in their own favor by imposing a series of piecemeal defeats upon us. They could erode the *status quo* by nibbling away at it bit by bit, without ever once facing this country with the one kind of challenge for which it was prepared. According to Henry Kissinger:

> It can be argued that the fear of all-out war is bound to be mutual, that the Soviet leaders will, therefore, share our reluctance to engage in any adventures which may involve this risk. But because each side may be equally deterred from engaging in all-out war, it makes all the difference which side can extricate itself from its dilemma *only* by initiating such a struggle. If the Soviet bloc can present its challenges in less than all-out form it may gain a crucial advantage. Every move on its part will then pose the appalling dilemma of whether we are willing to commit suicide to prevent encroachments, which do not, each in itself, seem to threaten our existence directly but which may be steps on the road to our ultimate destruction.
>
> To be sure, we shall continue to insist that we reject the notion of "peace at any price." The price of peace, however, cannot be determined in the abstract. The growth of the Soviet nuclear stockpile is certain to widen the line between what is considered "vital" and what is "peripheral" if we must weigh each objective against the destruction of New York or Detroit, of Los Angeles or Chicago.

American strategy, in short, suffers from an internal contradiction: it has so much power at its command that our governments are, and will be, fearful to employ it lest its use spell the end of our civilization as well as that of the enemy.

As the growing capacity of Soviet strategic air power increasingly neutralized SAC, American diplomacy became paralyzed. In 1950-51, during the Korean War, we were already unwilling to risk an attack upon China; in Indochina in 1954, we showed the same reluctance for the second time. And in 1956, during the Hungarian revolt, we even reassured the Soviet Union that we had no intention of either intervening to stop its repression of the Hungarian people or allying ourselves with any "liberated" satellite state. The Administration apparently believed that in the absence of such an explicit American renunciation of force in this instance, the

Soviet Union might unleash nuclear warfare. With its security belt in Eastern Europe collapsing—Poland, too, was striking out for a measure of independence from the Soviet Union—the Russian leaders, fearing American intervention, might be desperate enough to take the ultimate step. The American position foreshadowed the time when possibly even Europe would no longer be worth the cost of a total war any more—when only an all-out attack upon the United States itself would unleash SAC. Certainly, our allies in Europe grew increasingly doubtful that the United States would risk suicide in order to repulse Russian probes in Europe. They feared that as our vulnerability increased, the threat of massive retaliation would decline in Soviet eyes—as it had already done outside Europe. If Russian challenges were then not met, faith in America's protective power and willingness to live up to its commitments would be destroyed, and Europe left defenseless. If this day ever came, the Common Market and NATO would collapse, and the United States, strategically isolated, would face the Sino-Soviet bloc in essential control of Eurasia and Africa, Mac-Kinder's World-Island.

Massive Retaliation and NATO

The question raised by the Soviet buildup of a nuclear deterrent force—whether the United States would continue to defend Europe with strategic air power—was further underlined by the lack of sizable shield forces on the Continent. The original tasks assigned to these troops were twofold: first, to assure the Russians that an attack upon Europe would break the trip-wire and unleash SAC; and second, to implement the "forward strategy" and hold the Red Army at the Elbe. The former function was a very necessary one at a time when the Russians could not yet hit the United States. The Russian leaders might have believed then that this country was bluffing—as long as America was not attacked, she would not precipitate a total war for the sake of defending Europe. American troops were placed on the front line to assure them that we meant exactly what we said. But this function was now obsolete. For if the Russians believed their action would provoke American retaliation, they would obviously strike the first blow at the United States.

The second task perhaps still had some validity, although it, too, was becoming increasingly obsolete. Ground operations in Europe would hardly play an important role in World War III, if that calamity should ever be precipitated. The strategic nuclear exchange would then be decisive. If the Russians won that exchange, there would be no point in attempting to stop the Red Army. But if the Russians lost it, the Red Army would be in no position to advance. It seemed difficult to believe that the Soviet forces that managed to survive the initial nuclear holocaust would be at all able to wage a "broken-backed" war. The *minimum* damage inflicted upon the Soviet Union would make any further mobilization impossible; Russia's cities and industries would be destroyed, and most of her population would be either dead, injured, or living under radioactive clouds. The survivors could not be expected to be greatly concerned with the attainment of any political-military objectives. The shield forces, in short, were unlikely to have any significant effect upon the outcome of such a war.

The third and newest operational assignment provided for NATO forces seemed, therefore, to be its principal one: to conduct limited operations and thereby deter less than total challenge. It was preposterous to assume that the United States would continue to risk suicide *no matter what the level of Soviet provocation.* Would we really be willing to initiate an all-out nuclear war if the Russians seized a small portion of Turkey? Would we really precipitate a total nuclear exchange if the Red Army or satellite East Germany troops seized all or part of West Berlin or a small enclave of West Germany? Would suicide in these instances be preferable to accepting limited losses? Only a capacity for limited war would allow the United States and her allies to escape this dilemma. In the words of General Norstad, the NATO commander in the late 1950's:

> In an era of nuclear plenty and of delivery means adequate in number and in effectiveness, the NATO shield provides us with an option more useful than the simple choice between all or nothing. Should we fail to maintain reasonable shield strength on the NATO frontier, then massive retaliation could be our only response to an aggression, regardless of its nature. There is

real danger that inability to deal decisively with limited or local attacks could lead to our piecemeal defeat or bring on a general war. If, on the other hand, we have means to meet less than ultimate threats with a decisive but less than ultimate response, the very possession of this ability would discourage the threat, and would thereby provide us with an essential political and military maneuverability.

But it was exactly this capacity to respond to limited challenges that was missing in Europe, thus reinforcing the reliance upon massive retaliation. In a large measure, this was a result of the Eisenhower Administration's determination to "maximize air power and minimize the foot soldier." The Army was cut from twenty to fourteen divisions, and even then it received only relatively small sums for the modernization of its equipment. In 1956, the Chairman of the Joint Chiefs of Staff, Admiral Radford, even proposed an 800,000-man reduction in military strength. This would have left only a small task force in Europe and limited the Army's function at home primarily to a civil-defense mission. As a fighting force, the Army's days certainly seemed numbered. It was the strong protests of our allies, especially of West Germany, that prevented the adoption of this proposal. Nevertheless, Radford's proposal was symptomatic of the Administration's policy.

The impact upon NATO of this de-emphasis on ground power was immediate. It quickly became obvious that the NATO goal of ninety-six divisions—thirty-five to forty of which were to be in the front line on D-day—would remain unfulfilled. It was therefore decided that NATO forces should be equipped with atomic tactical weapons; fire power was to be substituted for manpower. The new force level was established at thirty divisions. But this goal remained elusive. The British soon decided to follow our example of relying almost completely upon strategic air power, and in 1957 they announced that the British Army would be cut back in size and that it would be equipped with "atomic rocket artillery." British forces in Germany were correspondingly reduced. In the meantime, the French had withdrawn almost their entire army stationed in Germany to suppress the nationalist rebellion in Algeria, and the Germans, too, had cut their force level from 500,000 to 325,000 men. (Only American forces remained steady—at five divisions and three armored units.) By January of 1960, NATO had only seventeen or eighteen ready divisions.

Apart from the numerical deficiency of NATO ground forces, their equipment with atomic tactical weapons raised the same question as did SAC: Would they be used? Would NATO not grow increasingly reluctant to rely on these forces to respond to Russian moves? When the original decision to equip Allied forces with atomic weapons was taken, it was believed that the Soviet Union would have few, if any, atomic tactical weapons. Thus, the damage caused by our weapons could be absorbed—particularly since East Germany and Poland would have to absorb most of it, and Soviet and satellite troops would have to suffer the atomic blows. The picture changed, however, because the Western powers were not the only ones to equip their forces with these arms (the Germans began to move in this direction in 1959 with the acquisition of American missiles, and the French, too, are re-equipping their army). The Russians, too, acquired these weapons and thereby ensured that their use would be reciprocal. In these circumstances, the advantages that atomic arms were supposed to confer upon the West began to diminish, if not to disappear.

Nuclear weapons would not protect Europe; they would devastate it. Europe is densely populated; its cities are too close to one another; civil, military, tactical, and strategic targets are all intertwined. A nuclear ground war would be a catastrophe for Europe, probably spelling the end of European civilization. The distinction between a limited atomic war and a total atomic war is thus meaningless. In Operation Carte Blanche, a military exercise conducted in 1955 to demonstrate the effectiveness of tactical atomic weapons, an estimated 1.7 million Germans were killed, 3.5 million wounded, and an unknown number affected by radiation. And in Exercise Winter Shield, held in February, 1960, "the theoretical casualty toll [according to Hanson Baldwin, military editor of *The New York Times*] ... was tremendous. ... Nuclear weapons delivered by gun and missile and atomic demolitions were used so extensively that an observer wonders—had Winter Shield been war—whether any integrated armies would have been left to fight." In brief, the use of these atomic weapons might be unacceptable politically. Even militarily, as a substitute for manpower, their value was questionable. An atomic war would be fought by highly mobile, self-sufficient units. Each of these units would have tremendous fire power. But one or two hits by an opposing force similarly armed would wipe out the entire unit. This would necessitate its complete replacement. Tactical atomic weapons would therefore seem to require more, not less, manpower. Finally, there was certainly no reason to believe that such weapons would be of greater benefit to the defense than to the offense. Both sides could use them with equally deadly effect. In any case it was a matter of simple logic that a big atomic army would have a major, if not decisive, advantage over a small atomic army. Thus, despite the trend within NATO toward atomic weapons, there were overwhelming political and military reasons why, even with a larger shield force, NATO's willingness to fight a limited tactical atomic war would be a doubtful quantity. As such, it did *not* allow the West to escape the dilemma of suicide or appeasement.

The irony of this situation was that atomic weapons were justified by our alleged numerical inferiority in manpower. Yet, the United States and her allies actually held a superiority of manpower over the Soviet Union and its European satellites. In terms of conventional warfare, the West retained a comparative advantage. To be sure, a Soviet attack with atomic weapons would leave us no choice but to respond in the same manner; but if the Russians or East Germans attempted a push with conventional forces, did it necessarily follow that this was to our *disadvantage?* A limited war in Europe was surely meaningless unless it also limited the devastation. While NATO had to be prepared to wage war with atomic tactical weapons if the opponent did, the alliance also —if it wished to survive—had to offer the Europeans the prospect of defense without a nuclear holocaust. Such an alternative did not exist in the late 1950's. The concentration on massive retaliation—on NATO's sword—had reduced the apparent necessity of raising sufficient ground forces and strengthening the NATO shield. This, in turn, reinforced the need to stake our survival on each issue, no matter what the level of provocation, since we were left with no weapon but strategic air power with which to respond to each Soviet challenge.

The Berlin Retreat

The Berlin issue therefore precipitated, as Khrushchev had intended, what the French aptly call a *crise de confiance* within NATO. For the Eisenhower Administration was convinced that the threat of unleashing SAC would deter any Soviet actions in Berlin; indeed, it was so convinced of this that it specifically ruled out the possibility of a ground war in Europe. It refused to call a partial mobilization or reinforce NATO ground forces. On the contrary, it continued to reduce the size of the Army and the Marine Corps. It seemed as though the Administration, by deliberately rejecting any other means than SAC for defending Berlin, was trying to persuade Mr. Khrushchev that we meant what we said. For if we consciously ruled out any alternative to total nuclear war, and at the same time told the Soviet leader over and over again that we would stand firm, he would have no choice but to believe us. In short, by leaving itself with no alternative to all-out war, the Administration was trying to restore the credibility of SAC as a deterrent.

However, few Western actions—and especially American ones—were calculated to impress Mr. Khrushchev with NATO's unity and resoluteness. For our almost exclusive reliance on SAC has always had a bipolarizing effect upon the alliance. When SAC seems to work, the Europeans are delighted, relax their own defense efforts, and even indulge in the luxury of criticizing our alleged warmongering. But as soon as it appears that massive retaliation may not be effective, the Europeans on the one hand apply pressure upon the United States in order to restrain us from precipitating a total nuclear war, and on the other hand are fearful that we will no longer protect them because we will not accept the risk of war. Given the nature of American strategy, European reaction was inevitable. When the possibility arose that the United States might bomb China during the Korean War, Britain, France, and the other NATO nations declared that they would not support such American action. This was one of the reasons for the Truman Administration's rejection of General MacArthur's strategy. The government was unwilling to undertake any unilateral action which might disrupt the alliance in Europe, the area it considered most vital to American security. In Indochina, the possibility that the

United States might intervene with nuclear air power had the same effect—though not on France, of course. If this opposition—especially that of Britain—was not the principal deterrent to our intervention, it was certainly an important consideration. American determination to defend Quemoy and Matsu was faced with a similar lack of support in Europe.

Thus, in each of these cases, either all our NATO allies or those not immediately involved opposed any American action that might result in World War III. This pattern was to be repeated with Berlin. The Adenauer Government wanted to stand fast. In its opinion, any change in Berlin's status was tantamount to appeasement. The West, Adenauer constantly stressed, must maintain its rights and obligations in Berlin: "That is a principle which must not be shaken. Everything else would be a capitulation of freedom to dictatorship, followed by new demands today, tomorrow, or the day after." A demonstration of Western weakness in Berlin, he warned, would set in motion a chain of events that would be disastrous for all of Europe: the dissolution of Germany's links to Western Europe, the disintegration of NATO, and Soviet domination of Europe.

The French Government supported the German stand. For France had long sought a united Europe in order to supplement her own strength. De Gaulle, like Adenauer, thought of Europe as a future world power. Since this power was to be founded on the Bonn-Paris axis, France was unwilling to see any changes brought about in Europe that might endanger West Germany's existence. The alternative to Franco-German unity was a bleak one. President de Gaulle had stated: "Being without means of action, that is to say, of destruction, equal to those in the hands of the Americans and the Russians, and thus of power to try to impose her policy, she [France] might try to keep outside the [great power] conflict and in the last resort of war. . . . This would amount to France's giving up her reasons for living in an attempt to keep her life." France and Germany therefore had to cooperate, for West Germany's integration into Europe was the prerequisite for France's ability "to keep her life."

In brief, both Germany and France were opposed to discussing the Berlin and general German questions with the Russians. The strongest pressure for such talks came from the British. It was upon them that the consequences of American massive retaliation had the greatest impact. In an age of nuclear parity, the British argued, it was better to negotiate than to fight; negotiations should at least first be tried in order to see whether the problem could be solved by means other than a war which would risk national survival. The West's objective was to deter Russia from taking actions which would destroy or threaten its security—without precipitating a global holocaust, if possible. Total war was a weapon of last resort; massive retaliation should be unleashed only in the extreme situation in which the opponent had proved completely inflexible in his demands and had left the West with no other honorable way to preserve its security. Only then should the Western powers take a position which would risk their own destruction as well. The British had never been happy—to put it mildly—with Secretary Dulles' brinkmanship. It frightened them, and this fear was increased by its failure in Indochina. What if the Russians, like the Chinese before them, considered the Administration's threats of massive retaliation a bluff because the policy had lost its credibility? If they did not take the American threat seriously and pushed forward with their plan, they might precipitate the very crisis which SAC was supposed to prevent. The deterrent would have failed to deter; indeed, it would have been responsible for a Soviet miscalculation which could bring most of the world down with it.

Britons had for years felt that American policies were on the whole too rigid, too much influenced by a strong—and immodest—sense of self-righteousness. The British had been far more inclined than the United States toward approaching the Russians in an attempt to negotiate with them on the various issues which had given rise to the cold war. To some extent, this belief that Britain was the "great conciliator" between rival power blocs was a hangover from the days when Britain had held the balance of power; and alleged American rigidity and occasional belligerency reinforced this nostalgia for bygone days. If Britain was to play a leading role in NATO—and all Britons assumed that their country should —it could do so only if it acted as a mediator attempting to bridge the gap between the two inflexible superpowers, while simultaneously trying to prevent the outbreak of an all-out war. The different ideological nature of the Soviet regime did not strike Britons with the same sense of horror and moral revulsion as it did Americans. Britain had for centuries maintained diplomatic relations with nations of whose form of government she disapproved. Advocating the reduction of tensions was thus not only a means of capturing the government or staying in power, but also a means of asserting Britain's leadership and prestige within NATO and on the world scene—which would, of course, also reap electoral advantages.

The initial American position on Berlin wavered between the inflexible German and French line and the more elastic British stand, although it gradually moved nearer to the latter. On the one hand, the United States was determined to stay in Berlin; on the other hand, having stated that it would defend Berlin by massive retaliation, it simultaneously sought to escape the consequences of its own military strategy. This it could do only by granting concessions. Shortly after the presentation of the Soviet ultimatum, Secretary of State Dulles talked of accepting the East Germans as "Russian agents" at the checkpoints on the routes leading into Berlin. The Secretary also declared that the reunification of Germany could be brought about by means other than free elections—a statement which seemed to clearly indicate abandonment of the long-time American position on free elections for a reunified Germany. The Administration, already pressured by the British, also accepted the standing Russian call for a summit conference. But it insisted—and here it departed from the British and Russian positions—on the prior fulfillment of two conditions: withdrawal of the Soviet six-month ultimatum, and a Foreign Ministers' conference to lay the basis for a settlement of the Berlin and the general German issues. The purpose of a "meeting at the top" was, in the Administration's opinion, essentially to ratify decisions already reached at a lower level; Eisenhower definitely rejected a meeting which would settle nothing and end in a fruitless propaganda debate.

The Russians reluctantly accepted the precondition of a Foreign Ministers' conference, and at the same time denied that the six-month ultimatum was an ultimatum. But they refused to budge from their position at the Foreign Ministers' marathon held in Geneva in the spring and summer of 1959. It was the West that offered the concessions. In the first place, the United States allowed an East German delegation to sit in on the deliberations. The Soviet Union had threatened not to negotiate at all if the East Germans were not permitted to attend; the United States and Britain, wishing to resolve the Berlin crisis without war, surrendered. Thereby, they took a step toward the *de facto* recognition of the Soviet puppet regime. Moreover, the West abandoned its plan for the reunification of Germany at the first sign of Soviet opposition. By this plan, the Western powers would have agreed to the establishment of a Big Four Commission aided by the two Germanys to discuss a peace treaty with a united Germany and an electoral law for all-German elections. No agreement could be reached on this plan, because among other things the Russians insisted that the Commission be composed of an equal number of representatives of the two unequal parts of Germany, and that it exclude the Big Four powers. The Foreign Ministers therefore took up the problem of an interim settlement for Berlin. In order to achieve such an arrangement, the West offered two concessions: first, the West would not arm its forces in Berlin with nuclear weapons and would not install missile bases in the city; and second, the Allies promised to curb their propaganda and intelligence activities in their sector if the Russians would halt similar (and anti-Western) activities in their zone. These proposals were unacceptable to the Soviet Union.

The Russians simply refused to renew their endorsement of Allied rights in Berlin, and reasserted that they would end the occupation regime. The Allies thus failed to obtain the Soviet guarantee they sought, but the fact that they had attempted to arrive at an interim arrangement for Berlin at all, and were willing to grant concessions to obtain it, is eloquent testimony to the dilemma in which American strategy had placed them. For, in effect, the Western powers—in this case, actually America and Britain—were willing to transform the Western position in Berlin merely in return for the withdrawal of the Soviet threat to the city. In an attempt to extricate themselves from the dilemma of suicide or surrender, the two countries were placing themselves in the humiliating position of calling into question their well-established rights in Berlin.

Khrushchev's bellicosity and rigidity were thus paying handsome dividends. The more menacing he sounded and the more inflexibly he stood, the greater the number of voices in the West who called for more Western "flexibility" and "new approaches" to the Soviet Union on the whole problem of Germany. Policies which had almost become "untouchable" over the years were suddenly placed in flux simply because of the Soviet threat to cut Western communication lines into the city. The Soviet game, as Henry Kissinger has pointed out, was a very shrewd one, indeed: it was to induce Western public opinion to forget that the cold war was the result of Soviet objectives and policies, and to create the impression instead that the cold war was merely a question of personalities. This technique held highly dangerous implications. If the Soviets could succeed in persuading the people of the West that serious international tensions stem from certain individuals, then in each Soviet-provoked crisis the West would be tempted to look inward; it would place the blame for the crises and their inherent dangers on its own leaders, and set up a clamor for "new approaches" and the abandonment of "old," "inflexible," and "dangerous" policies in order to relieve the tension.

During the Berlin crisis, the West was torn apart by precisely this kind of demoralizing controversy. The British, and particularly the British press, denounced Chancellor Adenauer's "rigidity"; the Germans, in turn, accused the British of "appeasement." Franco-British relations did not descend to the same depth of mutual suspicion and bitterness, but they did cool off considerably, especially after France failed to accept Britain in the Common Market on her own terms. And both Adenauer and De Gaulle demonstrated increasing suspicions of United States intentions and resolution. America's apparent willingness to discuss Berlin with the Russians seemed to the French and German leaders to show little American conviction or courage to uphold its previous position; to them, Eisenhower was showing far too much flexibility.

As if to prove Khrushchev correct that his threats of war against the West would have rewarding consequences, and to confirm De Gaulle's and Adenauer's apprehensions, President Eisenhower issued an invitation to Mr. Khrushchev to visit the United States in September, 1959. This invitation represented a major Soviet tactical victory, no matter how great the desirability that the two leaders should sit down and try to resolve the Berlin crisis. For the President had very definitely stated that he would not attend a summit conference unless the Russians first withdrew their ultimatum on Berlin, and second, met the Western powers at a Foreign Ministers' conference which would arrive at a basis for agreements. The Russians had done neither. Before the deadline of May 27, 1959, arrived, the West was already attempting to negotiate about Germany and Berlin at the Foreign Ministers' conference; when the opening session failed, the West resumed its efforts after a recess in order to postpone any Russian action; and when this session failed, the United States invited Mr. Khrushchev in still another attempt to delay the day when the Russian leader might carry out his threat to cut Berlin's "umbilical cord." While the deadline was thus postponed formally, the threat to Berlin was not withdrawn, and the Western powers were continuing to negotiate under duress. Moreover, the Foreign Ministers' conference had been unfruitful, and Soviet pressure on Berlin remained omnipresent. President Eisenhower therefore retracted his conditions. To be sure, the Administration did not call the meeting between the President and Premier Khrushchev a summit conference, but reality cannot be eliminated or disguised with words.

Khrushchev's warlike gestures and obduracy had, in brief, obtained for him not only a summit meeting but a summit à deux. This is exactly what he had long sought—a two-man meeting which excluded the other Allied leaders. Such a conference would show his equality with the American President and convincingly demonstrate to the world Russia's status with the United States as one of the two great superpowers. It would also help achieve another goal: to deepen the divisions within Western ranks. For such a conference was meant to suggest America's unreliability to her allies, especially France and Germany, by increasing their apprehension of a separate United States–Soviet agreement at their expense, and conversely, to persuade President Eisenhower that the crisis was caused by the rigidity of certain Allied leaders who were opposed to the "normalization" of relations. It is noticeable, for instance, that after the conference had ended, the President described the Allied position in Berlin with the same word Khrushchev constantly used—"abnormal." This seemed to imply agreement with the Soviet contention, though, in fact, the real abnormality and cause of the crisis was the Soviet occupation of East Germany. Perhaps the President, who together with the Secretary of State (Dulles' successor, Christian Herter) again referred to Berlin several times with that descriptive term, meant something quite different than did Khrushchev; perhaps "abnormal" to them meant only the peculiar situation of Berlin, divided within itself and lying 100 miles inside the Communist zone. But this differentiation was unimportant in terms of the world-wide impression it gave. By using the word "abnormal," the President and Secretary Herter appeared to support Khrushchev's position and unwittingly strengthened the latter's diplomatic hand. If the Allied position in Berlin was indeed "abnormal," the Soviet demands then seemed "reasonable" and the Western powers should alter their position to "normalize" the situation. This heedless use of a single word was characteristic of the manner in which Khrushchev was being allowed to set not only the pace of the negotiations, but also the context within which these took place. In any event, the President's use of the word "abnormal" only roused German and French distrust of the United States to new heights and caused De Gaulle to hold out successfully against an immediate summit conference, largely because of a genuine apprehension of American weakness. France was thus able to explode her own atomic bomb, which bolstered French prestige, and the Franco-German hand was strengthened against both the United States and Russia.

The Eisenhower-Khrushchev meeting was, in retrospect, justified with the argument that the two men reached an agreement by which the Soviet Union withdrew its threat to take unilateral action in Berlin, in return for American willingness to negotiate on the problems of Berlin and Germany at a four-power summit meeting. For American policymakers, this meant another postponement of the day on which they would have to decide the painful question of whether Berlin was worth the cost of a total war. But if the Administration believed that the crisis had been ended, that from then on it could leisurely negotiate on these issues and, if the Russians did not accept its terms, preserve the *status quo*, it was soon disabused of this notion. In December, 1959, Mr. Khrushchev reiterated his threat to sign a separate peace with East Germany. On New Year's Eve, at a Kremlin reception, he reportedly accused the Western powers of stalling in Berlin. And shortly thereafter, in January, 1960, he told the Supreme Soviet: "If all our efforts to conclude a peace treaty with the two German states fail to be crowned with success, after all, the Soviet Union and other willing states will sign a peace treaty with the [East] German Democratic Republic with all the consequences proceeding from this." This position was reaffirmed by the Warsaw Pact nations in their official communiqué issued at the end of their conference in early February; and between then and May, it was reiterated on a number of other occasions. The Berlin crisis was still very much alive. So were Allied differences. Germany and France still opposed any concessions to the Soviet Union. Adenauer and De Gaulle, in fact, wanted to scrap the Foreign Ministers' record of 1959—that is, they wished to retract the tentative concessions offered to the Russians in Geneva. But Britain and the United States did not agree with this stand. Their position was that the long negotiations of the Foreign Ministers could not be ignored and that the French and German attitude that any talks on Berlin should "start from scratch" was unrealistic. The Anglo-American position prevailed and provided the basis for the negotiations to be held at the summit conference in May, 1960.

Shortly before the scheduled Paris meeting, however, an event took place which was to shatter the summit conference after only one session and further postpone future negotiations on Berlin. On May Day, 1,300 miles within Soviet territory, the Russians downed an American U-2 "spy plane" loaded with photographic equipment for the gathering of intelligence data. The Eisenhower Administration reacted to this unexpected and unhappy turn of events with considerable diplomatic ineptitude. When Khrushchev initially announced only the shooting down of the U-2, our government responded that the plane had been engaged solely in meteorological observation and speculated that the pilot must have flown off his course after suffering a blackout caused by a failure of his oxygen equipment. But the Soviet Premier had shrewdly held back his trump cards, waiting to hear precisely what our explanation would be. He then revealed the real mission of our flight and produced an alleged confession by the pilot. At this point, the Administration reversed itself. In a move unprecedented in diplomatic history, it admitted that Khrushchev had been correct, that the U-2 pilot had been taking aerial photographs of the Soviet Union, and that it had lied in its previous announcement. Nor did the Administration stop there. For some still unexplained reason, our spokesmen claimed that similar flights had been sent into Russian skies for several years, and they strongly intimated that such flights would continue. The reason advanced was, to be sure, legitimate enough: Soviet secrecy made it necessary to gather information by this means in order to prevent a surprise attack. But it is one thing to be caught red-handed in spying and to admit it; it is quite another thing to assert that you will continue to do so in the future. In effect, the United States claimed the *right* to fly over Soviet territory (one need only imagine the uproar in this country if the Russians were to announce calmly that they had the right to fly over American soil and take photographs of our military installations).

Such a challenge could hardly have been left unmet. As Walter Lippmann has pointed out, for the Soviet Premier to have bypassed this claim would have been equivalent to acknowledging to the world, to his people, to his domestic enemies, and to his allies that he had surrendered to the United States the right to violate Soviet territory. Khrushchev could not have survived such an admission. The alternative course he took was to strike a belligerent pose in Paris. He launched a blistering personal attack upon President Eisenhower, demanding from him a personal apology for past U-2 flights, a promise that no such flights would be undertaken in the future, and punishment of those responsible for the spying operation (apparently, since the President had accepted full responsibility, Khrushchev meant that he should punish himself!). Eisenhower's promise that no more reconnaissance missions would be undertaken during his term of office—another reversal of the American position—did not satisfy Khrushchev; he apparently considered this to mean merely a temporary suspension. The other conditions demanded by the Soviet Premier were, of course, rejected outright by Eisenhower. Khrushchev thereupon suggested that the summit conference be postponed for a period of six to eight months, and he bluntly told Eisenhower that he would not be welcome if he came to the Soviet Union in June to return the Premier's previous visit to the United States. In short, behaving like a jilted suitor, Khrushchev said that he wanted nothing more to do with Eisenhower and that he would wait to negotiate the Berlin problem with the next administration. A new crisis had been put off for a little while longer.

But if the Russians were unwilling to risk the final test, they had shown once more that they were not hesitant to push the issue to a point just short of war. If the United States upheld the *status quo,* it had demonstrated once again the caution inherent in American postwar policy, a caution which in this crisis bordered on appeasement. The fact that the United States did not reject outright the Soviet demands, the manner in which it questioned its own position in Berlin, the way in which it retreated diplomatically, the concessions it offered in the name of flexibility—all demonstrated a lack of will power and sense of purpose which augured ill for the future. Former Secretary of State Acheson, in condemning the Eisenhower Administration's entire handling of the Berlin situation, saw the crisis in its true perspective: "The plain truth is that to negotiate about Berlin with the intention of coming to terms is only a polite misleading phrase for a retreat and an acceptance of Russian terms. It is a device for cloaking defeat with the appearance of consent." Any deal with the Russians on Berlin's future, he emphasized, would be worse than the one the Allies had held before and would open the city to annexation by the Communists. "It is so easy to confuse or to use this word 'negotiating' as a cover for surrender. . . . If to negotiate means to put the façade of consent upon defeat, then I think it is not something which should recommend itself to us. . . . The essential thing is what you confer about—not whether you should confer, but what you confer about." This was especially so since the United States was actually being asked to confer about the disengagement of American forces in West Germany and not just in West Berlin. "What disengagement means is that the whole attempt to create a counterforce [in Europe] to the Soviet force is ended. We cannot create such a counterforce with ground forces in Europe and in the U.S. separated by the Atlantic Ocean. . . . Khrushchev says, 'This is a matter on which compromise is possible. I don't have to cut all your throats; I only need to cut half of your throat.' This is the kind of thing into which we are being led by the incredible view that any sort of negotiating is good *per se.*"

But this view was, above all, the result of the mid-twentieth-century American dilemma. For if we invoked our strategy of massive retaliation, we would be committing suicide; and if we wished to avoid that risk, we would have to surrender. In these conditions, negotiations became an attempt to stall for time, as well as a means to inform the Soviet Union that the United States intended to honor its commitments and that the Soviets had better desist. The question was whether they would believe our verbal declarations of firmness—and if so, how much longer they would believe them—at a time when our strategy was becoming less credible. Our power could be preserved in Berlin, and in other spots around the world, only if the United States showed the requisite determination in the face of Communist challenges. Yet this determination was being undermined "from within" by the nature of our strategy.

The Lessons of Nuclear Blackmail

The basic lesson of Berlin was that American strategy was too inflexible. An all-or-nothing option was no option at all. If the United States had been reluctant to unleash SAC before the development of the Soviet Long-Range Air Force, it was even less likely to do so in a situation of mutual deterrence. Before the United States had become vulnerable to attack, the threat of an American first strike being launched against the Soviet Union might have been credible to the Soviet leadership and might therefore have acted as a deterrent to aggression. But this threat was no longer very credible when, to implement the threat, the United States would have to risk committing suicide.

This lack of credibility would, moreover, be reinforced by the change-over from bombers to missiles which began in the late 1950's. The significance of this change was that it would *stabilize* mutual deterrence. Bombers, located at known sites, are highly vulnerable to surprise attack. Thus, even in a situation of mutual deterrence, the possibility that many or most of the enemy's bombers might be surprised and destroyed on the ground remained an incentive to attack. If they could be destroyed, the retaliatory attack by a small remnant force might not be fatal to the attacking nation. In a crisis situation, this possibility could tempt either side to launch a pre-emptive strike in order to forestall a possible blow by the other side—even if the other side actually had no intention of striking. But solid-fuel missiles, like the Air Force's Minuteman, can be widely dispersed and protected, or "hardened" underground, instead of being concentrated on a few bases, as bombers are; and the Navy's Polaris missiles can be moved underwater (or on the ground) so that the enemy will at no time know where to strike them.

The importance of the dispersion, the "hardening," and especially the mobility of missiles is that a surprise attack is deprived of its rationale—although, on the other hand, missiles actually make such a surprise attack more feasible than ever before because of their high speeds of approximately 18,000 m.p.h. But this is not really a paradox. When the opponent's retaliatory power consists entirely or primarily of mobile, solid-fuel, long-range missiles, it is impossible to know where to hit him in order to destroy his retaliatory capacity. Obliterating his cities will benefit the aggressor very little if the enemy still retains this capacity. Surprise, therefore, no longer confers any significant advantage to the side that strikes first. Indeed, there is no need any longer to hit pre-emptively since enough of the missiles can survive an initial strike and still retaliate fully against the aggressor in a second strike. A first strike in these circumstances is completely irrational. But if missiles tend to stabilize mutual deterrence, they also increasingly deprive American threats of massive retaliation of their credibility.

The results of American strategy during the 1950's were likely to be threefold. First, it would create the possibility of war by miscalculation. Since an intentionally launched total war was suicidal, a miscalculation would be the most probable cause of war. And an American all-or-nothing strategy could lead the Soviets to commit a miscalculation. If the United States, for example, at some point in the future were determined to stand resolute in the face of a Soviet challenge, the danger would be that the Communists might not believe that the United States really intended to risk an all-out war. It is one thing to be firm, another to be foolish. The Russians might therefore discount American threats of massive retaliation, as the Chinese did in Indochina; and they would be inclined to discount them because, from a rational point of view, they would think that the United States would prefer acquiescence in a limited loss to its own total destruction. Repeated warnings might therefore have little deterrent impact in the future. The very fact that such warnings were necessary, and that they were so constantly repeated, would cause them to be suspect. If there were no reason for doubt, there would be no need for the frequent reassurances. Soviet nuclear blackmail threats could thus have one of two results. If the Russians discounted American threats of massive retaliation in response to their demands, they might keep up the pressure. If their estimate was correct, they would then win whatever issue was at stake. But if their estimate turned out to be wrong, they would have plunged the world into World War III by a miscalculation. Neither possibility can be termed a "happy ending."

A second result of an all-or-nothing strategy would be a possible increase in the number of limited Communist challenges—both nuclear blackmail attempts and limited wars. The Communists could be fully expected to exploit the American alternative of suicide or retreat. General Maxwell Taylor, who served as Army Chief of Staff under Eisenhower, but resigned in protest against the policy of almost exclusive reliance on strategic air power, wrote in the late 1950's:

> For years it has been predicted that in a period of mutual deterrence the Soviet would indulge in a rising level of provocations. In 1959, we are in such a period, and many episodes have verified the prediction. The Communist tactics in Taiwan [Formosa], the Middle East, Berlin, and Laos [where Vietminh army units apparently invaded Laos territory, only to withdraw as U.N. observers arrived on the scene] provide examples of the growing use of military power to support an aggressive course of action under the conditions of cold or limited war. As the Soviets become more assured of their superiority in general-war weapons, particularly in intercontinental ballistic missiles, if they sense American timidity, they may be expected to press harder than ever before, counting upon submissiveness arising from our consciousness of weakness. They will not believe, nor will our friends, that we will use our massive retaliatory forces for any purpose other than our own survival.

Increasingly, areas formerly considered of "vital interest" to American security might become of only "secondary interest," not worth defending at the cost of our nationhood and our comfortable way of life. At the moment of crisis, it might seem better to accept a limited loss by making some suitable denial of the value of the area surrendered. In the long run, of course, a series of such piecemeal defeats would turn the balance of power against the United States. At some point, the United States would be compelled to take a stand to prevent a further deterioration of its position. But the Soviets would hardly believe that the American commitment of defense was a firm one. Not only is massive retaliation not credible, but the United States, despite previous verbal vows of defense, has backed down before and preferred to accept a number of losses rather than commit suicide. However, in this instance, the United States would be willing to accept that risk. The Soviet challenge would then have precipitated a war by miscalculation. Thus, by its reluctance to fight limited wars, and by its reliance on massive retaliation, the United States would ironically have brought about the very total war massive retaliation was supposed to deter.

Finally, massive retaliation foreshadowed a possible disintegration of America's foremost alliance, NATO. Our European allies had joined NATO in order to gain the protection of American power, particularly SAC; but now that SAC was an instrument of the last resort—to be used only if the Soviets did the improbable, that is, launched a full-scale attack upon NATO, which was unlikely without a simultaneous strike against the United States itself—who would protect them? This was not a question of the cowardice or "softness" of an Eisenhower or any future President. Rather, it grew out of the very nature of alliances in an era of nuclear plenty. Which ally could genuinely be expected to stake its very survival for the defense of its allies' interests? More specifically, how would the United States respond to limited Soviet demands in Europe? If the United States did react with an all-out response, Europe would be "saved from Communism" by being reduced to rubble and ashes. On the other hand—and this seemed more likely—if the United States was unwilling to risk its existence for specific issues the Europeans deemed vital, then the alliance would become meaningless and the Europeans would need to acquire their own national deterrents. Yet this diffusion of nuclear arms within the alliance in turn would threaten to disintegrate NATO even further since the United States did not wish any of its allies to trigger it into war. Thus, by the end of the 1950's, the policy of massive retaliation had reached a point of diminishing returns.

VII. THE UNDERDEVELOPED
COUNTRIES, NEUTRALISM, AND
AMERICAN INTERESTS

The Revolution of Rising Expectations

"Four areas in the world," Guy J. Pauker has written, "are at present or potentially major power centers: the United States, the Soviet Union, Western Europe, and Communist China. In all four, productivity is on the increase, and the political system performs relatively well its integrating and decision-making functions. Despite major differences among them . . . these four areas are likely to be in a position to play major roles in political, economic, and cultural international affairs in the coming decade. In contrast, the Middle East, Southeast Asia, tropical Africa, and Latin America are apt to remain power vacuums during this period, owing to their lack of unity, political instability, economic stagnation, and cultural heterogeneity. It seems highly improbable that ten years from now any of the areas mentioned above will cease to be, respectively, a power center or a power vacuum."

Such a power vacuum is, however, very dangerous. For as it did in the eastern Mediterranean and in Western Europe immediately after the war, Communist power will attempt to flow into the void; in fact, Sino-Soviet attention has already been attracted, and efforts have been exerted with precisely this aim in mind. What this means is simply that the United States must take the lead, as before, in formulating policies which will create situations of strength among the underdeveloped countries of Asia, the Middle East, and Africa.

These underdeveloped nations are commonly characterized by three features. First, they are—with the exception of the Latin American ones—countries that have emerged from

Western imperialism or colonialism since World War II. This domination had been exercised in one of two forms: either as direct rule by the colonial power, or as indirect rule by the native aristocracy in alliance with the colonial state. Still, the essence of colonialism is not the manner in which the ruling nation exercised its power, but its political, economic, military, and cultural predominance over a backward territory. By the beginning of the twentieth century, the European states had extended their imperial holdings to two-thirds of the globe. But after 1900, these empires began to collapse. After World War I, Canada, South Africa, Australia, and New Zealand achieved self-government, and the British Empire began its transformation to a Commonwealth of equal and independent states. But it was World War II that struck the final blow at colonialism. By the end of the war, two decisive factors were at work: the nationalist movements throughout the colonial world were surging forward, and the colonial powers had been immeasurably weakened in strength and prestige. With the exhaustion and collapse of Europe after 1945, one after another of the colonial territories in Asia, the Middle East, and Africa, sought and gained their independence, though at times not without a severe struggle.

It is one of the strangest—and certainly, one of the most ironic—paradoxes that the disintegration of Western colonialism affords the most eloquent testimony to its success. For the Western powers, including America in the Philippines, justified their imperial domination in terms of bringing the backward peoples of the earth the benefits of Western democracy, medical science, and technology. It was the "white man's burden," or duty, to educate the natives so that one day they could govern themselves. If the French did not share this goal for their colonies, they did envisage admitting the native peoples to full-fledged French citizenship once they had been properly educated. It might well be said that the colonial powers taught their lesson too well. They ruled their colonies autocratically, while simultaneously propagating the virtues of democracy and the ideals of the British, American, and French revolutions. It was in the name of these revolutions that the Western powers first came as colonizers; it was in their name, too, that the nationalist movements challenged their rulers and asked them to practice what they preached.

The leaders of these nationalist movements had invariably been educated in Europe or America, or in Western schools in their own country; Nehru of India, Mahomed Ali-Jinnah of Pakistan, and Kwame Nkrumah of Ghana are outstanding examples. They fought the European powers in terms of the very principles of democracy and national freedom that they had learned in the West. They saw that these principles were incompatible with imperialism; thus, colonialism had in it from the beginning the seeds of its own destruction.

The second feature that characterizes most of the nations that have so recently gained their independence is their lack of administrative and political cohesiveness. Generally, the peoples have no single common culture or language; tribes are opposed to one another; different areas are in conflict with one another. There is in these nations no natural loyalty to the state, no tradition of cooperation except, of course, in the one overriding issue of eliminating the colonial ruler. But once that struggle for independence ends, power tends to fragment. Thus, colonial India distintegrated violently into Hindu India and Moslem Pakistan following independence, the Congo fell apart when the Belgians withdrew, and Cyprus divided into Turkish and Greek factions. Even where actual disintegration has not occurred, religious, linguistic, and racial differences and antagonisms tend to tear apart the fabric of these states with their lack of any history of nationhood. "Nation-building," indeed, becomes their first task.

The absence of the kind of strong sense of national consciousness that is taken for granted in the West is reflected in the manner in which many of the leaders of the new countries build themselves up as symbols of nationhood. It is not too difficult for them to do this, since their prestige is usually high as a result of the roles they have played in leading the nationalist movements for independence. But the task is an essential one. With Louis XIV, they must say, *"L'état, c'est moi."* For they *are* the state; without their presence as its symbol, their nation would not hold together as a unit. Furthermore, they also often crush the opposition party and place their countries under one-party rule.

Such policies may seem undemocratic, but they are to some degree necessary. Loyalties in the new nations are less to the state than to ancestors, family, village, or tribe. Wherever the opposition represents these centrifugal forces, an

American-style democracy cannot be permitted to operate, for it would lead not just to a change in government, but to the disintegration of the state! The alternatives facing the leaders of these countries are not democracy or dictatorship, but statehood or disintegration. Thus many of the leaders of the recently emerged nations have emasculated the spirit of the parliamentary system of government bequeathed to them by the colonial powers; the conditions for democracy are simply not yet ripe. Other nations have not even bothered to preserve the façade of parliamentary institutions, but have replaced them outright with military governments. Thailand, Egypt, Iraq, and Burma are only a few examples; other governments may not be overtly military in nature, but they function similarly, as in the case of Indonesia's "guided democracy."

The third, and most commonly cited, feature of these countries is their economic underdevelopment. Extreme poverty, illiteracy, malnutrition are the characteristics of their peoples. Rarely in these nations does the annual per capita income attain the $100 level. In Asia, the average during the 1950's was about $50—compared with the U.S. figure of more than $1,500. Or take the Arab world at that time: in Saudi Arabia, the annual per capita income was $40; in Egypt, it was $67, and 80 per cent of the population lived on the verge of starvation. Ninety per cent of the Arab peoples were affected by malaria, tuberculosis, trachoma, hookworm, or venereal diseases—all the result of a lack of even the most elementary sanitation, contaminated water, insects, malnutrition, lack of medical care and facilities, and sheer ignorance. There were only 9,200 doctors to take care of 46 million Arabs. The infant mortality rate was up to 50 per cent in Yemen, and about 35 per cent in Iraq and Syria. Life expectancy in Iraq was only 29 years, and 46 in Egypt. Eighty per cent of all Arabs were illiterate. The consequences of this high disease and death rate, of course, posed a major handicap to economic development. A large percentage of the children who were given food would nevertheless die before they reached the age of production; illness and chronic hunger curtailed the output of those who survived.

Yet economic development remains *the* essential task confronting the new nations—for political, not economic, reasons. Industrialization modernizes—that is, it transforms a backward, traditional, agrarian society into a twentieth-century, industrial, urban community. Its effects are several. Industrial strength gives a nation military strength. Any nation-state must obviously be concerned with its defense. But for a new nation particularly, "power" comes ahead of "profit." This power is not primarily important for purposes of attack, although in certain instances it may be; rather, power becomes a symbol of the new nation's sovereignty and independence, and a means of acquiring the status and respect already possessed by the older members of the international society of nations. In addition, industrialization consolidates the rather tenuous bonds holding the infant nation together as a political entity. Industrialization requires a high degree of specialization. The resulting division of labor between the various sectors of the economy located throughout all regions of the country and the need for all these branches of industry to cooperate therefore forges new cohesive links and places the still fragile political union upon the base of an interdependent economic union. Finally, industrialization can create greater welfare for all of the nation's new citizens. This, too, is a fact of great political significance. The people are familiar only with their immediate surrounding area, and they are loyal to this region; national loyalty is unknown. Consequently, the newly formed nation must prove to them that it can offer something they could not otherwise attain. This "something" is an improvement in their standard of living. By achieving this, the nation demonstrates its utility and, in turn, receives from its people the popular support and allegiance it needs to survive and grow.

Yet the question confronting the new countries is whether they can develop themselves economically. The answer will to a large extent depend upon whether their economic progress will be faster than their population growth, or whether their "population explosion" will eat up any increase in national income. The world population in January, 1960, was 2.8 billion. United Nations experts predict 6 to 7 billion by the year 2000. India's birth rate would allow her to build a city the size of New York every year; and China's new population would permit her to add another Canada annually. In 1900, there was one European for every two Asians; in 2000, the ratio will probably be one to four. In this hemisphere, there will, perhaps, be two Latin Americans for each North American. At that rate, the economic level of the underdeveloped nations will at best remain level, at worst decline. These countries may thus come face to face with the Malthusian problem: that is, the constant hunger and grinding poverty which result when the population grows faster than do the means of subsistence. More than 150 years ago, the Reverend Malthus, who was also an economist, predicted this fate for the Western world—unless the population growth were limited by either "positive checks" such as wars or epidemics, which result in a high death rate, or by "preventive checks," which result in a low birth rate. Yet, despite the huge population increase since 1800, the West has made great economic progress: agricultural production has provided a plentiful supply of food, and industrial production has raised the standard of living to heights never before attained. The West's recent history would thus refute Malthus' gloomy prediction.

Unfortunately, the conditions which confront the underdeveloped nations are quite dissimilar from those experienced by the West. One of the chief differences is that the Western countries had far smaller populations when they began industrializing, and their population increase did not outdistance the economic improvement. But India has set out on her industrial revolution with a population of more than 400 million, which is expected to double in the next 30 years. China already has 600 million, and is expected to have the staggering total of 1 billion people by the close of this century. In Egypt, the population is rising so fast that some experts have predicted that completion of the Aswan Dam will only allow her to remain at her present subsistence level. If the United States had a population density equivalent to that of Egypt, we would have more than 2 billion people, instead of our 180 million. Under these circumstances, we would hardly be a "developed" nation.

The European nations were also aided by the New World and by their colonial empires, which provided them with outlets to relieve their population pressures. About 60 million Europeans emigrated during the nineteenth and early twentieth centuries. The United States and Canada, rich in resources and fertile in land, easily absorbed millions of immigrants and still increased their living standards; Australia, New Zealand, and South Africa experienced similar population and economic expansions, although on a smaller scale. From 1650 to 1950, the European population (excluding Russia) increased by approximately 300 million. But today there are about 400 million people of European descent living outside Europe. If these millions could not have emigrated and if the mother countries would not have found many of their colonies profitable sources of cheap raw materials and labor, as well as of markets for their products, the West might be living in the same conditions as the underdeveloped nations. The colonies thus served Europe as a frontier similar to that of our own West, which absorbed population that might otherwise have overcrowded the Eastern seaboard and thus added materially to the nation's wealth. But the underdeveloped countries can find no such relatively empty and rich spaces to absorb their surplus populations. The 50,000 Puerto Ricans who immigrate each year into the United States hardly set a precedent. In any case, quite apart from the fact that it would take the enormous number of an estimated 25 million annual emigrants from Asia to keep that area stable, there would probably be too many racial barriers imposed upon their immigration. An alternative in some countries might be internal migration. In Indonesia, for instance, three-quarters of the population live in the island of Java, while Sumatra remains largely jungle. But habit, inertia, and deep roots make such extensive internal migration very difficult, if not impossible.

In the West, the Industrial Revolution made it possible to apply machinery to agriculture. This permitted a great increase in the food supply; efficient agriculture also meant that food could be produced by a smaller farm population. Excess labor on the land was thereby forced to go to the city, where it was used in the factories; this, in turn, accelerated the industrialization process. Quite apart from modern technology, however, Europe was blessed with sufficient sunshine and rain. Temperate lands are more favorable to food production than the tropical and monsoon areas in which many of the underdeveloped countries exist. Europe could thus grow sufficient food to feed its multiplying population; what it could not produce, it imported from the colonies and the New World in exchange for industrial products. This enabled some European countries to support larger populations than their domestic food resources would have permitted. By contrast, in the nonindustrialized nations, the majority of the population is still engaged in a primitive agriculture. Moreover, there is generally not sufficient land for any major agricultural expansion; and more intensive farming of land already under cultivation—that is, using better seed, more chemical fertilizers, and insecticides—may perhaps yield only enough to keep pace with the population growth. During India's first Five-Year Plan of economic development, about half of the new product was needed to feed new mouths. "If our population continues to increase as rapidly as it is doing," the President of Pakistan has said, "we will soon have nothing to eat and will all become cannibals."

If this statement is perhaps a little exaggerated, it nevertheless dramatizes the underdeveloped countries' problem of overpopulation. There are simply too many poor people. This might have been all right if the sleeping masses had not awakened—if they had continued to accept their miserable lot as natural and not suddenly become conscious that it was not a fate ordained by God but a man-made one, if they had not made this discovery and therefore demanded to eat more and live better. It is this "revolution of rising expectations" which creates the problem, for it will be impossible to fulfill these expectations unless there is a reduction in birth rates. The population pressure keeps the masses living close to subsistence; and such widespread poverty makes it very difficult, and perhaps completely unfeasible, to accumulate enough capital to stoke industrial growth.

In the West, the birth rate declined after 1850; with industrialization and the growth of cities came the spread of literacy and knowledge of artificial birth-control techniques. Malthus was thus right even for the West because preventive checks were adopted. But Asia has not yet reached this level of economic development, and knowledge of birth-control methods is likely to spread only very slowly. First of all, in Latin America, the Philippines, Vietnam, and Ceylon, the influence of the Roman Catholic Church is strong; and although there have been indications that the Church is beginning to re-examine its attitudes, at present it remains opposed to artificial birth control on moral grounds. The rhythm method is too hard for illiterate people to understand; in any case, even if the Church were not opposed to artificial means of lowering the birth rate, contracep-

tives are generally too expensive for those living in utter
poverty. Nor are the alternatives of sterilization or self-con-
trol in marriage likely to be greatly favored or widely adopted.
There is also another very powerful reason why artificial
birth control is not going to be too successful in the underdeveloped areas for a long time yet: children in many of these
countries are a religious or social—and even political—necessity. Moslems, for instance, believe that children are a "gift
of Allah"; the childless couple is pitied or despised. The
woman does not even establish herself with her husband or
his family until she has borne a son. A Hindu needs a son to
perform certain rituals after his death. Moreover, since death
comes at an early age and strikes many in the underdeveloped
countries, there is a genuine fear of *too few* children. Extra
hands are needed to work in the fields or to support their
parents as they grow older. Children are thus often a substitute for social-security payments or endowment policies.
And in some countries, such as China and perhaps Ghana,
there may be no desire to cut the birth rate because their
leaders are politically ambitious internationally. Still, in
most underdeveloped countries, there is a desire to lower the
annual increase in population. The Indian Government has
instituted a public education campaign in family planning
and in financing research to discover a cheap and effective
means of contraception which the untutored can use. It is
even considering sponsoring a law permitting sterilization.
And the Japanese Government, because the situation has become so desperate there, too—a population of nearly 90 million with 0.15 acres of arable land per person and a food
supply below minimum—has legalized abortion.

It is doubtful, however, that the birth rate will signifi-
cantly decline in most of these countries during the next
crucial decade or two. This means that the pace of economic
development must surpass the fast-rising populations. Econ-
omists seem to agree generally that an annual investment of
12 to 15 per cent of the national income is needed to transform a static agrarian economy into a modern, dynamic,
industrialized economy in which capital accumulation begins
to sustain itself. But these countries simply do not have that
kind of capital. Internal savings in sufficient amounts cannot
be squeezed out of peoples living at subsistence level—at

least, not without totalitarian controls. An alternative means of obtaining capital is to earn it by trade. The underdeveloped areas are exporters of primary products or raw materials, such as coffee, tea, rubber, and tin. It is precisely this fact which limits their earning capacity; for these exports rise or decline with every fluctuation in Western prosperity. A major Western recession like the one in 1957-58 lowers the demand and price levels of natural resources; the resulting losses of income may well exceed the Western aid extended during the same period. Furthermore, the market becomes glutted with certain items because of overproduction or substitution. In the former case, a nation seeking to raise its income increases its production, but the fact that its competitors do the same only results in lowering world prices; in the latter case, the Western industrial nations, whose ever-increasing demand for raw materials was supposed to furnish the capital for economic development, no longer need them because of the development of synthetics. The lack of stabilized international commodity prices, similar to the parity prices paid to American farmers, plus the inventiveness of modern technology thus hampers the prospects of financing industrialization via trade.

Foreign investment is the third source of capital for economic development. In the past, this burden fell primarily upon private capital, although even during the nineteenth-century days of *laissez faire* economics, governments loaned much of the money needed for projects and services which, while very necessary for economic development, did not produce immediate returns; these included services like education and such projects as construction of roads, railroads, and harbors. In its days as the world's leading power, Britain exported about 7 per cent of its national income each year. America's economic development would have been neither as rapid nor as extensive without British investments. In order to match those investments today, the United States would need to invest approximately $28 billion per year—more than the underdeveloped countries could absorb annually. Private capital has, in any case, been in short supply for the kind of long-range development that the underdeveloped nations need. Approximately two-thirds of private American investments outside the United States have been made by a small group of oil companies to build refineries and to discover and pump out oil fields in Latin America and the Middle East.

The reasons for this lack of private Western—and especially American—capital for foreign investment are not hard to find. The American economy has been booming—so much, in fact, that wealthy Asians, Middle Easterners, and Latin Americans have frequently been investing their capital in our growth rather than in that of their own economies. European capital has concentrated on the rebuilding, modernization, and expansion of its own capital plant. Private capital is drawn to investments which will return sizable and relatively speedy profits. And this is perhaps the basic reason that private funds are so small: because public funds are so small. Businessmen cannot be expected to invest in hospitals, ports, schools, and roads. The returns from such projects are insufficient; and even if there were any profits, it would take too long to reap them. The major burden or responsibility for developing the climate for economic growth therefore falls squarely on Western governments. The first step in promoting more private investment abroad has to be taken with public funds; it is these funds which can raise the economic level of underdeveloped nations to the point where they will begin to attract private capital. Optimists who feel that even this first stage of economic development can or will be undertaken by private funds might recall that even in the West the speedy economic growth of the nineteenth century, financed largely by private enterprise, rested upon an economic base developed by the mercantilist state; in brief, it was political authority, the state, which initiated the process that transformed the underdeveloped Western economies into the highly modern, industrialized economies we know today.

In the present underdeveloped countries, the state again must play a leading role in economic development. This is necessitated by the very lack of capital, which requires governments to allocate funds to those projects which will be most beneficial; governments must establish priorities so that money is not wasted on secondary matters. Even more important, the government must play a leading role in order to prove to its citizens that the nation can and does offer them a better standard of living. This is not primarily a question of socialism versus private enterprise, but a question of nation-building. But all this presumes that the underdeveloped countries will receive the necessary public funds. If they do not, their economies will continue to stagnate and quite possibly may fall below the subsistence level. This would breed strong resentment and bitterness, a condition rife for Communist exploitation. The Communists could then—in fact, they already do—point to the Soviet experience and say: "In 1917, Russia was also underdeveloped, but now, within the space of one generation, it has become the second most powerful industrial country in the world. You, too, can be industrialized quickly and live a better life." To people who already suffer from chronic hunger and poverty, it will not matter greatly that the Soviet Union and Communist China achieved industrialization by means of totalitarian governments that brutally squeezed the necessary savings out of the people; the loss of liberty will not mean much to people who have never known it anyway, who have lived for centuries under authoritarian governments, whether domestic or foreign. The eastern Rimlands of Eurasia and Africa could thus be conquered from within. And since Western Europe, a peninsula of the Eurasian continent, could not continue to live in freedom once the rest of the World-Island had fallen under Communism, the United States would be strategically isolated. This country can, in brief, lose the world by default, without a shot ever being fired. This may very well happen if the American response to the challenge of the underdeveloped countries remains inadequate.

Western Economic Aid as an International Income Tax

Any American policy toward the underdeveloped areas must start with the recognition that the future of these countries will play an important rôle in the survival of the United States. America cannot allow the gulf between the rich and poor nations to widen—for the same reason that this gap could not be allowed to exist *within* each of the Western nations 100 years ago. The two situations are, in fact, so amazingly similar that the lessons of the previous experience can easily be applied to the present international division of wealth. As the Industrial Revolution gathered momentum in each of the European countries and America, it created a privileged minority which owned most of the wealth. The distribution of income was, to say the least, unequal. Laborers, including a very high percentage of children and women, worked fourteen to sixteen hours per day, six or seven days a week, earned little beyond what was considered a living or subsistence wage (and sometimes less) and lived in overcrowded slums. The rich got richer, and the poor got poorer. This trend was so obvious that Disraeli talked of England not as one nation, but as two. But the prevailing *laissez faire* philosophy argued that nothing could be done to alleviate this situation. Government intervention, whether to end the grosser forms of exploitation such as child labor or to redistribute the income to help the poor lead a decent and dignified life, was rejected as contrary to the "iron laws of economics." Any outside interference with the workings of the market would stifle the private incentive and initiative which stoked the competitive capitalistic system. These "laws," which condemned a large section of the population to a hopeless and miserable existence, received even further support from Darwin's theory of evolution, with its emphasis on the "struggle for survival" and the "survival of the fittest." This philosophy, adapted by Herbert Spencer and called Social Darwinism, argued very simply that the rich were wealthy because their success in the competitive struggle had demonstrated that they were the most fit; conversely, the poor were destitute because they were unfit. It never occurred to Social Darwinists to ask themselves whether everybody had had an equal start or opportunity in this struggle. Perhaps this question was not asked because the Darwinian answer seemed so eminently right that it would be pointless, even silly, to doubt it—particularly since it apparently had God's approval. For it was He who must have endowed the rich with their superior talents and withheld these abilities from the poor. It was upon the men of wealth that human progress rested. Poverty, malnutrition, disease were admittedly evils, but they could be corrected and abolished only by the long-term evolution of the human species which would ensure that only the superior qualities of man would survive. Social legislation to support the unfit—that is, political interference with God's purpose, the laws of nature and economics—would at worst burden society and assure its stagnation, and at best slow down the evolution toward the healthy and wealthy paradise of supermen.

These philosophical justifications for leaving the poor very poor, if not to die, were rejected in all Western societies after holding temporary sway. The long working hours, the unsanitary and unsafe working conditions, the teeming slums were a blot on the West's conscience. Indeed, they were a disgrace to Christian nations who prided themselves on their humanitarian traditions. How could they justify condemning men to lifelong poverty and misery no matter how hard they worked? It was also politically shortsighted and economically foolish. Politically, the division of people into "haves" and "have-nots" could only end in revolution, with the bourgeoisie being overthrown by the working classes, or proletariat; or, if it surrendered its democratic beliefs and values, the bourgeoisie could perhaps retain its power by establishing an authoritarian government and crushing any proletarian protests and uprisings. Neither of these alternatives was a very happy one for the ruling middle classes. Nor did this policy of squeezing the workers for maximum profit make sense economically, since the less money people have, the fewer things they can buy. Thus, social justice made sense —morally, politically, and economically.

In every Western society, government in the late nineteenth century began to intervene increasingly in the economy. While all governments—national, state, and municipal —were involved, it was national governments upon whom the main responsibilities devolved. They regulated business and took antimonopoly actions; they passed minimum-wage and maximum-hours legislation and abolished child labor and "sweatshop" working conditions; they helped trade unions to organize so that the workers could bargain collectively with their employers for better wages and terms of employment; they took measures to counteract the sometimes violent swings of the business cycles; they redistributed the income with the progressive income tax; and during depressions they resorted to unemployment insurance, public-works programs, and other "pump-priming" projects to increase the purchasing power of the people, thereby stimulating renewed demand and production. These measures, especially in the United States, widened and raised the base of wealth, giving rise to the twentieth-century mass market. They also led to a discovery so simple and yet so hard to understand that Europe, particularly continental Europe, is just learning it: namely, that a worker is also a purchaser. If he is paid a good wage, he will also buy the goods he produces. This is profitable all around: the worker (except in France and Italy) is economically satisfied and therefore has a vested interest, politically, in the social and economic order; capitalists earn handsome profits by selling volume at reasonable prices, and they retain their social status and political control.

It is this same problem of an inequitable distribution of income which once again plagues the world. Only this time the problem does not exist within nations, but *between* nations. The rich countries are becoming wealthier, the poor ones more poverty-stricken; at best, the latter remain roughly at their present inadequate economic level. The iron laws of economics and nature seem to hold the same fate in store for them that they once did for the Western working classes. Has the Marxist prophecy that the exploited proletariat would overthrow the bourgeoisie been defeated domestically only to reappear internationally and defeat us on the global plane? Will the poverty-stricken nations of the world, the international proletariat, rise up in revolution against the privileged and wealthy Western countries, the international bourgeoisie? The answer to these questions is probably yes—unless the Western powers, and especially the United States, apply on a global scale the same principle which was so profitable at home, the principle of social justice.

Recognition of the need for such action will, in turn, call for a long-range plan and sustained effort to start the under-developed economies on a steady rise to the point where they can become self-sustaining. Most estimates seem to agree that the maximum these underdeveloped nations could annually absorb would be between $2.5 billion and $3.5 billion. Of this sum, the United States would contribute about $1 billion to $2 billion a year. A Marshall Plan program of this type would thus cost the United States a maximum sum of $8 billion to $10 billion, depending upon whether it covered a period of four or five years. This sum is smaller than that involved in the Marshall Plan for Europe which, it will be recalled, was no larger than our liquor bill over the same period of 1948-52. In late 1959 and early 1960, the United States even proposed that the European nations of the Inner

Six and Outer Seven, plus Japan, join with us and Canada in establishing a committee to coordinate aid programs to the underdeveloped areas. The proposed name of this group, whose European members are Belgium, Britain, France, Italy, Portugal, and West Germany, is the Organization for Economic Cooperation and Development. Certainly, until now the efforts of the United States, Britain, and France—the only highly industrialized Western powers that have undertaken sizable programs—have fallen far below the required needs; and while the United States demands that the increasingly prosperous and wealthy nations of Europe share with it the task of economic aid, the American pressure seems to have been stimulated not by a desire for a large-scale joint Marshall Plan program but a desire to lighten our already inadequate efforts.

What is probably required is, as Barbara Ward has suggested, a progressive international income tax by which all the advanced Western nations would contribute 1 to 2 per cent of their annual national income for this development process. The Western powers, to be sure, have been moving in this general direction for years. United States efforts have been divided into two kinds of assistance, technical and economic. The technical assistance involves such programs as sending agronomists to the underdeveloped nations to teach farmers how to get their hens to lay more eggs or to show the farmers irrigation techniques to increase their crop yields. Though this is a laudable and necessary effort, it does not meet the problem of capital development. Nor was it meant to when President Truman launched the Point Four program (so-called because it was the fourth point in Truman's 1949 Inaugural Address). The program recognized the existence of the problem, but at the same time attempted to limit American efforts. Point Four was the logical answer in these circumstances, since technical aid is not expensive. But at no time did Point Four ever meet the real issue of large-scale industrial development. Economic aid has simply been puny in comparison to both the needs of the underdeveloped countries and America's huge capacity. The term "economic aid" is, indeed, a misnomer. Since 1950 and the outbreak of the Korean War, most economic aid has, in fact, been military aid. Moreover, since Western Europe's recovery, most of this aid has been channeled to Turkey, Pakistan, Vietnam, South

Korea, and Nationalist China. This, then, constitutes the major part of the annual "economic aid" program. The sum that is left is used for economic assistance. But there is another snag. A good part of the remaining sum is devoted to what is called "defense support"; this provides money to sustain the economies of our allies like South Korea or Vietnam, who, in the absence of this support, could not maintain their standing armies. Only the final sum remaining after all these deductions is employed for the fundamental task of capital development, and of even this amount, almost half is used for technical assistance.

What is missing—and this is *the* essential prerequisite—is a recognition of the extent and urgency of this problem; if the problem is not met, the results will be disastrous to the survival of freedom. There is still not a sufficiently widespread awareness among either political leaders or the American public as a whole. The latter, particularly, enjoying affluence at home, remain blissfully unaware and abysmally ignorant of the problem. Far too frequently, the problem of economic aid is seen only as indicative of American generosity. In short, it is seen not in terms of American security but as charity. More often, the entire economic aid program has been subjected to increasingly heavy criticism in Congress. President Eisenhower frequently talked of the task of economic development in terms that strongly suggested that the leading role should be played by private enterprise—which is, of course, impossible since the conditions for massive private investment do not yet exist in the underdeveloped countries. This is not to deny private enterprise a role—indeed, an important role—but the principal responsibility in the initial stage of development falls on public investment. Only governmental funds can create the economic conditions that will later attract large-scale private money. Poverty and destitution certainly will not. Governmental investment thus remains a prerequisite to private investment.

The United States, if it wishes to ensure its survival, *cannot* afford to do less than is demanded by the situation. A Marshall Plan for the underdeveloped world is not just desirable; it is absolutely necessary. And just as governmental intervention in the domestic economy and the redistribution of income laid the foundation for the politically unified and economically prosperous Western nations, so aiding the poor nations can only prove advantageous to the West. Politically, it would help check Communism, which attempts to exploit the hunger and misery of these peoples who comprise two-thirds of the world's population. Economically, it would broaden markets for Western products; the underdeveloped countries already are buying five times as many American goods as in 1938 and twice as many as after World War II. Militarily, it is important because many of the strategic goods the United States stockpiles for military purposes (rubber, tin, lead, zinc, chrome, copper, bauxite, magnesium, and uranium) come from these areas. And morally, such a program would live up to all that is decent and fine in the Western tradition.

By acting in accordance with that heritage, we will be protecting and perhaps extending freedom in the world, instead of allowing the global balance of power to be turned against us by default. As the British historian Macaulay asked long ago, "When will people learn that it is the spirit we are of and not the machinery we employ that binds us together?" This may be somewhat exaggerated—since the spirit by itself is not enough and people's actions rarely, if ever, lack an element of self-interest—but it seems probable that if the United States is true to its own best spirit, it will protect its security as well as that of the rest of the non-Communist world. For as the underdeveloped countries gain in economic strength and welfare, they will also acquire political confidence. As their conditions improve, the memories of Western colonialism will fade and their attitude toward the West will become less hostile. For the need to be anti-Western will diminish as their peoples realize their respective nations' benefits and their allegiance becomes nationalized. Conversely, the new states' sense of nationalism is likely to be directed increasingly against the Communist world if Russia and China, because they do not wish to see strong states on their periphery, exert pressure upon them. In any case, the very facts of the new states' independence and sense of nationalism is likely to pose a barrier to Communist expansion.

First, however, the West must help these nations modernize. But this requires not only Western economic funds but Western support for social reform. The nationalist revolutions direct their opposition not only against the dominating foreign ruler, but also against the ruling class. In colonies ruled directly, such as India, the imperial powers usually abolished the traditional system, but in territories where they ruled indirectly, it was via the native aristocracy. The Middle East is an example of such an area. As a result, most of these countries have been split into two groups when they gained independence. The first is the ruling minority, composed of the landlords, tribal chiefs, and great merchants, fronted by an old-regime king. Usually, this group has been educated in the West, has acquired Western culture and manners, and therefore it has nothing in common with the tradition-bound masses of peasants who live on their land; nor does it have much contact with them. The second group, which constitutes about 80 per cent in most underdeveloped nations, encompasses the peasants, villagers, small artisans, and shopkeepers—those whose efforts have been concentrated largely on the sheer struggle for day-to-day survival. It is this group, which has for centuries borne its hardships silently, that has awakened and is now demanding a better life. For generation after generation, these people—who might truly be called *les misérables*—accepted their condition as if it was God-given rather than man-made. Suddenly, they have become aware that they can change their lot. It is the growing urban middle class that voices these resentments against the old way of life and proclaims the new aspirations most articulately and loudly. Change, change, and more change is the demand of the day.

Without such a social change—that is, the overthrow of the old feudal ruling class—long-range economic development will be inhibited. For instance, American farm experts have been sent to nations where the *ancien régime* still survived. The peasants were to be brought the benefits of American science and technology. But the Americans found, to their great surprise, that the peasants were not interested in acquiring this knowledge which would help them increase their annual crop. The reason quickly became obvious. If the peasants raised their yield, almost all the increase would go to the landlord, the moneylender, and the tax collector. There was, in short, little incentive for the peasant to work harder or apply new techniques. The limits to what the American specialists could achieve were thus set not by science, technology, or professional knowledge, but by social and political conditions. Assistance programs that should have been successful because they made sense by Western criteria could not produce the expected results when applied in societies that had not yet attained the West's level of social and political development. Economic growth must, therefore, be accompanied by a social transformation; and the change of the social structure is basic to this. It is really a matter not of "reform" but of revolution, for the crucial issue relates to power: Who controls the nation—the old ruling class, committed to the preservation of the traditional, religiously oriented, pre-industrial society, or those who seek to secularize, modernize, and industrialize the nation? One thing is certain: No ruling class yields its dominant political, social, and economic position without a struggle.

Yet, an understanding of class struggle and social politics is somewhat alien to the United States. America has avoided the kind of domestic conflicts over basic values that Europe experienced and which now plague many of the underdeveloped nations. Americans are, indeed, so overwhelmingly committed to one of values—middle-class values—that divergences, real or apparent, are likely to be condemned as "un-American." "Americanism" is an absolute. Deviations are "sinful" and must be rooted out so that the "American way of life" will remain pure and unadulterated. The principal challenges to these values have come not from within the system, but from outside our borders, and the United States has reacted to foreign threats—German, Japanese, Communist—in two ways: internally, by a hunt for "subversives" that each time has infringed upon civil liberties and endangered the security of our freedoms; and externally (that is, up to the present Communist threat), by the total destruction of the hostile regime so that American principles could continue to live untainted. Thus, domestically, the Communist threat in the early 1950's led to McCarthyism, a search for heresy in which the end goal of eliminating alleged un-American attitudes and behavior justified any means, including disregard for "due process of law," which is the basic guarantee of all our civil liberties. At times, this hunt went to frightening lengths, as when the United States Information Agency actually burned books that might be suspect. At other times, it became so ridiculous that it would have been funny if the implications were not so frightening—as when a member of an Indiana school board suggested that *Robin Hood* be banned since it was obviously a "pro-Communist" book in which the hero took from the rich to give to the poor. In foreign policy, our reaction to the Communist threat to the American way of life was to support almost any "anti-Communist" regime. Thus, the United States associated itself with traditional regimes whose days were numbered because they had alienated mass support: Bao Dai in Indochina and King Faisal in Iraq were just two examples of such regimes. The fact that these countries' governments were pro-American and anti-Communist qualified them in our eyes as "democratic," or at least potentially so; and by the same token, we opposed internal movements to overthrow them and condemned these as Communist or pro-Communist. This attitude was typical of our American absolutism and inability to understand the deeper social struggles of Asia and the Middle East. In the attempt to contain Communism—that is, to preserve the global *status quo*—the United States became committed to the domestic, social, and political *status quo* in these countries. Thus America, in seeking stability, is paradoxically trying to preserve freedom by supporting ramshackle autocracies that are unrepresentative of their peoples' aspirations. But this internal contradiction within our alliance system must eventually resolve itself. Our support for traditional regimes only bottles up the social and political resentment and ferment even more, thereby adding to the explosive forces that must someday burst forth and further upset the global balance of power.

Frequent American identification with social reaction and repressive policies has thus harmed our own cause. Not only has it led us to support regimes living on borrowed time, but it has driven—or is driving—the nationalist movements of the middle class and the peasants into the arms of the Communists, who, unlike us, do understand the concept of class struggle. In the competition between the United States on the one hand and Russia and China on the other (and these two powers began to compete with one another as well by the late 1950's) for the allegiance of the people living in the underdeveloped areas, the Communists hold a distinct advantage: They possess a genuine ideology of social revolution. The entire orientation of Communists is the class struggle; social conflict is the spectrum through which they view the

world. That it is not our own is amply revealed by the way in which our policies give the Communists opportunities to identify themselves with national independence and social progress.

American aid should therefore be conditioned upon social reform. This should, however, be the only major precondition for aid. All too often in the past, American dollars have been offered with the explicit or implicit assumption that the recipients should associate themselves with U.S. cold-war policies; that even if they do not formally ally themselves with us, they should often thank us for our generosity, praise us for the morality of our anti-Communist stand, and certainly refrain from criticizing us. The United States has been reluctant to give dollars to nations who would not join our side. After all, can any nation really be neutral in a struggle between right and wrong? Is not democracy good and Communism evil? If countries want our money, surely the least they can do is to fight with us "the battle of the righteous." Why, indeed, should we help those who are afraid or unwilling "to stand up and be counted"? And what is really wrong with attempting to win friends and allies with economic aid? The answer, perhaps, is "Nothing"; but it simply does not work. An economic aid program cannot achieve its purposes unless its aim is fully shared by the recipient; it must coincide with his aspirations. And the basic aspiration of the underdeveloped countries is to concentrate their attention and energy on internal matters, to raise their standard of living and strengthen their independence, and to minimize their involvement in the cold war. They therefore prefer to remain neutral in the struggle between the West and the Communists. For the present, they prefer to avoid all "entangling alliances." Any attempts to use economic aid as a means of forcing them into the American alliance system can only fail and set back our goal for their development.

In taking their neutral position, the underdeveloped nations are only following America's own experience. After we had gained our independence, we, too, abstained from all entangling alliances and preoccupied ourselves with internal developments; as an underdeveloped country ourself, we were very much aware that our newly realized independence meant very little until we had gained economic and political strength. Moreover, having just thrown off the shackles of colonialism, we had no desire to be once more tied to the European powers. For we knew that if we joined any alliance system, the European powers would again have a large voice in our affairs, simply because we were the far weaker party. We would become involved in their quarrels and wars; and this would mean that we would have to maintain a sizable military establishment, which, in turn, would divert much-needed capital from our economic growth. It was for these reasons that Washington, in his Farewell Address, advised the country to isolate itself from Europe's conflicts until it was strong enough to "choose peace or war, as our interest, guided by justice, shall counsel." It was for the same reasons that John Quincy Adams, when he was Secretary of State to President Monroe, advised against accepting the British bid for joint action against the Holy Alliance if it attempted to re-impose Spain's control over her former Latin-American colonies. The United States, Adams said, refused to become a cockboat in the wake of the British man-of-war. Adams knew that he could safely reject the British bid, since Britain's own interests would make it necessary for her to oppose the Holy Alliance—economically, because she had trade interests in South America, and politically, because a Holy Alliance powerful enough to extend its power across the Atlantic was a coalition strong enough to dominate the European continent and threaten Britain's security. Adams therefore unilaterally declared the Monroe Doctrine with every confidence that the British Navy would enforce it.

The underdeveloped countries of the world, with one or two exceptions, feel exactly as the United States did in that earlier period and for similar reasons; just as we could trust our safety to the British, who would oppose any power or group of powers seeking to dominate the world, the new nations of the world are aware that America must protect them if it wishes to contain further Soviet and Chinese expansion. The Monroe Doctrine is today a global doctrine. It may not have been explicitly stated, but it is silently understood and accepted by the neutral nations. If at times they criticize our policies and occasionally question our wisdom, this is no more than a repeat of our favorite pastime of "twisting the lion's tail." Only it is our tail which is being twisted this time, and the game, therefore, is no longer so enjoyable; indeed, since we want so much to be liked, if not loved, by the rest of the world, it hurts our vanity. But just as we wanted the British to protect us, so our current critics, however loud or frequent their comments, expect America to preserve the balance of power which safeguards their own independence as well.

This policy of nonentanglement for the underdeveloped countries is dictated in addition by their lack of national cohesion. The divisive forces in the new nations are far stronger than they ever were in the early United States. Yet even the young Republic had to be careful for, quite apart from the strength of state and regional loyalties, the nation soon became bitterly divided between the Jeffersonian supporters of the French Revolution, who emphasized its democratic character, and their Federalist opponents, who stressed the Revolution's terror, bloodshed, and attack upon religion and property. Later, with the arrival of massive waves of immigrants in the nineteenth century, involvement in Europe's quarrels posed a more serious danger to the bonds of unity. Allegiances to the "old country" would have badly divided the country, as they tended to do even as late as the World War I period. The new citizens first had to be "nationalized," or "Americanized"; their sense of identification as Americans in fact depended upon alienation from—and opposition to—the Old World. Still, the United States, for all its internal schisms, was born as largely a middle-class society with capitalistic and democratic values. The new nations born since 1945 are less fortunate; they suffer from intense class, religious, linguistic, ethnic, and racial differences of a kind and intensity that the American Republic has rarely experienced. Not surprisingly, therefore, these new nations generally flaunt their anticolonialism more vigorously than the United States ever did. The waving of the "bloody flag" of colonialism and the assertions of a nationalistic spirit seem to provide a means of forging the new nations into a "more perfect union." Since the only nationalism they have ever known was the nationalism they exerted against their former ruler, it is the West that is the obvious target of nation-building. Their lack of national consciousness thus makes it mandatory to stress nationalism, and this reinforces their need for a policy of nonentanglement. Any demand on our part that these nations "stand up and be counted" by aligning themselves with their former masters in the West in return for aid funds is likely merely to force them into a coalition with the Communists.

This would, in turn, pose a new threat to American security, already threatened increasingly since the Communist bloc, especially the Soviet Union, entered the foreign-aid field by extending large credits to such geographically or politically important nonaligned nations as Egypt, Syria, Iraq, Afghanistan, India, and Indonesia. Such aid has enhanced the Communist appeal, which was already strong because the Communists, not burdened with any colonies themselves, constantly preach anticolonialism and give their support to independence movements. Although the Communists, of course, do this to weaken Western power in the world, their position is nevertheless very pleasing to all nationalist movements and newly independent nations. To be sure, the Russians have their "colonies" in Eastern Europe (and, like colonies, these have increasingly sought to gain a greater measure of self-rule). But Europe is far away from Asia and Africa; in any case, it is natural that nationalists in these countries should be preoccupied with the kind of colonialism they still know or only recently experienced. Nor is America's own record of anticolonialism a sufficient rebuttal, since the United States for its own security is allied with European states who were, and in several cases still are, colonial powers.

Economic aid also enhances the attraction of Communism because, in granting loans, the Russians do not attempt to compel the underdeveloped countries to take sides in the cold war. The Communists rarely even mention war; in fact, they praise their recipients for being "peace-loving." The Russians thereby give the impression that they genuinely respect the neutral position of the new states. In contrast, the United States has at times tried to use economic aid as an instrument for forcing the uncommitted nations to surrender their neutrality and align themselves with this country and the West. This has made American purposes suspect, for the new nations fear that American policy may represent a new form of colonialism by which the United States, through alliances, wishes to use them as pawns in the cold war. The annual debate on foreign aid in Congress has made it crystal-clear that the funds this country provides for economic and technical assistance, small as they are, are voted solely because of our fear of Communism.

This explains the third element of the Communist appeal. Whereas the United States seems to grant aid very reluctantly and only for the negative purpose of stopping Communism, the Soviet Union extends aid with a positive message. The Russians constantly point to their record of economic development. Their claim is that they have become the world's most powerful industrial nation. This claim draws great attention in the backward areas of the world, whose peoples are in a great hurry to industrialize. Rightly or wrongly, they see in modern technology the answer to their poverty, and they want to build their industrial establishment within one generation. The Soviet experience is thus a meaningful one for them, and in many ways more meaningful than the Western one, since development in Europe and America took several generations. Was not the Soviet Union also an underdeveloped country only 40 years ago, when America was already the world's leading industrial power? And is not the steel mill which the Russians have so gladly offered to construct not evidence of the industrial successes of Communism in only four decades? This is precisely what the Soviets want the people of underdeveloped areas to think, for these countries have a choice of only two means of implementing economic development—democratic or totalitarian. If the former fails to raise the economic level quickly enough to meet the aspirations of their masses, they will almost surely turn to totalitarian methods. If the United States and the West cannot adequately respond to the "revolution of rising expectations," it will be the Communists who will profit. If the underdeveloped countries—or at least their more influential members—turn Communist, the impact on the world balance of power will be disastrous. And the possibility of this happening is further enhanced by the continued discrimination which prevents American Negroes from realizing their full measure of civil rights. To a world in which the vast majority of the population is colored, the segregationist practices of the South (and often of the North as well) seem to be flagrant violations of the democratic principles of freedom and human dignity so often proclaimed by the United States. The peoples of the underdeveloped areas not only claim equal status as nations, but also seek equality as human beings; when they hear about segregation in America, they can only be reminded of the old days when the white

man treated them as inferiors simply because of the color of
their skins. In short, the civil-rights issue in the United
States is a contributing factor in the alienation of the underdeveloped countries.

The challenge posed by the nationalistic and social
revolutions raging through two-thirds of the world, therefore, must be accepted. It has to be faced in all its stark
reality and ominous implications. Anti-Communism will not
suffice this time. America will have to identify itself with the
aspirations of the rising nationalist movements. This, in
turn, will require that the United States overcome the limitations imposed by its system of values and its domestic experience. There is no guarantee that we will be capable of
achieving this at all. It can only be predicted with relative
safety that if our international involvement since 1945 has
not yet taught us the necessity for complementing power
politics with social politics, then it is high time we learned it.
The United States can no longer rely primarily on military
containment of the Communist sphere. In the underdeveloped
areas, the cold war is reflected as basically a conflict of social
and economic statesmanship. Thus, the United States must
strive for the creation of a new world order in which America
and the West can not only be safe, but flourish—a task re-
quiring us to make a major effort to lay the foundations of
free societies that can afford to grant their citizens political
freedom, economic opportunities, and social mobility. All
our dollars and technical skills will have little effect if the
"common man" feels that our help is only benefiting the
privileged few while neglecting him. In short, the very essence of American society is being tested, for the Communists
are challenging this country in terms of the principles and
purposes on which the United States was originally founded.
If the United States fails to live up to its own ideals at home,
and if it fails abroad in the attempt to help the new societies
create a better life for themselves, then democracy will have
failed its historic task. And unless the United States learns
this elementary lesson quickly—and responds effectively—it
will lose the world by default. For time is not necessarily on
the side of the United States and the West, as American
policy-makers have all too often assumed in the past. Time is
neutral, and it will reward only the nation or side that grasps
its opportunities and exploits them successfully by mobiliz-

ing all available moral and material resources. It cannot be said that the United States made this effort during the 1950's. But the Soviet Union did. Its military power rose sharply, its economy grew rapidly, and its scientific performance startled the world. Soviet achievements thereby challenged the complacent American assumption that democracy was the inevitable wave of the future; and they posed the uncomfortable question as to whether American values—and American principles of political and social organization—were indeed adequate to meet the decade ahead, the crucial "decade of development" of the 1960's, during which it would be necessary to forge a new partnership between the northern and southern halves of the world and turn the "revolution of rising expectations" into a "revolution of rising satisfactions."

VIII. THE CHALLENGES OF THE 1960's

The Legacy of the 1950's

Could the United States transcend its own experience and change its way of looking at the world, and do so quickly enough? This was the single most important question that confronted this country during the 1960's. Upon its answer would depend not just American and free-world security, but the non-Communist world's survival.

American democracy was actually faced with three questions, all of which demanded speedy answers: Would it continue to regard peace and war as two mutually exclusive states of affairs? Could it end the divorce between force and diplomacy? And finally, could it understand the social revolutions occurring in many of the underdeveloped nations? Perhaps it was expecting too much of any people that they change their way of life and the values of several generations within the short span of one or two decades. Old beliefs and traditions are not surrendered easily or altered lightly. Still, the chances were that unless this could be accomplished, these traditions would serve to excuse this country into disaster. The world would not stand fast while we reluctantly and slowly adjusted our preconceptions. Indeed, the challenge for the 1960's was whether we could make this adjustment quickly enough to grasp and cope with the problems that faced us in the world.

First of all, the United States could no longer afford to regard power as evil. For the consequence of this attitude had been that we had attempted to abstain from power politics during peacetime in order to remain morally pure. But once we had been attacked and were compelled to resort to force, we applied it absolutely in order to absolve ourselves from sin. Only the nobility of our purposes—above all, the aim to eliminate power politics forever and spread the light of democracy—could justify the use of this immoral instrument war. The guilt feelings induced by our employment of power could be relieved only if the power we applied was righteous power. The resulting distinction between total peace and total war was deeply ingrained in the American people. Thus, containment had within it from the beginning a built-in reaction, for it was a policy of "neither war nor peace" which promised no speedy end to America's involvement in foreign affairs. The last years of the Truman Administration made very apparent the profound emotional distaste for waging a conflict which did not allow the public either to preoccupy itself with domestic concerns or to pose in its favorite guise of a noble and unselfish crusader on behalf of moral principles. If the people could not conduct an all-out war to eliminate the Communist threat and power politics for all time, they preferred to retire from the sordid international struggle, to remain untainted by the evil ways of the rest of the world, and to concentrate on their individual material needs and wants. By 1952, the country therefore sought relief from the vigorous exertions and frustrations of the seemingly endless cold war—frustrations which were heightened by the loss of China, the atomic monopoly, and the hard-fought but inconclusive Korean War. The nation realized, of course, that it could not withdraw completely into its own shell, that a return to pre-World War II isolationism was impossible. But it did want to minimize the energies devoted to foreign policy and maximize attention on domestic affairs and the pursuit of individual material welfare. The result was the election of General Eisenhower to the Presidency. His Administration faithfully mirrored this popular desire for cutting political and economic commitments. The Eisenhower Administration spent eight years reducing the share of the national income spent on public purposes, especially for defense. To be sure, the national government spent more money in 1960 than it had a decade earlier under Truman, but this sum was a smaller portion of a much increased national income. The consequence of this reduction of expenditures, as Walter Lippmann has bluntly said, was a decrease of American power and influence in the world. According to Lippmann:

. . . During these years [1953-60] of private prosperity, the

President has been presiding over the loss of American primacy among the great powers of the world. . . . We have fallen behind and are not holding our own in terms of national power, in all-over military capacity, in the competition to pioneer outer space (in which the United States is, according to testimony, three to five years behind *if* the Soviet Union suspends its own space program!), in the comparative rate of economic growth, and in education, which is the life-giving principle of national power.

Why has this happened? Why are we challenged in this way when, in fact, the Soviet Union has a gross national product which is less than half of ours and a standard of living about a third as high as our own? Why is this richer country being pressed by a poorer country?

The reason, at bottom, is that in this period of cold war, the President has adhered to a principle which would probably no longer be suitable even in a time of total peace. He has adhered to a principle which puts private comfort and private consumption ahead of national need. . . . The challenge of the Soviet Union has been demanding an increase, not a reduction, of the share of the national income devoted to public purposes. We are falling behind in the race because we are not allowed to run.

The Soviet economy is growing at a rate which, estimated conservatively, is 6 per cent per annum. Our economy has been growing at a rate of less than 3 per cent. The Soviet economy is half as big as ours, but it is growing twice as fast.

This means that this year's increment of increase is about $12 billion in the U.S.S.R. and about $15 billion in the United States.

But, and this is the crux of the matter, the U.S.S.R. will use most, not all, of the $12 billion increase for national purposes, for armaments, for productive investment, for foreign aid, and for national education. We, on the other hand, are acting on the Eisenhower principle, and are spending a greater share of our $15 billion increase for private purposes, for the making of consumer goods and of the factories and facilities connected with the making and use of consumer goods.

That is why the national power of the Soviet Union is forging ahead of the national power of the United States.

It was characteristic of the 1950's and the desire to flee from international responsibilities into domestic comfort and unconcern that at the time the Russians shot their first Sputnik into space, the Ford Motor Company produced the new Edsel automobile. And nothing could have been more symptomatic of the prevailing mood than the public debate during 1960 of America's "national purpose." A nation that debates its purposes at a time when nothing should be more clear is a nation that has lost, even if only temporarily, a clear vision of any larger purpose than private selfishness, self-indulgence, and the preservation of the *status quo.* The election slogan of the 1950's, "You never had it so good," was the cry of the satisfied, not the disturbed. Americans seemed to prefer self-deception to facing the brutal realities of the world and the increasing danger of the nation's global position. If one judged by the public debates, the chief concern of the American people seemed to be the balanced budget. Most Americans—led by President Eisenhower—apparently regarded this as the pre-eminent goal of government. Surely, nothing could have been more symbolic of the lack of popular awareness of the national purpose and the overriding individual concern with the accumulation of material objects and the enjoyment of affluence. A predetermined annual budget—one stating *a priori* that so and so much can be spent, and no more—is not a budget that can ask what public purposes need attention and what must be done to fulfill them. Its only real question is what can the country afford. And the answer will always tend to be conservative. Moreover, the justification will constantly be the same—that the government must live within its income or risk bankruptcy.

Ironically, no reason had ever been advanced that paid less attention to the nation's own empirical behavior. For the basis of the American economy is, in fact, credit. The individual buys goods he cannot at the moment pay for; he therefore buys on installment because he calculates that he can pay off the balance with his future salary. The consumer, in short, does not ask first what he can afford at the time; he first determines his need, and then he counts up his future income. Nor could an industrial corporation operate on an annually balanced budget. Hopefully anticipating installment buying and ever larger markets for its products, it plans the expansion of its facilities. This costs millions, sometimes billions, of dollars; if it means a deficit one year because the amount of invested capital exceeds the annual revenue, the corporation nevertheless spends the money because it expects future profits to increase and more than compensate for the current deficit.

Yet, the government is expected to act in a way that most American individuals and industries have long ago rejected, even if they still pay lip service to the tradition of "a penny saved, a penny earned." The government is not permitted to ask first what the needs of the country are, internationally and domestically, and then to plan the requisite budget on the assumption of increased future revenues. It is expected to balance its budget each year, *irrespective* of the nation's needs. If there is not sufficient money, the need will remain unattended, or at least inadequately attended. To be sure, this will lead to a crisis in the future, as the problem grows worse; and then a crash remedial program will cost far more than if the problem had been met at an earlier stage. A penny saved and earned becomes a dollar thrown away in the end. But that is, of course, in the future. It seemed at times during the 1950's that America's cult of the balanced budget had become this nation's equivalent of the totalitarian country's worship of the leader. But whereas in Russia the leader had a purpose that he pursued with vigor and skill, in America the balanced budget had become the national substitute for purpose, betraying only a lack of faith in America, in its political system and economy—and in its capacity for sufficiently speedy economic growth to provide the future revenues to pay for present deficits.

The distinction between war and peace at a time the Communists were pursuing a strategy of "neither war nor peace" was not the only aspect of the American approach to foreign policy that hampered the conduct of this policy. Another aspect was the continued separation of force and diplomacy. Admittedly, during the days of America's atomic monopoly, our all-or-nothing strategy may have helped to deter the Soviet Union from precipitating World War III. But even this is subject to doubt. Russia had suffered extensive damage and terrible losses in her fight with Nazi Germany, and she was hardly in a position to wage another global conflict so soon after the second one had ended. Moreover, if the United States had not possessed the atomic bomb, she would have had to remobilize her conventional forces, especially the Army, to balance Soviet power. In any case, whether or not the atomic bomb was responsible for preventing another world war, the Soviet explosion of an atomic device in late 1949, many years ahead of American expectations, precipitated a crisis for our strategy because it foreshadowed a drastic shift in the global strategic balance. Russia's atomic explosion, in effect, presaged: first, the possibility of a Soviet nuclear retaliation in the near future; second, a delimitation of the objectives for which the United States would be willing to invoke SAC; third, an even greater Soviet willingness to assume risks, since SAC's neutralization reduced the risks Russia would incur from limited probes and demands; and fourth, in the absence of a capacity to wage limited warfare, a growing American hesitation to oppose such expansion, as in Indochina, or to stand completely firm on its rights, as in Berlin. In short, the United States would become increasingly fearful of employing its military power to answer Communist challenges; but a diplomacy unsupported by force spells impotence. As Henry Kissinger has stressed: "In a society of 'sovereign' states, a power can in the last resort vindicate its interpretation of justice or defend its 'vital interests' only by the willingness to employ force. . . . The motive force behind international settlements has always been a combination of the belief in the advantages of harmony and the fear of the consequences of proving obdurate. A renunciation of force, by eliminating the penalty for intransigence, will therefore place the international order at the mercy of its most ruthless or its most irresponsible member." It would, in other words, create a political vacuum into which the Soviet Union and Communist China could move without fear of retaliation. This situation demanded that in the age of nuclear parity the United States find some means of employing force that allowed it to escape the dilemma of suicide or appeasement. Policy and power had to be harmonized. This could be achieved only if the United States raised the requisite limited war forces. Their possession would be the best guarantee that such kinds of conflicts would not happen, just as a total-war force was the best deterrent to all-out aggression. But this limited-war capability had to be accompanied by a willingness to fight such conflicts—which demanded a basic change in the American approach to war. "All of us assume almost without question," Bernard Brodie said, "that peace is better than war, but it is curious and interesting that we do not have the same consensus that limited war is preferable to total war. One reason is that some people apparently still entertain fantasies of total war which have the United States doing all the hitting while receiving few if any nuclear bombs in return." Only when this notion was rejected for the nonsense it was would the American people feel compelled to reconsider their attitude toward total and limited wars and adjust their thinking to the realities of the world.

Lastly, America had to meet the problem posed by the anticolonial revolutions of the underdeveloped nations. Being the product of an anticolonial revolution, we have long prided ourselves that, more than any other nation in the world, the United States could understand their aspirations for freedom and help them with advice on how to establish a democratic system of gocernment. Unfortunately, our political definition of freedom was not sufficient. The real issue was whether the United States could supply the new nations with capital funds and with a social message that could compete with the appeal of Communism. The peoples of these countries wanted to move from poverty to industrialism within one generation, in order to achieve their aspirations for a higher standard of living and a better way of life. And in those nations where the traditional society had not yet been overthrown, this desire was accompanied by an acute class struggle. The nationalist movements sought not only emancipation from Western political domination, but also freedom from internal rule by traditional aristocracies, sheiks, big merchants, and *ancien régime* rulers. This problem of dealing with countries experiencing social revolutions thus posed a real dilemma for America: Could a people "born free" understand peoples who had had to struggle to become so? Could a country that had not itself experienced a social revolution understand nations where the focus of politics was the class struggle? A diminished military capability and an inflexible military strategy were not the only means by which the United States could lose the world; an inadequate response to the needs of the underdeveloped nations could lose it for us as well. Anti-Communism was no answer to the problems of a world in revolution. America had to make her belief in human dignity and liberty meaningful to the contemporary world—a world in which most people were not white—and this she could do only if she acquired a sophisticated understanding of social politics. It was here, perhaps, that American democracy faced its greatest challenge, precisely because its grasp of social politics abroad was even more lacking than its understanding of power politics in the international arena.

The challenge for American foreign policy in the 1960's was thus to adapt its traditional view of the world to contemporary realities. This was neither an easy task to accomplish nor a goal to be achieved quickly. Nations, like individuals, guide themselves by their experience. How then do they cope with unprecedented problems for which their experience has not prepared them? In good part, this is a matter of trial and error. At first, they react in terms of past habits. But when time and time again this approach bears little fruit, they normally reappraise their approach and adjust themselves more or less accurately to their environment. Thus, the reaction of the American people in the early 1950's to their intensive and extensive involvement in foreign affairs was hardly surprising. If peace *was* the normal state of affairs and if *all* problems, including those of foreign policy, could be solved, why was it that the cold war continued and continued without any end in sight? If the question is never *whether* problems can be solved, but only *how,* was the inability to win the cold war not the fault of those in power? Surely, if foreign policy was merely a question of the right technique, plus having a will to win, then the real issue was that our political leadership lacked either competence or determination, or both. Thus the initial reaction was to weed out those who lacked the will to win; the assumption was that there were traitors within the government. Clearly, someone was hobbling our power and thereby favoring the Communists, because they, the policy-makers, were either Communists themselves or Communist "dupes." A second, somewhat less extreme reaction simply assumed incompetence on the part of the leadership. This dictated a change of leaders, from those who held a "defeatist" attitude to those who believed in a "red-blooded" and dynamic American policy of "liberation" for Eastern Europe which would "roll back" the Communists. But no liberations occurred, and the cold war did not end. This time, however, no one could attribute it to a lack of either patriotism or will. The President was the commander who had led the American and British armies to victory in Europe.

Thus, by the late 1950's, it had become necessary to re-think former attitudes toward foreign policy. Clearly, victory in the cold war was far from being won. Perhaps the lives of nations were, after all, like those of individuals. They, too, found it impossible to resolve all their problems and had to learn the hard way sometimes that the art of living was the ability to learn to live *with* problems. Problems are rarely resolved completely; more often than not, they are isolated, contained, or moderated. There are no quick, simple, or easy answers to life; no brave words or tough postures will produce a magic solution. Furthermore, just as it is impossible to resolve all of our individual problems, so it is impossible to achieve all our goals. However able or rich or influential we may be, we are not all-powerful; nor do we exist in isolation. Rather, we coexist with other men who have their own goals and interests, some of which conflict with ours; but this does not mean that we normally live in a state of either total war or complete harmony. Quite the contrary: We live in a twilight zone between war and peace; we settle our differences by a process of bargaining in which we exert pressures and counterpressures, offer rewards and counterrewards, and learn to compromise. In brief, most individuals learn to adjust to "reality" and cope with the world as it exists, not as they wish it were; only neurotics live in a constant dream world. Most individuals also learn that their "power" is limited and that some of their goals are therefore beyond their reach. Consequently, they set themselves more limited aims that can be realized. Failure to adjust their goals to their "power" condemns them to lives of eternal frustration. By 1960, many Americans were learning that these simple truths applied to nations as well.

Three men in the early 1960's, indeed, have testified to the changes in American attitudes. The first was President Kennedy. From the beginning of his administration, Kennedy emphasized that "the torch has been passed to a new generation of Americans—born in this century, tempered by war, disciplined by a hard and a bitter peace, proud of our ancient heritage," and presumably more able to understand the world of the mid-twentieth century. In his speeches, Kennedy, the "great articulator," stressed a number of themes over and over again. First, there would be no quick international solutions:

> There is no single, simple key to this peace—no grand or magic formula to be adopted by one or two powers. Genuine peace must be the product of many nations, the sum of many acts. It must be dynamic, not static, changing to meet the challenge of each new generation. For peace is a process—a way of solving problems.
>
> With such a peace, there will still be quarrels and conflicting interests, as there are within families and nations.

Second, we could not continue to view the cold war in simple black-and-white stereotypes that made negotiations with the Soviet Union unthinkable lest we be tainted and outmaneuvered. While we had "wholly different views of the world, its freedom, its future," we also had a common interest in avoiding suicidal war. Thus we had to deal with the Soviet Union:

> While the road to peace is long and full of traps and pitfalls, there is no reason not to take each step that we can safely take. It is in our national self-interest to ban nuclear testing in the atmosphere so that all of our citizens can breathe more easily. It is in our national self-interest to sell surplus wheat in storage to feed Russians and Eastern Europeans who are willing to divert large portions of their limited foreign exchange reserves away from the implements of war.
>
> It is in our national self-interest to keep weapons of mass destruction out of outer space—to maintain an emergency communications link with Moscow—and to substitute joint and peaceful exploration in the Antarctic and outer space for cold war exploitation. . . . Let us always make clear our willingness to talk, if talk will help.

Third, we also intended to keep up our strength, and especially to adopt a flexible strategy: "We intend to have a wider choice than humiliation or all-out nuclear action." Fourth, and finally, we had to help the new nations develop themselves: "If a free society cannot help the many who are poor, it cannot save the many who are rich." Moreover, the United States would respect their nonalignment: "We shall not always expect to find them supporting our view. But we shall always hope to find them strongly supporting their own freedom."

If President Kennedy articulated these themes and shaped his policies in accordance with them, it was President Johnson who, after Kennedy's tragic assassination in late 1963, seemed best fitted to continue the adaptation of the United States to its environment and to deal with the problems confronting this country in realistic terms. For Johnson is the "great pragmatist." He is, in the best sense of the word, a politician to his fingertips. However noble his vision—for instance, of the Great Society—he will not allow his enthusiasm to carry him away; he does not waste his time or energy supporting lost causes. Politics, it has been said, is the art of the possible. For Johnson, who has spent more than half of his lifetime in the capital and might well be called Mr. Government, this is a credo, not a cliché. He first clearly identifies the array of conflicting forces on the political scene, calculates their relative strengths, and then, as in a football game, decides upon his strategy. He does not expect total victory for he recognizes that opposing forces exist and that one is best able to advance one's cause by bargaining and compromise. His favorite quotation comes from Isaiah: "Come, let us reason together." In this process, two points are significant. First, one does not usually condemn one's opponents as immoral while claiming a monopoly of virtue; self-righteousness makes compromise impossible for it leads to rigid positions. Second, one has to know both how to use power and how to be aware of the limits of power—and therefore the purposes that can realistically be achieved. One always distinguishes between those interests which are vital and those which are secondary, and one always has to be prepared to defend "vital interests," even at the risk of strong criticism from other nations, and to sacrifice the lesser interests for the more important. One thing is quite clear about Johnson: He does not live in a dream world of simple answers and ready solutions, and he is not likely to shout "Stop the world, I want to get off" when he faces difficult and frustrating problems. Having gained his stature and recogni-

tion because of his outstanding ability as a domestic states-
man—for a great politician is a domestic diplomat who, by
means of the bargaining process, ensures that the competing
interests and forces in a society coexist peacefully—Johnson,
with his pragmatism and flexibility, appeared to be the right
man in the White House in a period during which the
United States is adjusting to the world "as it is."

How far the American people may already have adjusted
was perhaps indicated by the overwhelming defeat of Senator
Goldwater in the 1964 Presidential election. Besides winning
Southern racist votes, the Senator captured mainly the votes
of rock-ribbed Republicans who would probably vote for
Walter Reuther if he ran on the Republican ticket. But
millions of Republicans voted *for* President Johnson and
against Senator Goldwater. This is all the more surprising
since Goldwater espoused very traditional themes in both his
domestic and foreign-policy pronouncements. In the former,
he attacked the evils of "big government" and lauded individualism and private enterprise. Yet his very criticisms demonstrated the "cultural gap" between what Americans frequently enunciate and how they actually behave. Few of the
farmers who heard Goldwater, for example, *really* wanted to
reduce the size of the government or to practice free enterprise; they rather liked their price supports. Yet many of
these farmers had probably themselves denounced the big-
ness of the Federal Government and lauded individualism in
the past. But now they were fearful that Goldwater would
really do what they had themselves often advocated—namely,
eliminate price supports and restore real private enterprise
and individual initiative by ending wicked Federal "interference." The traditional Republican states of the Midwest
all voted for Johnson.

It was particularly in foreign policy, however, that Goldwater presented himself as the advocate of the old ways—not
because they were old, but because they were right. Victory
could be won, he maintained; it was simply a matter of will
power. If the requisite will were there, no obstacles were so
great that they could not be surmounted. If the United States
really wanted to win, it could; once it made up its mind, that
was that. The way to win was simply *to win*. The continued
problems caused by the outside world could be solved easily
and quickly. "Why not victory?" asked the Republican candi-

date. The postwar Democratic Administrations, as well as the Eisenhower Administration, had been unable to attain a cold-war victory because they had pursued a "no-win" policy; they had lacked the determination to vanquish. Explaining how he would win the war in South Vietnam, candidate Goldwater said simply that he would turn to the Joint Chiefs of Staff and tell them: "Fellows, we made the decision to win. Now the problem is yours." He and his cabinet would supply the will. For the Chiefs, victory would thereafter be a matter only of technical accomplishment. But most Americans, by 1964, had begun to learn that life was no longer that simple. Goldwater represented the last, desperate crying-out against this new world of the mid-twentieth century which the United States did not make but had to live in, and in which its traditional patterns of thinking and behavior no longer sufficed. Johnson, on the other hand, represented a willingness to abandon outmoded patterns of thought and to learn new ways in which to cope with the world as it existed. Johnson's landslide victory suggested that a vast majority of his fellow countrymen were also willing to learn rather than cling to the old ways in a doctrinaire and rigid manner.

How disastrous it could be to cling to those old ways, and how necessary it was to adjust in order to act effectively, had nowhere been better illustrated than in Southeast Asia.

Southeast Asia, Neutralism, and Limited Warfare

In 1961, the United States was suddenly confronted with the consequences of the disastrous 1954 brinkmanship policy in Indochina, which had ended in the agreement to partition Vietnam and neutralize Laos and Cambodia, and in the establishment of an International Control Commission (composed of Canada, India, and Poland) to supervise these arrangements. From the beginning, though, three factions struggled for the domination of Laos: the neutralists, led by Prince Souvanna Phouma; the pro-Communist Pathet Lao, a guerrilla force whose base of operations was the northeastern provinces; and the anti-Communists, led by General Phoumi Nosavan. For the first four years, Prince Phouma sought to follow a neutralist path—to remain free from both American and Communist entanglements and blocs and to form a coalition government that would unite all Laotian factions. After lengthy negotiations, Pathet Lao representatives joined the government, but cooperation with them soon began to be impossible. The Prince resigned, charging the Pathet Lao with bad faith. The result was that the anti-Communists gained control of the government, denounced Laos' neutrality, and sought to defeat the Pathet Lao. The Eisenhower Administration, happy with this turn of events, supplied the new right-wing government with economic aid, military supplies, and a training mission for the Royal Laotian Army. In early August, 1960, however, paratroop Captain Kong Le and his American-trained men overthrew the government in an attempt to conclude the fratricidal civil war; to achieve this goal, Kong Le restored Prince Phouma to the Premiership. For four months, the latter tried to form a Government of National Unity—a coalition of the pro-Communist, neutralist, and anti-Communist factions—in order to end "the killing of Lao by Lao." But a conclusion of the fight against the Pathet Lao, plus the Prince's apparent friendliness to Russia and China, alienated the pro-Western elements, who established their headquarters in southern Laos. Since most of the Royal Laotian Army had followed General Nosavan, Prince Phouma became almost completely dependent upon the Pathet Lao for his support.

American concern over this evolving situation was understandable. For Laos' geographical position—surrounded by Burma in the northwest, Communist China in the extreme north, North and South Vietnam in the east, Cambodia in the south, and Thailand in the west—is a crucial one. The danger of a Communist-controlled Laotian government was therefore a danger to American security interests in the whole of Southeast Asia. The Communists would be in a position to take over South Vietnam, since they could then bypass the heavily guarded 17th Parallel and infiltrate their guerrilla forces to overthrow the pro-Western Ngo Dinh Diem via Laos' eastern jungle trail. They would also be able to exert greater pressure against Cambodia, Thailand, Burma, Malaya, and Indonesia. American power and prestige were thus once more at stake in the "gateway to Southeast Asia."

The Eisenhower Administration therefore swung its support behind General Nosavan and sent him military supplies. Nosavan now began his drive on Vientiane, the administrative capital, which he recaptured in early December, 1960. Prince Phouma and most of his cabinet fled to Cambodia, and the United States pledged its full support to the new anti-Communist Laotian Government of Prince Boun Oum. This did not, however, end the Laotian crisis; rather, the crisis now entered its most crucial stage. For at this point, the Soviet Union began to play a more active part in the struggle. It continued to support Prince Phouma, whose government, it claimed, was the only legitimate Laotian government, and it began to airlift arms and ammunition to the Pathet Lao and the Laotian Army forces that followed Captain Kong Le. Help was also apparently received from North Vietnamese advisers, technicians, artillery experts, and forces; both North Vietnam and China threatened open intervention.

The U.S. response was to warn the Communists against such intervention, but the real danger stemmed from the fact that the Pathet Lao suddenly took the military initiative, consolidated its grip on the three northern provinces on the Chinese frontier, and extended its power. By the middle of March, 1961, the situation was critical. The Communist forces were well trained and supplied and demonstrated a will to win superior to that of the larger Royal Laotian Army. It seemed only a matter of time until the Communists would overrun the entire country.

The Kennedy Administration, upon assumption of office, thus faced an unenviable set of alternatives: to avoid intervention and place the whole of Southeast Asia in jeopardy, or to intervene in an area whose mountains and forests favored the guerrilla warfare in which the Communists had proved themselves past masters. The President therefore sought out a middle way. First, he reversed the Eisenhower course of establishing a pro-Western Laotian government; Kennedy made it very plain that the American objective was a genuinely neutral and independent Laos. Implicit in his statement was the American acceptance of a coalition government. Since this aim coincided with that of Prince Phouma, whom the Soviet Union was backing, the reversal of American policy offered the best means of avoiding a military clash. On the other hand, Kennedy warned the Communists that if they continued their attempts to take over the country, if they did not agree to a cease-fire, the United States would intervene to fulfill its obligations as a member of SEATO. The seriousness of the President's words was reinforced by the movement of naval units toward Laos. Simultaneously, British Prime Minister Macmillan, acting in close cooperation with Washington, proposed that Britain and Russia call for an end to the hostilities, revive the International Control Commission to supervise the truce, and, upon cessation of the military conflict, convene a conference to negotiate a political settlement guaranteeing Laos' neutrality (that is, its establishment as a "buffer zone"). But the Russians stalled. While they accepted the British proposal, they implied that the international conference should be called before the cease-fire; by this tactic, the Soviets obviously expected to delay the cease-fire as long as possible, thereby enabling the Pathet Lao to strengthen and advance its position. Not until a month later was the date for the cessation of hostilities set; and when that day came, it was met with new Communist drives.

In the final analysis, the British proposal was really nothing more than an Anglo-American face-saving formula. At best, a difficult limited war had been avoided, but the price that the West paid was a high one: another major political and psychological defeat. It was 1954 all over again: the threat to intervene that turned out to be a bluff; the public and Congressional unwillingness to become involved in "another Korea"; and lack of an American capacity to fight a limited war, especially an unconventional or guerrilla one. And the excuses for inaction were also the same: The United States should not get "bogged down" on the Asian mainland; the terrain was not favorable for American intervention; France and, as usual, Great Britain were opposed to intervention; China, with her huge manpower resources, might intervene; the native army hardly bothered to put up a fight; and finally, the national government was not popular with its own people.

But what these excuses indicated was clear: SEATO had been unable to protect Laos because the United States under Eisenhower and Kennedy had failed to fulfill its obligations. America's strategic position in vital Southeast Asia was allowed to deteriorate even further because the United States would apparently act only when *all* conditions were favorable. Unfortunately, Moscow and Peking were not very obliging. They refused to expand in areas whose geographic location and terrain rendered effective and conventional American military counteraction relatively easy. They also declined to expand in a clear-cut, aggressive manner, á la Korea, that would arouse the American public and unite the principal Western allies to meet the common threat. But the result of the failure to act in Laos not only allowed Communism to advance another step; it also had the effect of weakening SEATO itself. SEATO's Asian members increasingly questioned the value of the alliance. In Pakistan and Thailand, neutralist sentiment rose in response to America's inability to protect the area; and in the Philippines, the government leaders openly questioned whether America would ever do more than talk and back up its strong words with vigorous action. Eisenhower had not; neither had Kennedy.

By contrast, Harry Truman began increasingly to stand out among the postwar Presidents as *the* man of decision and courage. Almost all the same reasons for nonintervention had existed in Korea, a country that the United States had not ever been legally sworn to safeguard. American public opinion had hardly been enthusiastic about fighting; our army had been meager in size; our allies had not demanded American action; and Russian or Chinese intervention had been a definite possibility. But Truman had held American security interests in Asia as paramount, and he had therefore responded to the limited challenge. But in Laos there had not been a similar response. SAC's tremendous nuclear power had once more been shown to be totally useless for any action short of all-out war. And in view of American unwillingness to become engaged in a limited war, American foreign policy had suffered another defeat. Communism had made one more advance as the balance of power continued to shift against the United States. If the 1961 Cuban invasion was the Kennedy Administration's most dramatic failure, the Laotian defeat—which was, in fact, the failure of both the Eisenhower and the Kennedy Administrations—was likely to prove the more damaging one in the long run. For if American foreign policy were to operate in the future according to past precedent, it would be only a question of time until South Vietnam and Thailand would fall, thereby increasing Communist pressure on Malaysia, Indonesia, Burma, and India.

It still remained for the United States to recognize the clear lesson of its failures in Southeast Asia; that peace could not be the pre-eminent American objective when the nation's vital interests were threatened by external aggression or internal subversion; that, if indigenous forces could not cope with these threats, the United States had no alternative but to intervene directly and locally; and that charges that American intervention would be on the side of an undemocratic government could not be permitted to prevent American action, for internal conditions could not be ameliorated and popular government developed, no matter how large American foreign-aid programs were, until *security* had first been established. In the final analysis, it was America's responsibility—and hers alone, since British and French help was doubtful—to defend native governments unable to deal by themselves with seemingly domestic revolts, which were, in fact, organized and supported by the global Communist movement. And threats of Chinese intervention had to be risked, for to accept every Communist threat at face value could only result in the paralysis of American action. It was no longer good enough for American governments constantly to announce reasons why the Communists could do everything, and America could do nothing. The Russians and Chinese were not omnipotent; and if the United States was not omnipotent either, neither was it impotent.

Subsequent events in Laos and South Vietnam drove these conclusions home. In Laos, the neutralist government —based upon a coalition of the Pathet Lao, neutralist, and right-wing forces—soon broke down as the three began quarreling with each other. Above all, the Pathet Lao increasingly turned on Kong Le's neutralist forces with whom they had been in alliance against General Nosavan. The Communists thereby eroded the only base of support for Prince Phouma's government. Too late, Kong Le reunited with the right-wing forces; Le's troops were badly defeated in a series of engagements, and General Nosavan's troops proved worthless. Thus the danger of Communist expansion in Laos, which was to have been forestalled by the "neutralist" government, became once more a key issue. Phouma now turned to the United States for help, and he received it. The Laotian Air Force received American planes, and American jets went along on bombing raids of Pathet Lao positions. The Communist forces subsequently withdrew from some of their advanced positions, but the question remained as to what the

United States would do if the Pathet Lao should launch any major drive that the weak government forces could not hold. Thus the prospect of a limited war arose once more.

This prospect became even more likely as in neighboring South Vietnam, the Communist Vietcong, again supported by North Vietnam and China, stepped up its attacks against the government in Saigon. These attacks had actually begun in 1957, but the Eisenhower Administration comforted itself at that time with the delusion that these Communist troops were merely remnants stemming from the Vietminh's war against the French. All that the South Vietnamese Government had to do was to mop them up. Characteristically, in its preoccupation with conventionally fought wars, Washington proceeded to train the South Vietnamese Army as though its principal purpose was to defend South Vietnam against a military attack launched southward across the 17th Parallel. The United States, in short, was thinking in terms of an invasion like the one launched by North Korea and a military war like the Korean War; the only difference was that this time the war would be fought completely by the South Vietnamese without the involvement of American troops. Thus the Eisenhower Administration misunderstood the events occurring under its very eyes. The clashes between government forces and the Vietcong were the beginning of an attempt to take over South Vietnam; and this attempt was being made by means of a guerrilla war—precisely the kind that Mao Tse-tung had always engaged in, and naturally the very one that the United States had not prepared the South Vietnamese forces to wage.

A guerrilla war is anything but the traditional type of Western warfare. Its aim is to capture the power of the government from within, and to do so by eroding the morale of the army and undermining popular confidence in the government. To achieve this objective, it is not necessary to inflict complete defeat on the government's forces and to compel them to surrender unconditionally. Indeed, until the final stage of the war, guerrillas do not even meet these forces openly, and then they do so only to apply the *coup de grâce*. Guerrilla forces fight a guerrilla war because they are compelled to; in the initial phases, they are the weaker side militarily. Guerrilla war is therefore a protracted conflict in which the guerrillas resort to hit-and-run tactics—here, there, everywhere—and engage only smaller and weaker government forces whom they can defeat. In order to cope with such tactics, year in and year out, the government troops must be dispersed to guard every town, every hamlet, and every bridge against possible attack. Unable to come to real grips with the enemy and impose a heavy defeat upon him as in a conventional and set battle, suffering defeat after defeat, however small, the army is subject to great loss of morale and its mood becomes defensive.

Although such tactics gradually weaken the military strength of the army, the guerrillas' main effort remains directed at the civilian population. As they are the weaker side, their principal aim becomes to win the allegiance of the population away from the government. Without popular support, the government will simply collapse. The guerrillas proceed to do this in two ways. First, by their increasing control of the countryside, where the vast majority of the population live, and by their defeats of government forces, they demonstrate to the peasants that the government cannot protect them. The execution of the village headmen, who are generally government representatives, and of any persons who may have helped the government forces proves this most vividly. Second, and even more important, the guerrillas exploit any existing popular grievances. Communist guerrillas do not pose as Communists, and they do not receive popular support because they are Communists. The populace will support them because it believes the guerrillas will oust the government with which it is dissatisfied and that a new government will meet its aspirations. Mao Tse-tung has said that guerrillas need the people as fish need water; without popular support, the guerrillas would not receive recruits, food, shelter, and, above all, information on the government forces' disposition. Thus, in contrast to conventional warfare in which each army seeks the destruction of the other's military forces, in guerrilla warfare the guerrillas seek to win the support of the people. A government that has the allegiance of its population does not provide fertile soil for guerrillas; the outbreak of guerrilla warfare is therefore one indication that a government is unpopular. The guerrillas gain the support of the peasantry because they successfully represent themselves as the liberators from colonialism or foreign rule, native despotic governments, economic deprivation, or social injustice.

Counterguerrilla war is therefore not a purely military war, but is a political war as well. While the defeat of guerrillas in the field must be vigorously pursued, the principal task is to tackle the political, social, and economic conditions which bred the support for the guerrillas. Fundamentally, counterguerrilla warfare is therefore an extremely difficult and sophisticated form of war to wage—far more so than the traditional clash of armies—because the war cannot be won without thoroughgoing reforms. Yet these have to be carried out in the midst of battle. Such a war is also likely to take years; five to ten years is not at all out of the ordinary. And finally, it takes approximately fifteen counterguerrilla fighters to one guerrilla—in short, a sizable army, and one trained not in conventional fighting but in counterguerrilla tactics. What all this means is that the United States will find such wars extremely difficult to fight. America likes its wars "strictly military." A war that is concerned primarily with social and political reforms—and thus opens itself up to all the usual domestic criticisms of "socialistic," "pro-Communistic," and "do-gooder" reforms—runs completely counter to the American approach. Its length would also cause great frustration because the United States likes to get its "boys home by Christmas"; not a lengthy, drawn-out affair, but a quick and happy ending à la Hollywood is the American way of fighting. If this new kind of warfare did not yield swift and successful results, the American temptation would be either to pull out or to seek a short-cut to victory by purely military action.

By late 1964, the United States confronted these alternatives. For years, the United States had supported Ngo Dinh Diem, whose increasingly authoritarian rule and aloofness from his people had alienated them. By the time he was overthrown, in 1963, the Vietcong already controlled much of South Vietnam; the social, political, and economic reforms needed to win the war had all too long been neglected. The successor governments all proved to be unstable, and were not able to rally popular support for a vigorous prosecution of the war against the Vietcong. Diem, in short, may have been overthrown too late for the situation to be saved by counterguerrilla warfare. Increasingly, therefore, the United States considered the possibility of extending the war to North Vietnam in order to end the guerrilla war in South Vietnam. For North Vietnam was directing the war and sending both men and military supplies to the South, although most of the guerrillas were South Vietnamese. The first U.S. air attack on North Vietnam came in retaliation to Communist PT-boat attacks on some American destroyers; the next strike, too, was retaliatory in response to a Vietcong attack on American personnel. But after that, American air attacks were no longer regarded as purely retaliatory. Apparently, Washington simply decided that it could neither withdraw from the war nor suffer further defeat. Either eventuality would inflict an irreparable loss of prestige on the United States, convince Peking and Hanoi that the United States was a "paper tiger" that could not counter expansion through guerrilla warfare, and thereby only encourage them to institute further guerrilla wars against other Southeast Asian countries.

On the other hand, the United States also wished to avoid large-scale air *and* ground warfare involving American troops. Washington therefore began to attack North Vietnamese military targets with greater frequency and gradually extended its attacks farther northward, closer and closer to Hanoi. The purpose was clearly not primarily military. For guerrillas can live off the land and capture many of their weapons from their enemies; and, in any case, the sustained American attacks on Chinese supply lines in North Korea during the Korean War had shown that air power alone was unable to stop the flow of supplies southward to the fighting zone. The aim of the attacks was political—to persuade North Vietnam and China to call a halt to the war. The gradual extension of these attacks was intended to stress the fact that the United States meant to protect South Vietnam and would not withdraw; that the price Hanoi and Peking might have to pay for victory would be disproportionally costly (for the former, it would mean the possible destruction of its cities; for the latter, a probable major land war in which the United States might not again permit China to wage war behind a "privileged sanctuary"); and therefore that they had better desist. Were they any more eager to fight another Korea than the United States? That was the question Washington posed for them as it escalated the guerrilla war, extended it from South Vietnam to North Vietnam, and threatened to conventionalize it.

The Kennedy-Johnson commitment to South Vietnam and the apparent willingness of the United States to engage in limited conflicts, if necessary, were signs of a change in attitude from the more traditional all-or-nothing approach to war. One of President Kennedy's first tasks, indeed, had been to make American strategy more flexible. The limited-war forces were boosted by raising the size of the army, and their mobility was increased by supplying them with more and speedier air transportation. In addition, regional commands covering virtually every area of the globe were established. And the Eisenhower stress on tactical atomic weapons was de-emphasized in favor of conventional arms. Finally, Special Forces to deal with counterguerrilla warfare were trained. In South Vietnam, these Forces were assigned as "advisers" to the South Vietnamese Army. Increasing attention was also focused on the political and social aspects of guerrilla warfare. In brief, events in the field had made it clear to U.S. policy-makers that first, we needed both the willingness and the capacity to fight limited wars, and second, we could no longer fight wars as strictly military conflicts unencumbered by "extraneous" political considerations. Thus, in the area of warfare, too, the United States had to learn to supplement power politics with social politics. The important point, however, was that it was learning this lesson in the early 1960's. Nowhere was this more clearly revealed than by the American response—the Alliance for Progress—to Castro's challenge in the Western Hemisphere.

Castro, "Castroism," and Social Politics

Cuba's revolutionary government had been established on January 1, 1959, after its leaders had overthrown the tyrannical Batista dictatorship. During his struggle against Batista, Castro had identified himself with both democratic government and social and economic justice and had gained widespread popularity among the Cuban people. This public support ensured the victory of his guerrilla army against the larger government forces. The Castro revolution

Commonweal

XII Century

N. Republic.

Commonweal Publishing Co.
232 Madison Ave.
NY, NY 10016

Commentary
165 E. 56th St.
NY, NY 10022

Christian Century Foundation
407 So. Dearborn St.
Chicago, Ill. 60605

was essentially a social revolution. In the opening months of its rule, the new government moved to remedy the conditions of the people by instituting land reforms and by building low-cost housing, schools, and clinics. But some features of this social revolution were bound to clash with the United States. Like Nasser in Egypt, Castro was highly nationalistic; whereas Nasser was anti-British because of past British domination, Castro was anti-American because of past American domination of Cuba. Although the United States had been instrumental in freeing Cuba from Spain, the subsequent Platt Amendment had granted this country the right to intervene at any time in Cuba for the preservation of Cuban independence, for the protection of life, property, and individual liberty, and for the discharge of Cuba's treaty obligations. By 1934, when the Amendment was repealed, the United States had intervened militarily three times; it also had established a naval base at Guantánamo Bay. American capital was even more effective in controlling Cuba. By 1956, the United States controlled 80 per cent of Cuba's utilities, 90 per cent of its mines and cattle ranches, nearly all its oil, and 40 per cent of its sugar. It was thus not surprising that the Cuban revolution should in large part direct its long-pent-up nationalism and social resentment against "Yanqui imperialism." America's support of the Batista dictatorship until the moment of its collapse only intensified this anti-American sentiment. "Cuba, si! Yanqui, no!" was the Castro regime's rallying cry, the ceremonial burning of the American flag its ritual, and the confiscation of American property its reward.

This anti-American nationalistic feeling—which, moreover, was deliberately fostered by Castro, as by Nasser, to increase the popularity of his regime—led to an increasing identification of Castro's government with Communism. Before long, the regime became a dictatorship with centralized control over all phases of Cuba's life. All parties were abolished except for one—the Communist Party, upon whose organizational strength Castro, unlike Nasser, had become increasingly dependent. It was simply a matter of debate as to whether the Communists dominated the government. The real point was that the Communists actively supported Castro's revolution, convinced that it was only a transitory stage to Communism, and that the Castro government linked itself to the Communist bloc—and then consolidated these political, military, and economic links. The Soviet Union supplied Cuba with vast amounts of arms and accompanying military advisers. Cuban airmen were sent to Czechoslovakia to learn how to fly Soviet fighters, and a large number of Cuban technicians were trained in Communist countries. Cuba's armed services soon ranked second only to America's as the largest in the hemisphere. Diplomatic relations were established with all Communist countries except East Germany; and economic agreements were signed with many of the same countries, including East Germany. Cuba's economy became integrated into that of the Communist bloc; 75 per cent of the island's trade was with countries behind the Iron Curtain. In January, 1961, the United States cut off diplomatic relations with Cuba. Castro was America's Nasser; if the former had only seized the Guantánamo base, the resemblance would have been complete—and America would have had to face its own "Suez."

There was no such crisis, however, to justify direct military intervention. But the United States supported an attempt in April, 1961, by a small force of Cuban exiles—many of them former Castro associates who had become disillusioned by the Premier's tyranny and his Communist sympathies— to land in Cuba and attempt to overthrow Castro. Plans for this operation had been begun during the Eisenhower Administration, and Kennedy decided to support them when he came into office. Intelligence estimates held that in six more months, Castro would have sufficient Soviet military equipment, including jet fighters, to make an internal uprising by the anti-Castro forces impossible. Intelligence believed that once the exiles had gained a beachhead, units of Castro's army would defect as a prelude to a popular revolt that would welcome the invaders as liberators. But when the American-organized and financed operation was launched, it turned out to be a dramatic and magnificent failure. No mass uprising met the 1,500 men who were landed; and the rumors and press reports, which conveyed the impression of a major invasion, only made the failure appear to be even greater.

If nothing succeeds like success, it can also be said that nothing fails like failure. American prestige, already lowered by Russia's man-in-space achievement, sank to a new low. In Cyrus Sulzberger's succinct sentence, "We looked like fools to our friends, rascals to our enemies, and incompetents to the rest." The Administration had fallen victim to its own half-heartedness. The results of an unsuccessful invasion could have been predicted: an increase in Castro's domestic support, a revival of Latin American fears of "Yankee imperialism," a blunting of Kennedy's initially successful attempts to identify the United States with anticolonialism, and a loss of confidence in American leadership by our allies. And Soviet threats that overt American intervention would be met by Russian retaliation—threats issued only after it became clear that there would be no direct U.S. military support for the rebels—allowed Khrushchev to pose once more as the champion and protector of small nations in conflict with the West.

The United States had apparently not learned the one lesson that stood out clearly from Suez: that this kind of undertaking must be quick and decisive. The British and French had bungled because of the delay in their military operations. America had bungled because it launched a major foreign-policy move involving American prestige—whether we intervened directly or not—on the lighthearted assumption that a feeble beachhead operation would result in a mass uprising of Cubans against their government. But such an operation was bound to fail without adequate planning and preparation inside Cuba, without the binding together of the different anti-Castro factions, and amid conditions in which popular anti-Castro sentiment had not yet ripened. Under these circumstances, the overthrow of Castro could have been successful only if the Cuban exiles had received American military assistance; it surely was the only way in which, at the moment of the exiles' failure, American prestige, lowered deeply by America's failure in its own sphere of influence 90 miles off the coast of Florida, could have been recovered. As with Suez, the initial outcry among the underdeveloped nations and from the Communists would have been deafening. But a successful outcome would also have clarified to the Soviet Union and Latin America the limits of American patience and tolerance; in addition, it would have conveyed the impression that the United States could decide on its objectives and then—whether these goals were universally approved or rejected—carry them out promptly and effectively. The United States would probably not have been very popular for a while; but it would at least not have lost so much respect. The invasion had been a compromise between inaction and overt American intervention; the outcome was predictable. Castro survived, and Cuba remained a Communist base from which the Soviet Union could threaten the United States herself and subvert the security of the other nations of this hemisphere. The Soviets soon showed that they intended to use Cuba for both purposes.

In the fall of 1962, U.S. intelligence suddenly discovered, to its great surprise and consternation, that the Soviets were building launching sites for forty medium-range ballistic missiles. The very fact that Khrushchev had dared to move his missiles so near the United States, and apparently expected no counteraction beyond ineffective diplomatic protests, was a dangerous sign. The great danger of all-out war is war by miscalculation; to prevent such a miscalculation is therefore an absolute necessity. But American actions had seemingly convinced the Soviet Premier, the apostle of "peaceful coexistence," that the United States would not fight to protect her vital interests. He probably remembered Indochina in 1954. He certainly recalled more recent events: the desire of Kennedy to eliminate Castro, but his unwillingness at the moment of truth to send in American forces; the Kennedy threat to intervene in Laos and his subsequent failure to do so; and in Berlin, Kennedy's paralysis when the Soviets had on August 13, 1961, built the Wall and thereby ended once and for all the four-power occupation of Berlin and Western rights in East Berlin. In each instance, Khrushchev had seen the fear of conflict and the possible escalation of that conflict into nuclear war deter the United States. Thus, he came to believe that he could install his missiles in Cuba with impunity; the United States would rather accept this result than risk the use of force.

For Khrushchev, the stakes were high. American failure to respond to his move would have proved to her NATO allies what they feared already—namely, that the United States, having itself become highly vulnerable to attack, could no longer be relied upon for the protection of their vital interests in Europe. Inaction in the face of Soviet missiles installed only 90 miles away from the American coast would have emphasized this consequence of the nuclear stalemate in a most dramatic fashion. And the promised renewal of Soviet pressure on Berlin after our mid-term Congressional elections, together with the likelihood of an even more cautious American reaction than before, would only have reinforced this impression. This time, the Soviets would probably have issued an ultimatum to get out or else—and the "else" was the fact that the Soviets could for the first time cover a large part of the North American continent with their missiles, which would come flying in over areas where there was no adequate protection against them. The early warning systems against bombers and missiles were in the north, since a Soviet attack had always been expected to come in over the Arctic. American vulnerability to attack had therefore risen. Furthermore, the U.S. position in the Western Hemisphere would have been undermined as well. The sudden and unchallenged appearance of another great power in the area where the United States had long been paramount would have eroded America's authority and status and encouraged the spread of Castroism throughout Latin America. All anti-Castro forces, including the indispensable and all too few genuinely democratic reformers, would have been demoralized and perhaps paralyzed by Washington's inaction.

The political and psychological implications of Khrushchev's limited challenge were thus enormous, for the global distribution of power could well be gravely affected. But Khrushchev had for once overplayed his hand. He had raised the pressure on the United States too quickly and too near the United States herself for Washington to be able to avoid the test. Particularly if previous American actions and inactions had convinced the Soviet leader that he could "get away with it," it was imperative to disabuse him of this notion. Such confidence on Khrushchev's part could only be the result of a conviction that the United States no longer possessed the will to defend her interests. Such a notion was dangerous for, if it remained uncorrected, it could lead to an even greater challenge; and if the United States did respond, a violent clash, possibly a nuclear war, would be the result. Luckily, the Soviets had not committed themselves irrevocably in Cuba, and they were willing to suffer a serious loss of face in order to avoid a catastrophic clash; and fortunately, too, the United States stood firm from the beginning and made its determination clear to Moscow. For once, therefore, it was the Soviets who had to decide whether to fire the first shot—to break the American blockade of their missile-carrying ships—and thus risk a possible escalation of the conflict. And for once, the Kremlin backed down. But the challenge had been far too close for comfort.

Cuba also remained a base for subversion of other Latin American nations. In the long run, this could prove to be an even greater threat to the United States, for to the extent that Castro was successful, this would mean the establishment of anti-American and pro-Communist governments throughout the region. Cuba was the beachhead from which the Communists, by identifying themselves with nationalist aspirations and social injustice, could extend their penetration into America's own back yard—and thereby undermine the Monroe Doctrine. Possibilities of success for such penetration were enhanced by a number of factors: resentment against a history of past American interventions in the Caribbean and Central America; vast-scale private American capital investments and economic control of many Latin American economies; frequent American support for the privileged few who, usually closely linked to American capital, seek to preserve their position by ignoring social grievances and establishing right-wing military dictatorships; and finally, and above all, the sheer misery, grinding poverty, mass illiteracy, and constant hunger of the vast majority of the people, who, although they live in the country, are landless.

Latin America, in short, shares the two aspirations that are sweeping through all the underdeveloped areas: the urge for a better life for the mass of people who, dispossessed and exploited, are filled with deep and bitter social resentment; and the desire of countries to determine their own national destiny and become free of colonial rule—in this instance, America's. The United States has exercised its colonial domination by indirect means: usually an alliance with the native aristocracy or wealthy and privileged governing class. The absence of direct political and military rule may have granted Americans the self-righteous belief that they were free of Europe's taint of colonialism, but it has not disguised this fact from Latin America. The Monroe Doctrine turned the Southern Hemisphere into an American sphere of influence; America did not have to resort to direct rule. Invested American capital spoke louder than guns; and political orders were unnecessary when a nation was a "banana republic" or an economic satellite. The economies of Latin American nations remained backward, undiversified, and agrarian; they therefore continued to depend for a livelihood on the export of one or two raw materials to the United States, their largest market. In good years, they earned money; in bad years, the normal measure of unemployment, poverty, and hunger increased. Their very lives depended on the fluctuations of the business cycle, as well as, of course, their obedience to American political wishes.

In these conditions, the future success of Castroism will be determined by two factors. First, it will depend upon the Latin American governments themselves: whether they will undertake large-scale social and economic reforms or cling to their privileges; whether these privileged few will be wise enough to understand the need for internal changes or whether, like Chiang Kai-shek, they will prefer to commit suicide after fearfully clinging to their fading power for a few more years. Public pressure for change is rising. The only question is whether this change will be revolutionary or evolutionary. If the ruling classes remain hostile to reform and as irresponsible toward public welfare as in the past, Castro will be able to export his revolution. For wherever there is social injustice, Castro—or Communists speaking through a Castro—will find receptive audiences. The destruction of the *ancien régime* will in these circumstances appear as the sole way of gaining a job, a piece of land, or enough food. Revolution and a "radical solution" will seem the only hope for a better life. But even where governments will undertake social reforms, the danger of revolution will remain; for the failure to close the gap between the people's aspirations and their present miserable standards with sufficient speed will stir up further frustration and resentment. It is on this inability to remedy quickly the lot of the bulk of Latin America's population that Castro has placed his hopes for the future. If he were successful in just one country, it would encourage his supporters in other lands while discouraging his opponents. The revolution would then probably spread like a chain reaction throughout Latin America.

Secondly, the success of Castroism will depend on the effectiveness of an American policy directed toward alleviating the conditions that foster popular resentment in the Southern Hemisphere. Whether America will be able to lead this revolution, however, is another matter. For it is a task that will require American support of non-Communist left-wing movements and acquiescence in the expropriation of American property—both rather difficult in view of the false but popular identification of democratic "socialism" with revolutionary Communism, and because of the powerful influence in government of American industry and capital, which stand to lose their investments and cheap raw materials. Moreover, the United States will have to inject into the Latin American economies billions of dollars of primarily public capital in order to help them achieve a self-sustaining rate of economic growth, to develop conditions in which private capital is attracted to other projects than raw materials such as oil or iron ore, and to aid in the transformation of backward societies into modern, urbanized, industrial nations. Latin America's projected 50 per cent increase of population during the next twenty-five years—approximately 90 million people—only underlines the urgency of this developmental task. In the absence of an adequate effort, the already far too low standard of living will deteriorate even more. This can only ensure the success of future radical revolutions and the complete alienation of Latin America from the United States. Effective economic aid, in short, would require a towering effort, even greater than that made in postwar Europe. For the task in Europe was to reconstruct a continent shattered by war; but the resources, the skills, and the industries were already there. These are all absent from the Latin American nations. Europe was also a modern society; the Latin American nations are largely agrarian and their traditional ways have to be uprooted and their entire societies transformed.

It was to meet the challenge of the Latin American "revolution of rising expectations" that President Kennedy, soon after assuming office, called for an Alliance for Progress between the United States and the nations to the south. He pledged $20 billion of primarily public capital over the next decade to Latin America and, even more significantly, he placed great emphasis upon the need for social politics. In the absence of the necessary reforms, he realized, the possibilities of economic and political development were slight. Failure is, of course, a possibility, but it remains too early to make a judgment as to success or failure. But it should be noted that ruling classes have rarely surrendered their power, status, and prestige voluntarily. Will the fear of a Castro and of a radical revolution shock the Latin American ruling classes into recognition of their responsibilities to their own peoples? The fear of Castro certainly awakened the United States to the significance of social politics; but there are limits to what the United States can achieve if the leaders of a nation are determined to preserve the *status quo*. In the words of a veteran observer of the Latin American scene, Herbert L. Matthews:

> In the whole of Latin America, the rich are getting richer and the poor poorer. This is the worst, the most difficult and the most dangerous feature of the area. The Alliance for Progress was created primarily to tackle this essentially social problem, but social imbalances (as the United States is discovering in the case of segregation) are devilishly hard to correct.
>
> The most serious feature of this problem centers around agriculture and land reform. The frantic urge to industrialize that seized Latin America after the Second World War was, in part, satisfied at the expense of the agrarian sector. Yet virtually all the countries are from half to three-quarters agricultural. Latin exports are overwhelmingly agricultural and mineral.
>
> The abnormal and dangerous urbanization, caused by the flight of impoverished peasants from the rural areas to the urban centers, has led to some of the largest cities in the world and some of the worst slums. Countries with plenty of land were, and are, importing food at high cost.
>
> Most landowners are resisting the reforms that their governments and the Alliance for Progress desire. . . . Much will depend on whether the ruling classes see the need to make drastic structural reforms. Much, also, will depend on the state of the world and the world markets for raw materials, not to mention the ability of the United States to invest and to aid. The rise of dynamic revolutionary leaders is always possible—not another Fidel Castro, who is *sui generis,* but Latin America has always been a region where personalism plays a great role.
>
> There are revolutions and revolutions. The fascist-military type in Latin America comes from the right; the

socialistic-communistic from the left; and in between is
the sort of peaceful, voluntary, gradual but genuine type
of revolution which the Alliance for Progress is trying to
promote.

Latin America is such a dynamic area of the world that
it is bound to have revolutions. The only unknown factor
is: what kind?*

Thus, while military action by American forces could at any
time eliminate Castro, it is clear that eliminating Castro
would not eliminate Castroism—if only because most of
Latin America is in a revolutionary stage. The issue of Sino-
Soviet penetration in the southern half of this hemisphere,
while quite real, should not, therefore, be confused with the
real issue—the battle against economic poverty, political
privilege, social injustice, and human misery—even when
these two issues become intertwined, as they did in the
Dominican Republic in late April, 1965.

After 31 years, the cruel Dominican military dictatorship
of Rafael Trujillo had been overthrown in 1961; then, following a brief intervening period of political turmoil, Juan
Bosch, a man of genuinely democratic convictions, had been
elected to the office of President. Seven months later, Bosch
was overthrown by a military *coup d'état* whose leaders announced that they would re-establish a "rightist state." In
April, 1965, the pro-Bosch forces revolted against this right-
wing military government. But the leadership of this revolution—which, in President Johnson's words, began "as a
popular democratic revolution committed to democracy and
social justice"—swung increasingly, according to Washington, in a Communist direction. Communists were known to
be active in the anti-junta movement, and Washington feared
they would gain control of the pro-Bosch forces and that the
result would be a second Cuba in this hemisphere. President
Johnson was thus confronted with a double dilemma. The
rebels claimed that while Communists might support their
movement, their revolution was led by non-Communists who
only sought a return to constitutional government. On the
other hand, if the President waited and another Cuba were
established, this would clearly be detrimental to American
interests. Our inaction in the face of this possibility would

* *The New York Times*, March 15, 1965.

damage our prestige and encourage the pro-Castro forces in the hemisphere. But a preventive military intervention in the Caribbean would once more raise the old specter of American intervention, so common in the days before Franklin Roosevelt's "Good Neighbor" policy. Indeed, Latin Americans have been so opposed to U.S. intervention that they have refused to sanction it even when it might be used for democratic purposes—as, for instance, in 1960, when the Eisenhower Administration suggested to the Organization of American States that diplomatic and economic sanctions be imposed against the Dominican Republic until Trujillo permitted genuinely free elections in his country. The Latin American nations, often so critical of the United States for its support of right-wing regimes, on this occasion showed they preferred a continuation of such a right-wing regime to a violation of the principle of nonintervention. In 1965, however, the problem was not only that we would intervene but that our fear of a Communist capture of the Bosch movement would lead us to intervene on behalf of a right-wing military junta. In short, the United States would be siding with the very forces who supported the *status quo* and opposed the Alliance for Progress. At the same time, by opposing the non-Communist element in the revolt, which enjoyed widespread popular support in the Dominican Republic, Washington might drive many Latin Americans into a militantly anti-American, pro-Communist direction.

Faced with this dilemma, President Johnson decided that he could not afford to wait to see whether Juan Bosch—a rather weak political figure who remained in Puerto Rico throughout the course of the revolution fought in his name —could control his movement. Once a second Cuba was established, it would be too late to act; preventive action would at least keep open the possibility of democratic development in the future. Furthermore, by taking prompt and effective action, however unpopular it might be in Latin America, the United States would at least convey the impression—which it had failed to do after the abortive Cuban invasion—that when its interests were involved, it could and would act decisively; and that it would intervene unilaterally if the OAS hesitated to act when a revolution's "object is the establishment of a Communist dictatorship." President Kennedy had said in 1961: "Let the record show that our restraint is not inexhaustible. Should it ever appear that the inter-American doctrine of noninterference merely conceals or excuses a policy of nonaction—if the nations of this hemisphere should fail to meet their commitments against outside Communist penetration—then I want it clearly understood that this government will not hesitate in meeting its primary obligations, which are the security of our nation." Elaborating on this statement, Kennedy had added: "If Cuba should ever attempt to export its aggressive purposes by force or the threat of force against any nation in this hemisphere... then this country will do whatever must be done to protect its own security and that of its allies." It was this "Kennedy doctrine"—that the United States would intervene automatically against the threat of a Communist takeover in any Latin American country—which President Johnson implemented in 1965. Clearly, the principle of nonintervention, aimed against external aggression, was meaningless in a situation where the danger was internal subversion, and where all government authority which might have quelled a Communist attempt at seizure had disintegrated during the rebellion. The Dominican Republic, in short, was a classic instance where we were "damned if we did" and "damned if we didn't." If the United States had not intervened and our worst fears had been realized, we would have been criticized for our "weakness" and inability to take effective counteraction against the advancing Communist threat; but in the absence of this realization, our preventive intervention was also bound to be criticized as contrary to the spirit of the Alliance for Progress and a return to "Yanqui imperialism." Yet, if power politics is a necessary ingredient of America's Latin American policy, it should also be remembered that in the long run, the very conditions that precipitate Latin American political instability and revolutions can be ameliorated only by social politics.

The Congo and Nonalignment

Even American support for social politics will not, however, suffice. The United States must also respect the new states' policy of nonalignment. Castro, of course, does not fall into this category since he has unreservedly aligned himself with the Soviet Union. But this is not true for most of the leaders of the new nations. Just as we expect them to respect our commitment, we must respect their desire to be neutral. There is no reason why they should have to "stand up and be counted." They must remain nonaligned just as the United States once had to isolate itself from the Old World. The attitude "If you are not for me, you must be against me" is not a healthy one in the conduct of a foreign policy seeking to win friends and reduce the number of one's opponents and enemies. The essential point is not whether the new states are pro-American. It is whether they will defend their independence against all who seek to dominate them, including the Communists. Nonaligned nations should therefore be politically and economically supported by the West. They may not be particularly friendly toward the West, but this is not essential. What is significant is that their nationalism will also act as a barrier to Communist expansion. If the United States doubts this possibility, and believes that neutralism is "immoral" (as Secretary of State Dulles once characterized it) and pro-Communist, its policies can only drive the new states into the arms of the Communists— as almost happened when the Belgian Congo became independent on June 30, 1960. If this actually had occurred, the Soviet Union would have gained a foothold in the center of the vital African continent, with its 250 million people just emerging from colonialism.

The struggle in the Congo began the day Patrice Lumumba, leader of the nationalist party, became the country's new Premier and Joseph Kasavubu its first President. But almost immediately, the Congo began to disintegrate into disorder. First, the rich mining province of Katanga, upon whose copper and cobalt exports the Congo was largely dependent as a major source of revenue, split off into a separate state. In this venture, Katanga's President, Moise Tshombe, had the support of the powerful Belgian mining interests, anxious to protect their investments. Then the army began to revolt because it resented the continued presence of its Belgian officers and wanted them replaced with native leadership. In a wild spree, the soldiers began to attack white women (including nuns) and children. The Belgian settlers' reaction was to flee. Among their numbers were the experts the Belgians had expected to leave behind in order to help the Congolese in their early period of self-government. All public services now collapsed because the Congo lacked an educated native elite. The Belgians had never trained one in the false belief that this would prevent the emergence of a national leadership and the development of a desire for self-determination. On the day of independence, therefore, the Congo had only fifteen university graduates—that is, one for each of the Congo's 15 million population. In the civil service, there had been 500 natives but none at the policy level; and in the army of 24,000 men, there had not been a single native officer. Thus chaos reigned.

In the midst of this situation, the Belgians flew in paratroopers to protect their nationals. Lumumba, however, saw this move as a Belgian attempt to restore colonial rule, and he appealed to the United Nations to send forces to help him against the Belgians. It was at this point that the cold war was injected into the Congo. For the United Nations troops, whose composition did not include any of the great powers, did not compel the Belgians to evacuate their paratroopers or agree to Lumumba's demand that they help him re-establish control over Katanga Province. Secretary General Dag Hammarskjöld ordered that the international organization's forces were not to be involved in the internal squabbles of the Congo or employed by the different contending political factions for the purpose of gaining power over their rivals. This, however, had the effect of underwriting the divisions of the Congo, and the country could not survive without Katanga. Since no leader likes to preside over the disintegration of his nation—particularly when that disintegration is being encouraged by the former colonial power seeking to preserve a base of control—Lumumba now turned against the United Nations, bitterly attacked the Secretary General, and accused Belgium and the Western powers, especially the United States, of conspiring against him; in these attacks, Lumumba resorted increasingly to antiwhite racial appeals. When, on top of all this, Albert Kalonji of South Kasai followed the example of Moise Tshombe and declared that his province was also an independent state, Lumumba appealed to the Soviet Union for help to prevent the disintegration of the Congo. He received both Russian diplomatic backing and military supplies; several neutrals, especially the United

Arab Republic, Guinea, and Ghana, also extended their sympathy and support.

A touch of comedy was added to this disorder when President Kasavubu dismissed Patrice Lumumba and appointed Joseph Ileo to the Premiership. Lumumba, in turn, dismissed Kasavubu. The Congolese Parliament, trying valiantly to restore some sort of government, canceled both dismissals. It was the army commander, Colonel Mobutu, who finally resolved the matter by suspending the President and both premiers and establishing a "caretaker" government composed of the fifteen university students. He also infuriated the Soviet Union by driving out all Communist-bloc personnel, who had been aiding Lumumba. The Russians insisted that Lumumba was still the Congo's legitimate ruler and demanded his restoration; so did the neutrals, who supported this demand by threatening to remove their contingents from the United Nations army. This would have left the Congo in utter chaos. Nevertheless, the United States refused to budge and continued to give its support to Colonel Mobutu, in whom it saw the best means of eliminating Soviet influence in the Congo and possible Communist penetration into the heart of Africa—which had been made possible in the first place by the West's failure to support Lumumba's demands for the reunification of his country.

Soviet-American differences now became extremely bitter. The Russians, thwarted in the Congo for the time being, made two demands: the resignation of Dag Hammarskjöld and a change in the structure of the Secretariat. They advocated the creation of a triumvirate composed of one Western, one Communist, and one neutralist representative. In effect, this Soviet plan would have conferred upon Russia a veto power over the Secretary General's activities and thereby ensured that the international organization would not again be employed to counter Soviet interests. These Russian attacks upon Hammarskjöld and the United States became vitriolic when, in February, 1961, Patrice Lumumba was murdered. For the Russians, his death raised the prospect of a victory for the anti-Communist Kasavubu-Mobutu faction. They now called for the withdrawal of U.N. forces and announced that they would support the "legitimate" government of Antoine Gizenga, who had taken over the leadership of the Lumumba faction. For the West, this raised the danger that the Soviet Union would build up Gizenga's army as a pro-Communist and anti-Western striking force. Reportedly, military supplies were also being sent via the United Arab Republic. Nasser's interest, like Khrushchev's, lay in extending his influence to the area below the Sahara Desert. This threat of unilateral intervention in the Congo was quickly met by President Kennedy, who made it crystal-clear that the United States would not tolerate Russian—or U.A.R.— intervention.

The President's warning opened a new phase in Congolese developments. The initial act was to change the original U.N. mandate that limited the organization's forces to self-defense and prohibited them from interfering in internal Congolese conflicts. The troops were now authorized to use force if this were necessary to prevent clashes. This change in instructions met the united opposition of all Congolese factions, of course, because it involved the United Nations in their domestic affairs. But, on the other hand, it provided an incentive for these factions to try to settle their differences by peaceful means. The initial result was a meeting that merely confirmed the already existing dissolution of the Congo along traditional tribal and ethnic lines. The central government could not compel the seceding provinces of Katanga and South Kasai to reintegrate themselves into a unitary state; a confederation thus seemed the logical solution—except to President Kasavubu, for whom a solution that virtually scrapped all national institutions proclaimed his own impotence and the triumph of his rival in Katanga.

Kasavubu therefore called another meeting and then, in co-operation with U.N. troops, imprisoned President Tshombe, his Belgian advisers, and, later, many of the white officers of his army. These actions were intended to isolate Katanga's President and cut the basis of his power. And by aligning himself with the United Nations, Kasavubu expected to gain the upper hand militarily and enhance his chances of reunifying the Congo by increasing the pressure upon both Gizenga and Tshombe to back the central government. But as soon as Tshombe was released, he reaffirmed Katanga's independence.

By early 1962, the situation in the Congo had thus completed a full circle. Adoula, like Lumumba before him, had come to symbolize national unity; but unlike Lumumba, he had the support of the U.N. forces to put down any opposition to unification. The international organization, by reversing its original stand, had thereby finally adopted the very position Lumumba had originally requested—which, had it been adopted at the outset, might have avoided the subsequent turmoil that compelled Lumumba to turn for help to the Soviet Union and thereby led the United States to support a rival faction. In any event, the policy was finally adopted, although it was still to be many months before the country was "unified" through the deposition of Tshombe and his Belgian advisers and foreign mercenaries. But this task was eventually accomplished, although not without bloodshed. Ironically, this restoration of national order, accomplished with United Nations support, proved to be a posthumous victory for Lumumba. The new Premier, Cyrille Adoula, also turned out to be an advocate of a neutralist foreign policy. The result of American policy might therefore well be summed up as "Lumumbism without Lumumba." Nevertheless, the fact that the United States had finally supported the United Nations action to crush Katanga—and had done so despite the vigorous opposition of Belgium, Britain, and France, all of whom had economic interests in Katanga—demonstrated clearly that the United States had learned the essential lesson, namely, that if a new nation wished to be neutral it was to be supported in this wish. If Adoula had not received American and United Nations support, and had been unable to reunite the Congo, he, like Lumumba before him, would have been compelled to turn toward the Soviet Union. National unity and nonalignment were a far better and less dangerous alternative than national disunity, great-power interference, attempts to impose "their" factions upon the country, plus the possibility of a Soviet-American military clash.

The establishment of national unity remained the new state's first imperative, and this task was exceedingly difficult under conditions of foreign intervention, as Moise Tshombe was to discover for himself very quickly when the former secessionist was himself asked to form his government of "national reconciliation." Rebellion against the central government continued, but this time the rebels, who were largely the followers of Lumumba, were supported by the Chinese Communists. It was now Tshombe who had to crush this insurrection. The United Nations force having been withdrawn, however, Tshombe confronted an agonizing problem. The Congolese army was ineffective, and the other African states, who regarded Tshombe as a tool of the "imperialists" and a friend of white racists, refused to send African troops to his help. He therefore hired, as he previously had in Katanga, white mercenaries, largely from South Africa, and this only served to alienate him further from most other African states. As the mercenaries advanced against the rebel-held city of Stanleyville, however, a major crisis developed. The rebels threatened to shoot their hostages, mostly white (and Belgian, although some Americans were included), unless Tshombe in Léopoldville called off the advance. Since the central government was bent on suppressing the rebels— many of whom were quite primitive and believed in magic, and some of whom even practiced cannibalism—Tshombe called on Belgium and the United States, both anxious to save their citizens, to intervene. Although the mission carried out by Belgian paratroopers dropped by American planes was a humane one necessitated by the threats of the rebels to kill the hostages, many Africans saw the Western intervention as an attempt to keep Tshombe in power, and thereby in effect to keep the Congo in the grip of Western "colonialism"; the intervention was also attributed to "white supremacy" feelings—for, asked some of the Africans, where were the Western powers with their alleged humanitarian concern when Tshombe's white mercenaries shot or maltreated those whom they captured? Thus, the division between Tshombe and some of the African states grew more bitter, as did feeling against the United States. The more radical states —Ghana, Mali, Algeria, and the United Arab Republic—now began to send military aid to the rebels; so did the Soviet Union. The more moderate African states did not, however, forget that virtually all African states were faced with internal dissension and possible revolt, and they therefore remained loyal to the principle of the legitimacy of the national government. For them, this issue took precedence over their like or dislike of Tshombe. For the United States, this was also the principal issue, particularly since we had not been responsible for the appointment of Tshombe, with whom we had actually been in conflict earlier. Thus, while the struggle to transform the Congo's *pluribus* into *unum* continued

to plague the international scene—and it would seem doubtful that this struggle would have been quite as bitter or
divisive if Tshombe had not become Premier—the United
States had at least relearned an old and almost forgotten lesson—namely, that nonalignment is the position most new
nations adopt upon becoming independent states. Indeed, by
the mid-1960's, it could be said that the United States had
made significant progress in its adaptation to the world in
which it lived.

IX. POLYCENTRISM—IN THE EAST
AND THE WEST

The Franco-American "Split"

It is ironic, perhaps, that at the very time the United States was "learning the ways of the world," her authority to speak for the most powerful alliance she led was being questioned by the members whom she was leading—the states of Europe, particularly the Continental states. What they increasingly sought was to share Washington's authority to formulate NATO policies for Europe. The reasons they sought this authority were twofold. First, the European nations had recovered their economic health and political confidence; and their increasing integration into a political union has transformed them into the world's third potential superpower. To be sure, this union may not turn out to be the federation envisaged by the functional advocates; for the establishment of a European supranational authority cannot, as expected, be an automatic result of the spill-over process. The spill-over would work "automatically" only if all the member states agreed to form a federal union. But General de Gaulle opposed a union in which the Six would lose their individual identities. He therefore sought a political confederation in which power would remain in Paris, Bonn, Rome, the Hague, Brussels, and Luxembourg; the Six were, however, to coordinate their political policies through regular meetings of the chief executives, foreign ministers, defense ministers, and other ministers. Such a "Europe of Fatherlands" received tacit support from Chancellor Adenauer's successor, Ludwig Erhard, who opposed, as he put it, a Europe ruled by technocrats (the experts who possess supranational authority in the various functional areas that have been integrated). Britain, a prospective member, was also determined to maintain her "Britishness" if she ever entered Europe. But if Europe's future as a confederation or federation remained undetermined—and a confederation may, as in the case of the American Confederation, be only a stepping-stone toward federation—her future as a closer union was not in doubt, despite some of the contemporary differences among the Six. For Europe was no longer the weak, divided, and demoralized continent of 1945. Her power placed her right behind the United States and the Soviet Union as a superpower whose potential strength would be realized long before China's. In the early 1960's, therefore, Europe began with increasing vehemence to assert her equality with the United States.

When NATO had been formed, Europe had been almost powerless. The imbalance of power within the alliance resulting from Europe's virtually exclusive reliance upon the United States for her defense had placed Washington in a primary and Europe in a subordinate status. Washington's voice had been the voice of the alliance. It was Washington that had determined over-all Western foreign and defense policies. While Washington had taken into account her allies' objections and had on occasion adjusted her policies to their wishes, her voice had nevertheless remained the determining one. If France objected to West German rearmament, Paris could delay but not prevent it. If France and Britain acted to defend what they deemed their vital interests, as at Suez, and the United States disagreed and opposed them, they had to withdraw in humiliation. If France or West Germany denounced negotiations with the Soviet Union on Berlin, or criticized certain proposals that were to be offered to the Russians as dangerous to the defense of the city, they were ignored. For the final decisions were made in Washington in terms of what the United States defined as the West's vital interests. But once Europe had recovered, and even surpassed, her prewar strength, she considered herself as America's equal and demanded that she share more fully in the determination of NATO's political policies and strategic decisions.

This desire for equality with Washington—and with London, as head of the British Commonwealth—had, of course, been one of the original motives behind the French proposals for European integration. Not surprisingly, therefore, once a more equitable distribution of power had been restored within NATO, the French insisted that the political relationship between the United States and her allies must be changed, too; and they claimed to speak for Continental Europe. The subsequent Franco-American differences may well be ascribed to De Gaulle; but Gaullism, in the sense of what might perhaps be called a nascent European nationalism, is paradoxically both the product of America's postwar policy of rebuilding Europe and proof of its success. Just as once the youthful American Republic strengthened its unity by rejecting Europe, so the embryonic Europe of the Six is consolidating her bonds by opposition to her "outside" ally, America; and this opposition, moreover, is consistent with the changing distribution of power within the Atlantic Community. If De Gaulle did not exist, he would have to be invented; for Gaullism is the end product of American policy. The United States may not have been prepared for Europe's insistence on sharing authority when it sponsored Europe's integration. But this could only have been due to shortsightedness. It would have been unnatural for the Six not to rebel against their subordinate, or "satellite," status in an alliance controlled by Washington with its junior partner in London.

Besides equality, however, the Europeans also sought a voice in policy formulation because of fear. As the United States has become more vulnerable, they have had to ask themselves whether they could always rely—even five, ten, or twenty years ahead—upon American protection against limited Soviet challenges if the cold war continued for that length of time. Without nuclear weapons of their own, they would continue to be completely reliant upon American power for the most important aspect of their existence, their national security. But what would happen if the Soviets ever made demands considered vital by the Europeans but not by Washington, either because this was its true assessment of the demands or because it did not consider the demands worth the price of all-out war? Could Europe then do anything but seek to obstruct Washington's subsequent negotiations and compromise on these demands?

If positions were reversed, and France were the great Western nuclear power and the United States were dependent upon France for her defense, would Americans—the people, the Congress, and especially the President, whose sworn duty it is to defend the country—always wish to remain 100 per cent reliant upon Paris for America's security? Even if they felt that Paris' word was her bond today, would they feel that Paris would be willing to risk France's survival, say, five or ten years in the future, for an issue vital to the United States? What if, for example, the Soviets demanded the return of Alaska? To a French government, holding the line in Europe might appear vital and worth the risk of nuclear war; but Alaska, thousands of miles away from France, on the other side of the Atlantic, might not seem so important, or at least of sufficient importance to affect drastically the global balance of power in Russia's favor. Geography in this instance gives a different sense of perspective. Yet how could the United States defend Alaska without nuclear weapons of its own? Must it not therefore seek an independent national deterrent? Such a deterrent need not be as large or powerful as that of France, for its use would be threatened only in instances in which France might not defend interests Washington considered vital. If the Soviets in such a case should feel that France could be pressured into submission—for example, on Alaska, since, viewed "rationally" by Paris, it would not be worth risking France's existence—then America's small deterrent could help prevent the Soviets from overreaching and thereby precipitating a total war by miscalculation. For Moscow would believe that however "irrational" it might be for Washington to strike at the Soviet Union, the defense of American territory might cause the President to launch his small force. Admittedly, it could not knock the Soviet Union out, while the Soviets could completely destroy the United States. But the point is that the United States could still destroy a sufficient number of Russia's major cities and impose catastrophic damage and enormous casualties upon the Soviet Union. Would Alaska be worth that high a price to the Kremlin? In brief, America would not need more than a relatively small force. This force might not be able to deter the Soviets by threatening them with annihilation; nevertheless, it would clearly be able to exact a price in destruction completely disproportionate to the value of any American objective they might be seeking. Thereby, it could deter, if not the challenge, at least the war, for this force would constitute what the French call their own small deterrent, a *force de dissuasion*. The major contribution of such a force is to help minimize the opponent's possible miscalculation. And in the absence of any deliberate American or Soviet decision to launch a first strike—a decision unlikely to be taken since it would be tantamount to suicide for both nations—it is precisely this type of miscalculation that remains the most probable cause of war.

Since nuclear weapons play this triple role within NATO —as a symbol of great-power status and prestige, as a means of seeking and gaining a voice in Washington, and as a means of defense—it is clear why Washington's differences with the Europeans, particularly with France, have been concentrated on nuclear weapons. Only in the economic realm has the United States been willing to accommodate itself to the new Europe. The Six's bargaining power, derived from their common external tariff, was indeed an incentive for the United States to pass the Reciprocal Trade Expansion Act. Under this Act, the United States could bargain with the Europeans for across-the-board, rather than item-by-item, tariff cuts. Tariffs could be reduced by 50 per cent in this manner, and on items in which the United States and the Common Market conducted 80 per cent of the world's trade, they could be eliminated entirely. In short, the United States was anxious to cash in on the Six's expanding and increasingly prosperous market. Perhaps the Six might not be prepared to lower their tariffs this much at the outset. After all, it was their common external tariff, accompanied by the elimination of tariffs among themselves, that realized the common economic benefits providing the principal incentive for the business, labor, and farm groups whose support for the closer political union was essential. Nevertheless, in the long run, America could not but prosper by being permitted entry into a market that would be the equal to that of the United States.

But in the nuclear field, the United States was not willing to surrender its primacy and the accompanying political dominance that the virtually exclusive possession of nuclear weapons gave her. Partly, Washington had become too used to wielding the determining voice in the alliance, and consequently, when her protective capacity was questioned, she tended to react with hurt pride as if the issue at stake were a matter of American honor. Partly, too, Washington feared the diffusion of nuclear weapons, which would seem to increase the opportunities for accidents and miscalculations that might trigger nuclear war. And politically, it was feared that such a diffusion would tear the alliance apart since none of the members would permit one of the partners to decide on which issues to stake its survival. This was especially true for the United States, which for almost two decades had possessed the power to determine an issue on which the Europeans might have to die; but now that France, for example, could perhaps decide for which issues Americans might die, the United States balked. What this meant was that the issue of more than "one finger on the trigger" might rupture the American-European partnership. The bonds of internal cohesion of the "entangling alliance," and therefore the external security the alliance provided for its members, were thus coming apart under the pressure of this ominous question: How does an alliance preserve its unity in the nuclear age when each major crisis poses the risk that actions by one member may precipitate a nuclear holocaust for an issue that the other members may not consider worth so high a price? Washington was therefore insistent on maintaining its nuclear monopoly and political domination of the alliance.

It sought to do so in two ways. First, it supported Britain's bid to join the new Europe. Her membership, it was hoped, would mean that one of the leaders of the resurgent Europe would be a close friend who would act as the spokesman for the American point of view. This would result in a more harmonious American-European relationship. Britain had already achieved her national deterrent and, unlike France, whose atomic development was vigorously opposed by the United States, she had received extensive U.S. help. Britain's reasons for developing a deterrent were exactly the same as those stated by France in its quest for nuclear arms—namely, to gain prestige, security, and particularly a voice in Washington. Indeed, it was the "special relationship" between nuclear Washington and nuclear London that had been the incentive for France to follow Britain's lead.

Despite her possession of nuclear weapons, however, Britain's world position had changed radically by this time. Since the end of World War II, she had stayed out of all European integration schemes for two main reasons: first, because she considered her close ties with the Commonwealth and, more generally, her global interests as incompatible with integration into Europe; and second, to preserve her special position as America's closest ally. The only European organizations Britain had joined were those which committed America to Europe. On the other hand, Britain was so dependent for her livelihood on trade that she could not afford to be shut out of the Common Market. To reap its advantages, Britain had therefore proposed that the Common Market be included in a large free-trade area including Sweden, Norway, Denmark, Switzerland, Austria, and Portugal. Members would abolish the tariff barriers among themselves, but they would establish no common tariffs against third parties. The British purpose was clear: to eliminate tariffs on industrial goods, but not on agricultural commodities, which she received from the Commonwealth countries under preferential tariff arrangements. Thus, she wished to exploit the economic benefits of the Common Market for which she was in a strong competitive position. At the same time, she also wanted to maintain the advantages she derived from her Commonwealth association. France and Italy had objected strongly: Facing German competition was serious enough, without the addition of British industry. Germany was at least providing a large part of the capital for the Common Market's development. Britain was not proposing to make any contributions to the Common Market's funds. She wanted all the advantages of the new market, but none of its obligations. Faced with rebuff, Britain in 1959 decided to oppose the Inner Six by forming the European Free Trade Association, or Outer Seven (Sweden, Norway, Denmark, Switzerland, Austria, Portugal, and Britain), by hoping to sink the Common Market just after its launching. By including the Scandinavian countries, with whom West Germany did much of its trade, Britain hoped to deny Germany its northern export outlet and thereby compel it to pressure its Common Market partners to include her and her EFTA partners in an enlarged free-trade area. This would, of course, have destroyed the political purpose of the Common Market, for the closer union was being built up behind the common external tariff. But until the early 1960's Britain was basically hostile to a European political union and wished primarily to reap the economic advantage of the Six's union.

This was natural, considering that the Commonwealth— traditionally an outlet for British goods and in this respect

Britain's own common market—was buying fewer and fewer British industrial and consumer goods, and either manufacturing these themselves or receiving them more cheaply from the United States or Common Market countries. But by the early 1960's, with the memory of Suez still a reminder, Britain had also begun to realize the advantages of a European political union. Increasingly, in the scale of world powers, London's voice would be heard less and less in comparison with those of Washington, Moscow, Brussels (the new Europe's capital), and Peiping; nations would pay principal attention to these centers of power, not to a comparatively feeble London. Britain therefore sought entry into Europe. But De Gaulle and Adenauer were suspicious of Britain's bid. What they feared was that if Britain maintained her special relationship with the United States, Continental Europe would remain in its subordinate status in what they felt was an Anglo-American–dominated alliance.

The crucial issue for Britain was therefore to prove her loyalty to the Europe she had shunned at the time of ECSC, EDC, and EEC. Instead of shattering EEC, as she had tried to do, she had to demonstrate that this time she was wholeheartedly committed to the political aspirations of European union. This is exactly what she failed to do in a year and a half of negotiations. Entry into Europe meant accepting the Six's common external tariff, which would, in effect, have ended the preferential tariff relationship Britain enjoyed with the Commonwealth countries—and this tariff was the economic link that had become the Commonwealth's principal bond. Yet, month in and month out, Britain sought special arrangements. Some, though not all, of the Commonwealth countries, to be sure, needed a new outlet because of their very great dependence on the British market. But it would have been shrewder for Britain to accept the European tariff and, once having shown that she desired to be a part of the new Europe, then asked for any interim arrangements to help those Commonwealth nations in distress. By bargaining doggedly over every minor detail, however, and seeking special arrangements even for those countries who would not be hurt, such as Canada, Britain jeopardized her good faith in the negotiations and once more aroused the suspicion that all she wanted from the Six was the Common Market's economic benefits. Confronted by a choice between the Commonwealth and Europe, Britain hesitated, implying all too strongly a choice for the Commonwealth.

Her stand on the nuclear issue reinforced this anti-European impression. Since she was economically weak, Britain's only real bargaining point with the Six was, in fact, her nuclear force. If Europe was to have an economic and political identity, she also needed a nuclear one. As a great power, this was fitting; for international bargaining, this was essential; for her defense, in case of American nonprotection, this was vital. For France, still developing her nuclear deterrent, Britain's help in this area, plus the contribution of her bombers, would have been very important. By breaking her special nuclear relationship with Washington and offering her nuclear knowledge and deterrent to the new Europe, Britain would have shown that this time she was sincere in her application and that she wished to help build this greater Europe politically, economically, and militarily. But, in late 1962, at Nassau, Britain made her choice between Brussels and Washington in forty-eight hours—choosing, as usual, Washington, although it had just made a decision that would deprive Britain of her deterrent. London had found staying in the nuclear armaments race too expensive when bombers were being replaced by missiles. So she had sought and gained America's promise of the delivery of the still-to-be-developed air-to-ground Skybolt missile, which, because it was to be slung under the wings of bombers, would prolong the life of Britain's deterrent. But then the Kennedy Administration suddenly canceled the Skybolt because it had decided America's bombers were to be phased out and replaced by ICBM's. Because bombers were "soft" weapons, the backbone of America's deterrent strength was to be the "hard," or invulnerable, solid-fuel missile. At a hastily arranged meeting at Nassau, Britain's Prime Minister apparently warned that if he were not given a substitute for Skybolt, he would have to adopt a strongly anti-American position upon his return home in order to preserve his government's position after the public humiliation of this attempt to scuttle Britain's deterrent. His warning had its effect, leading to an American promise to supply Britain with the Polaris missile, for which Britain would build her own submarines and warheads. Thus London had made her choice. Faced with treatment virtually as an American satellite, and certainly not as Washington's equal, London could either continue her special relationship with America or contribute her nuclear force to Europe and help to develop a European deterrent. London's decision— supported by a United States that wanted Britain's deterrent to remain under American supervision—at the very time she was negotiating with the Six and trying to prove to them that in the future she would take her stand with Europe, ended the negotiations and Britain's bid for entry into the Common Market. Just as she had chosen the Commonwealth as between the Commonwealth and Europe, she had now made her choice between the United States and Europe. The logical conclusion of Britain's "special relationship" was De Gaulle's veto of Britain's entry in January, 1963.

The second American proposal to resolve the Atlantic crisis was the Multilateral Nuclear Fleet (MLF), whose purposes were to be threefold: First, it recognized Europe's determination to have greater authority in NATO policy determination and sought simultaneously to preserve the unity of the alliance. Second, it sought to isolate France. And third, it sought to forestall the emergence of a West German deterrent. Washington's great fear was that West Germany, following the example of France, would also seek to acquire nuclear arms since these had become the distinguishing mark of great power. Bonn's acquisition of nuclear weapons would have badly divided the alliance and perhaps driven some of the allies into neutrality. Why Bonn's desire for nuclear weapons should result from Paris' example, rather than London's, was never explained; if anything, it was the logical result, not of France's possession, but of America's policy of rearming West Germany. In any case, by granting West Germany the largest share of the MLF, the United States hoped to forestall a move by Bonn to gain its own deterrent.

Yet MLF was no solution at all. It would cost a lot of money, diverting funds that might be better spent on building up Europe's conventional limited-war forces. The whole scheme was useless because, while granting Europe the form of nuclear participation, it withheld the substance of that participation since the United States retained the veto over the use of the fleet's nuclear arms. Thus the MLF did not meet the European's aspirations and only intensified the crisis in the Western alliance. Moreover, Britain and Italy hardly disguised their dislike for such a politically futile scheme. If they did not participate, though, MLF would turn out to be an American-German venture that would threaten the cohesion of the alliance. MLF could not even meet West Germany's aspirations. To be sure, because she had been forbidden to produce her own nuclear weapons, Bonn favored the MLF. Unable to build her own deterrent, West Germany's goal had to be a NATO nuclear force in which she could participate; this was her only opportunity to gain control of nuclear weapons and acquire the prestige and importance that accompany their possession. Yet, as her Defense Minister made quite plain, unless the United States gave up her veto over the MLF's nuclear weapons, MLF could not satisfy West German's aspirations—or Europe's, for that matter. It could only stimulate further the very feelings it was supposed to eliminate—the Europeans' dissatisfaction with their subordinate status and influence and the West Germans' expectations for their own deterrent.

Thus, by the mid-1960's, NATO had arrived at a major crisis point. Only one thing about its future was certain—namely, that the relationship between the United States and Europe, particularly with the Continental Six, whom Britain might one day still join, would undergo a profound change. One way of viewing the American-French "split," indeed, was as part of a vigorous airing of transatlantic differences on this very matter. In this sense, the discussion of these differences denoted a great "constitutional debate" about NATO's next and more mature and equitable stage of existence. On the other hand, some might see the debate as an indication of a deep and abiding split between one superpower and a potential superpower that is not likely to be satisfied with a subordinate status and has ambitions and interests of its own, some of which are bound to conflict with those of the United States.

If this latter interpretation is correct, the transatlantic quarrel can be seen as a counterpart to the Sino-Soviet conflict.

The Sino-Soviet Conflict

The Sino-Soviet dispute stemmed from the increasing tendency of China, first, to assert her equality with the Soviet

Union, and second, to take independent actions in foreign policy. Peiping's first major opportunity for the former came during the East European crisis in late 1956. The Hungarian revolt had overthrown the Communist regime, and only intervention by the Red Army had kept Hungary within the Communist bloc; and Poland had also struck for a measure of independence from Russia under the leadership of a man whom Khrushchev had personally attempted to keep out of power. For a while, it looked as though Russian power in Eastern Europe might collapse. At this point, the Chinese came to Russia's rescue. They did so by issuing a statement approving of Russia's suppression of the Hungarian "counter-revolution" and by sending Chou En-lai to Europe to reconcile Moscow and Warsaw. In Stalin's time, such Chinese intervention in Europe would have had been inconveivable; now the Chinese were actually helping Russia stabilize her position in her own satellite sphere. They achieved this by stressing the unity of the Communist bloc under the leadership of the Soviet Union, and at the same time supporting the aspirations of the East European states for greater control over their domestic affairs. This position was not as incompatible as it might seem. The Chinese argued that the Communist states must stand together against the capitalists, and since Russia was the strongest Communist nation, she was the obvious leader. But Russia's primacy did not mean that the other Communist states could not take "different roads to socialism."

The idea that this assertion of China's independence might lead to a break with Russia gained support as China began to take a different stand on international issues with increasing frequency. For instance, during the Middle Eastern crisis in the summer of 1958, the Chinese sounded far more belligerent than the Russians. Admittedly, Khrushchev did not exactly sound like a peaceful dove, but he was using the crisis to compel the Western powers to meet him in a summit conference which would permit him to pose as the friend of Arab nationalism and the champion of all anti-colonialism. But while the Russians only hinted that they would send "volunteers" to help the Arabs in their fight, the Chinese openly threatened to send such volunteers. Moreover, as in Korea, they again called the United States a "paper tiger," thereby suggesting that our action in the

Middle East was a bluff which should be called. And when Khrushchev seemed willing to accept the West's counterproposal that the summit conference should be held within the United Nations Security Council, the Chinese apparently opposed this meeting—probably because Nationalist China was still represented in the Security Council. Perhaps they were also irked by the original Russian proposal that India join the summit meeting. This was a clever maneuver on the part of the Soviet Union, since India felt very sensitive on the colonial issue, and winning her support as the leading Asian neutralist power would be of obvious advantage to Soviet policy. But the Chinese could hardly have approved this idea, for it bolstered India's prestige and strengthened her claim to Asian leadership. In any case, Chinese pressure brought Khrushchev flying to Peiping, where the Russian leader dropped the whole idea of an immediate summit meeting.

In late 1959-60, the Chinese took further actions which were apparently in opposition to Soviet wishes. First, they crushed a revolt against their rule in Tibet; perhaps remembering Hungary, the Russians approved of this Chinese act. But it cannot be said that they similarly approved of China's disputes with India and Indonesia. The quarrel with India, which involved minor military skirmishes, was over the precise location of the Sino-Indian frontier in the Himalayan mountains. This was a clear test of strength, and the Chinese were apparently determined to press their point of view in an attempt to damage seriously the prestige of their main Asian rival for power. In Indonesia, the Chinese protested vigorously against Jakarta's action to end Chinese economic influence in Indonesia's rural areas. There are more than 12 million Chinese scattered throughout Southeast Asia; in many of the countries in this area, they constitute a sizable proportion of the population. Most of these Chinese are capitalists who earn their living as merchants or moneylenders; they thus occupy an economically strategic position. As successful foreigners, however, they are resented and envied. They have therefore generally turned back to China for protection; but this has availed them little, since China has traditionally been weak. Now that China is Communist, their position is ambivalent. As local capitalists, they belong to the class the Communists want to wipe out; yet, their first loyalty in the past has always been to the homeland, and China's new prestige has given them a new sense of national pride. In these circumstances, Peiping's championship of their case against the Indonesian Government was an effort to win their allegiance. The new regime wished to show them that, unlike previous Chinese governments, it could protect them. Perhaps it really had no choice but to take this stand. Inaction would have encouraged the other Southeast Asian nations to take similar actions, since they all feared the possibility that China might someday use the overseas Chinese for subversive purposes. In her attempts to assert China's new status as one of the world's five great powers and the leading nation in Asia, Peiping therefore took firm stands on both issues; and in neither case could she retreat without a considerable loss of prestige.

These actions were a shock to Asia. Up to then, the Asians had interpreted the Chinese Communist revolution largely in terms of their own experience. Chiang Kai-shek had been tied to the landlord class; his overthrow was therefore a blow for social progress. The Nationalist leader had also been allied to the West; his defeat was therefore an advance toward national independence. Now the Chinese were showing themselves to be aggressive in nature. This hurt the Communist cause in Asia, and no one realized it more keenly than Premier Khrushchev. He made no attempt to hide his annoyance. Few things could have mattered less to him than a few square miles this way or that on the Indian-Chinese frontier or the fate of Chinese capitalists who had long been residents of Indonesia. These matters were picayune in comparison to making a favorable impression on the underdeveloped countries; for the issue at stake was a triumph of Communism throughout the formerly colonial world and a shift away from the West in the global balance of power.

The Chinese did not really disagree. They merely believed that the Communist victory must be won in a different way. It was on this central issue of the proper strategy with which to win the global victory that Russia and China differed with increasing vehemence; and their "debate" focused on the two interrelated issues of war and peace, and policy toward the leaders—the so-called "national bourgeoisie"—of the underdeveloped countries. The Soviet position was that in a nuclear war the Soviet Union would not only destroy its enemies, but be destroyed itself; assuming that the United

States maintains its deterrent strength, Russian reluctance to precipitate all-out hostilities is likely to continue. The Soviet Union has built a great industrial complex—the basis of its power—and the Soviet leaders are unwilling to risk its destruction on the gamble that they can eliminate the United States in one blow. The rewards of such a gamble may be supreme; but failure would mean extinction. Russia has been quite willing to practice "nuclear blackmail" when the opportunity has seemed ripe. But it has shifted the main line of the Soviet attack upon the West's position to Asia, the Middle East, Africa, and Latin America; great energy has been devoted to the encouragement of the revolutions raging throughout the underdeveloped areas. The aim has been obvious: the establishment of friendly political relations with the nationalist regimes, whose emotional dispositions are generally anti-Western. The Soviet Union has intended to encourage their neutralism or nonalignment in the cold war.

This is clearly a tactical device. For if the Communists opposed their wish to remain disassociated from the cold war on the grounds that "if you're not with us, you must be against us," these new nations might be alienated and driven back into the capitalist camp. If their neutrality were supported, however, their separation from the West would be reinforced and world capitalism further weakened. This, it is expected, would eventually lead to Communist control of the entire World-Island (since an outflanked Europe could not survive alone on the Eurasian land mass). America's fate would then be sealed, even if the Communists were never to penetrate the Western Hemisphere through Latin America.

The Chinese Communists have a somewhat different point of view. They seem far more willing to use nuclear blackmail tactics than the Soviets, and thus run the risk of an all-out war. This attitude is probably shaped by a number of factors. China, with her gigantic population, could afford to lose 400 to 500 million people, for she would still have a population of 200 million or more. No other country in the world could survive such mammoth losses. Nor does China yet possess a large industrial establishment, as does Russia, whose destruction its leaders would be unwilling to risk in a total war. Since 1957—the year of Russia's first successful testing of an ICBM and of the launching of the world's first Sputnik—they have felt that the balance of power has turned clearly in favor of the Communist world; and they have advocated that this military strength should be used to destroy Western "imperialism." China's experiences in Korea, where she fought the free world's greatest power to a stalemate, and in Indochina in 1954, when the United States failed to intervene, reinforced her feeling that America was after all only a "paper tiger." "On the debris of a dead imperialism," Peiping has pronounced, "the victorious people would create very swiftly a civilization thousands of times higher than the capitalist system and a truly beautiful future for themselves."

Simultaneously, the Chinese have grown increasingly skeptical of aiding the new nationalist governments not under Communist control. Though often anti-Western, these governments are also bourgeois—and thus by nature anti-Communist. Economic aid and technical assistance therefore only build up nations whose true colors will sooner or later come to the fore. Consequently, the Chinese prefer to encourage the local Communist parties to seize power. In any case, the Soviet Union should channel her aid exclusively or primarily to Communist countries, especially to China.

These Sino-Soviet disagreements, severe as they may be, should be recognized for what they are: an argument over means—whether the West should be shot or strangled—rather than ends. And even this overstates the difference. Even if nuclear weapons did not exist, the Soviets would not necessarily be tugging at the leash eager to attack the West. Neither Lenin nor Stalin thought of the world revolution in exclusively, or even primarily, military terms. Khrushchev's policy of "peaceful coexistence" was hardly novel. The Communists have been coexisting peacefully with the non-Communist world since 1917. This coexistence is not, however, regarded as permanent. It will last only until the capitalist world is defeated. But Communists think of this victory in long-run historical terms; and history, according to them, is determined by economic forces. Hence the struggle will be conducted in primarily social and economic terms, not military ones. This does not mean that the role of military power is therefore unimportant. But its principal use is political—to harass, pressure, frighten, or gain limited objectives, not to precipitate an all-out war that would risk the security of the bastion of the world revolution. This was as true in the pre-nuclear period as it is in the nuclear one. And it is equally true for the Chinese as well. They may talk of several hundred million Chinese surviving a nuclear attack, but they also know that such a war would endanger Communist control of the country. They may talk of building a superior post-nuclear civilization, but they are also anxious to avoid any major clash with the United States. In Korea, they warned the United States several times not to advance to their frontier and they finally intervened only for the same defensive and security reasons that had led to America's intervention after the invasion of South Korea. In the Formosa Straits, they did not invade even the offshore islands when the United States openly supported the Nationalist troops on these islands. The whole Chinese approach is, in fact, that of protracted guerrilla warfare—in China itself, in North and South Vietnam, as well as in Laos—rather than direct military attack. Only in the last stage of a guerrilla war, when the government has already lost its popular support and the morale of its troops has been shattered, do the guerrillas finally resort to a conventional military campaign to administer the final blow. In the final analysis, for all the Chinese leaders' militant talk, they have acted with great caution. And for all his talk of peaceful coexistence, it was Khrushchev who threatened to attack London and Paris during Suez, who precipitated the Berlin crisis, who broke the test-ban moratorium, and who sought to install missiles in Cuba. The real difference between the Russians and the Chinese has not been that one favors peace and the other desires war. Rather, the key issue that has divided them has been how much pressure should be exerted against the United States, how far Washington could be pushed before it would react. Moscow's view has been that the United States could not be pushed as far as Peiping has asserted. Clearly, this is *the* vital question, and not only *between* the two Communist powers; in each crisis, this question is likely to split policy-makers *within* each country as well. For the answer determines both the opportunities that can be exploited and the consequences that may have to be suffered. If not much pressure is applied because of the high risks, then the gains will be small, if any; this is why the Chinese charge the Russians with betraying the cause through a cowardice that leads them to "kowtow" to the United States. If a great deal of pressure is exerted, the "profit" may also be far higher, but so are the risks; this is why the Russians accuse the Chinese of a recklessness that can end in suicide by provoking the United States. Wisdom in these circumstances counsels caution. In terms of American policy positions—for this issue of how much pressure can be exerted against the Soviet Union or China has also divided Americans—the Soviet position has increasingly veered to what might be called the Truman-Eisenhower-Kennedy-Johnson position, and the Chinese have assumed a position closer to that of Senator Goldwater, who claimed that the Communists would always give way if only the pressure on them were great enough. Similarly, the Chinese claim that the United States can usually be pushed backward, if only the push is sufficiently vigorous and sustained. Both Goldwater and the Chinese also accuse their opponents of pursuing "no-win" policies because they are fearful of using the threat of war against their respective enemies.

The issue of strategy toward the West and the underdeveloped nations is, furthermore, closely related to the issue of leadership of the Communist bloc. The Soviets have long dominated the Communist world. As the capital of the only Communist-controlled nation, Moscow has since the early 1920's controlled the international Communist movement; and it has been Moscow that has formulated the movement's policies. After World War II, it established control over the states of Eastern Europe, which were unable at that time to pursue an independent policy. Only Yugoslavia was not controlled by Moscow, and when it opposed Stalin's efforts to control it, Tito was read out of Stalin's empire. Communist China's birth—another state controlled by the indigenous Party—thus presented a real problem for the Soviets. Potentially far more powerful than Yugoslavia, China was determined to be Russia's equal, not subordinate, in the Communist bloc. Peiping therefore sought to share Moscow's authority to formulate bloc policies. But Khrushchev would have none of this. Moscow, like Washington, had too long defined the policies for its followers and thus become a poor alliance-manager. Instead of sharing authority with Peiping, Khrushchev acted as Stalin had—and ironically, he did so first on the issue of de-Stalinization! He had decided to de-Stalinize at home and within the bloc; China was expected to adopt the same policy. It was not that the Chinese had been particularly fond of Stalin, for they had not. Nor was it that the Chinese did not recognize the need for de-Stalinization, particularly some relaxation of the Soviet grip on the satellites and permission for each to travel its own "road to Socialism"; they did recognize this need. What offended the Chinese, and therefore initiated the Sino-Soviet dispute, was that Khrushchev pronounced policy for the entire Communist bloc without even bothering to consult them. Yet China was not a satellite, and as a great power, and potentially a superpower, she was determined to be Russia's equal and to share with Moscow the authority to formulate bloc strategy.

It was this conflict over authority, then, that was the essence of the Sino-Soviet conflict. If to this extent it is comparable to the Franco-American conflict, it has also proved to be totally different in one respect: Unlike the French and Americans, the Chinese and Russians have conducted their struggle in ideological terms. And because of this, the struggle has held more ominous implications for the continued unity of the Communist bloc. For paradoxically, the very ideology that bound them together also tended to divide them. On the one hand, Moscow and Peiping interpret the world through the same ideological framework; Communism provides both of them with a *Weltanschauung*. Both hold the same view of man, society, and history. They both see world conflict in terms of class struggle and the final triumph of Communism, and they both define capitalism as their common enemy. On the other hand, precisely because of the intimate relationship between ideology and action—ideology providing the analytic framework through which events in the world are analyzed, and defining the general purposes of the movement—ideology becomes a divisive factor. Moscow has long been the Communist Rome, and the ruler in Moscow therefore becomes the Communist Pope when he assumes power. But if an ideology claims to represent the truth, there can only be one correct interpretation of that truth. Thus, in fact, there can be only one center for the interpretation and application of the doctrine.

The implications for China were twofold. First, in order to compel Moscow to share its policy-making authority, Peiping had to attack Moscow on ideological grounds and try to show that Khrushchev was not correctly interpreting the doctrine, if indeed he was not a heretic. For the Soviet leader was asserting his right to define policy for the entire Communist movement on the basis of his faithful interpretation of Communist "theology." If the Chinese could demonstrate his errors and perhaps his unfaithfulness, they would in effect be undermining this claim. Second, no ideological-theological movement of this type can tolerate two Romes and two Popes. A schism might therefore develop, since one of the Romes and one of the Popes must indeed be heretical. Could the difference between "truth" and "heresy" be compromised in order to maintain a united front against the West? Probably not. On the other hand, could either Russia or China permit the bloc to split? Both states claim that Communism is the "wave of the future." They point to Poland, Hungary, Bulgaria, Romania, East Germany, China, Korea, Tibet, and Indochina as proof that Communism is sweeping irresistibly onward and that capitalism is decaying and disintegrating. This claim would be undermined if the two leading representatives of this future wave were to split. The Communist millenium could not be achieved if this happened; the world revolution would be set back irreparably as Russia and China split and all Communist parties aligned themselves with either one or the other of the two countries.

The question is, therefore, whether two ideological and revolutionary powers can work out some manner of joint decision-making within their common value framework. This is not primarily a matter of personalities, of the relationship between a Mao and a Stalin or Khrushchev. The same issue of decision-making, of course, confronts the NATO powers, too, but because they are not possessed by any revolutionary zeal, they are far more likely to resolve their differences empirically. National interests, unlike truth, are more amenable to compromise.

Pluralism and the Relaxation of Tensions

It is clear that in both alliances the leading powers are no longer in firm command. Increasingly, they have to bargain with their allies in order to win their support for particular policies; tougher give-and-take negotiations will replace Washington's and Moscow's former commands. By compelling the United States and the Soviet Union to bargain in this manner with their allies, both sets of alliances have gained built-in multiple restraints. The Soviets have even had to bargain with the Eastern European People's Democracies because, as a result of the Sino-Soviet conflict, these states have gained a degree of independence from Moscow in return for their support of Moscow against Peiping; indeed, it is doubtful that they can any longer be called satellites. Their conflict with the Soviet Union, moreover, has taken on a dynamic of its own. Romania is the most defiant of the People's Democracies; but none is as completely subservient as it was during Stalin's reign. Both American and Soviet diplomacy must therefore now be adapted to diverse external interests and sensitivities; and policy must be hammered out as a compromise between such a variety of interests. These restraints placed on American and Soviet power and leadership will grow even stronger as the world becomes increasingly pluralistic with the eventual rise of some of the larger underdeveloped countries to the ranks of great powers.

Yet, however true it may be that the world will in the future become more pluralistic, does this future also include a continuation of the cold war? Since the cold war results from the expansionist aims of Communist Russia and China, the question becomes whether events within the two countries will occur that will dampen their ideological messianism and revolutionary goals. It is often asserted that as both states become increasingly industrialized, they will become increasingly unconcerned with achieving a Communist world victory; indeed, Russia is sometimes already said to be more concerned with consolidating the security of her empire than with Communist global extension. The expectation of a Communist conversion to the *status quo,* of the adoption of a live-and-let-live attitude, is based largely on three factors. The first is that a complex industrial society requires for its operation a literate people, but that once men and women have been taught to think for themselves, they will begin to subject the propaganda they hear—and the system that issues this propaganda—to critical analysis. In short, in educating their subjects, the Communists may be sowing the seeds of their own destruction. Second, industrialism also undermines the one-party state because it creates a new ruling class—a managerial and technical elite that will gain a vested interest in the system because it will wish to preserve its high social status and the attendant material perquisites. This group—comprising engineers, scientists, technicians, and military specialists—will be a conservative or restraining force within the totalitarian system because it will oppose an adventurous foreign policy which might jeopardize its position. Third, as industrialization proceeds, it stimulates a widespread popular demand for more consumer goods, particularly because the past concentration of capital investment in heavy industry has meant that economic growth was not accompanied by a rise in the standard of living. There will, therefore, be pressure from below to satisfy this desire for more and better shoes and clothing, radios, cars, television sets, household appliances, and similar items. And this need to fulfill domestic consumer needs, in turn, means less capital for investment in heavy industry and the military forces.

Unfortunately, the history of the Nazis in Germany, short as it was, must place a damper upon these optimistic expectations. The Germans were the best educated, most cultured people in Europe; Germany was the most advanced industrial nation in the world after the United States; it possessed a vast and conservative managerial bureaucracy; and Germany had a high standard of living. It would therefore be wise to base American policy upon the pessimistic assumption that the Communist Party in Russia will be able to maintain itself in power. The security of America and the entire free world make this assumption imperative. If internal changes should someday occur, they would be most welcome, but one cannot formulate a policy to safeguard national survival upon the unlikely contingency that the opposing state will transform itself from within and thereby save us from our dilemmas, hard decisions, and even more demanding efforts. For it does not appear that this will occur.

The Communist Party in the Soviet Union seems to retain a tight control over the managerial and technocratic elite. There is, indeed, no reason to believe that a one-party dictatorship is incompatible with a modern industrial society. The somewhat greater Soviet production of consumer goods during recent years has not prevented the continued heavy investment of capital in heavy industry, the armed forces, and the space race. At the same time, however, the gradual improvement in the standard of living, plus such other measures as the relaxed police controls, have brought the regime a larger measure of popular support and thereby, in fact, strengthened its grip on Soviet society. The regime may, perhaps, have become somewhat less arbitrary, but it remains totalitarian nevertheless. The reforms instituted since Stalin's death in 1953 have not "democratized" the Soviet Union; they have merely modernized, or streamlined, the system so that it can be administered more efficiently.

Indeed, as Adam B. Ulam has argued, the emphasis on ideology will increase to the extent that the optimistic assumptions regarding internal changes within the Communist system are correct. If the "managerial revolution" does mean that a highly industrialized society renders the need for further one-party direction superfluous because it can, so to speak, "run itself," then it becomes all the more necessary for the Soviet leaders to justify maintaining their power. And their only remaining reason will be the fulfillment of their global mission to liberate mankind from capitalist chains. In other words, the cold war cannot be settled short of an ultimate Communist victory; for to accept a permanent *status quo* would be to surrender the Party leaders' sole remaining *raison d'être*. A static condition while capitalism continues to exist is therefore impossible. A revolutionary power does not surrender its revolutionary purposes. Communists will not cease being Communists—at least, as Khrushchev put it so characteristically, "until shrimps learn to whistle." Thus, the Communist challenge not only remains; it is more serious than at any previous time. It is global in scope; military, political, economic, social, and ideological in means; and total in aim. Khrushchev once told America, "We will bury you." Nothing would be more foolish than to laugh this remark off as a vain and silly boast; for Khrushchev meant not only to dig the West's grave but to supervise the funeral arrangements.

The expectation that changes within the Soviet system will democratize its totalitarian nature remains, nevertheless, characteristic of a society that believes that all "power politics" is merely a temporary phenomenon, that sooner or later "normalcy" must be restored, and that all problems can be solved if only the correct technique is employed. Moreover, the thesis that industrialization should give rise to democracy is, after all, "good Americanism"; it means, in effect, that the Soviet Union will follow the American pattern. This belief— that Russia, too, will become a society of suburbs, station wagons, and mass consumption—is, of course, the highest form of self-flattery for Americans. Certainly, it is a typical attitude. Throughout America's history, the emphasis has been on economic development for the public benefit. Concentration on domestic affairs is considered normal; attaining a higher standard of living and social status is thought to be everyone's concern. Americans find it almost impossible, therefore, to believe that any society would *not* give priority to economic development for the benefit of the individual. Sooner or later, it is hoped, the Communist "aberration"— stressing the development of those economic means that will increase Russia's power—must end. Then industrialization will be used for its "natural" function of providing more consumer goods and undermining the Communist totalitarian system. This faith in the effects of industrialization is indeed ironic, for it reflects the Communist faith in economic determinism. The difference is merely one of interpretation of the political consequences of the economic process. The American believes that industrialization will destroy totalitarianism and produce a peaceful democracy. The Soviet believes that industrialization will destroy capitalism and produce a peaceful Communist society.

Marx's prophecy concerning capitalist development has not, however, been borne out by the course of events. Nor are future events likely to follow the pattern of the modern theory of Communist development, for it ignores the most powerful teacher of all—history. Industrial development did not lead to democracy in the United States or Britain. In both countries, the foundations of democracy were laid in a preindustrial environment. It is, in fact, rather questionable whether industrialization per se leads to democracy. In its initial phases, industrialization in the West resulted in large-scale exploitation and misery. Capitalist accumulation made it necessary to keep wages low in order to reap maximum profits for further reinvestment and economic expansion. The result of this *laissez-faire* economics was a maldistribution of income and increasingly tense social dissatisfaction. Governments were powerless to remedy this condition because the prevailing attitude was that the governmental function should be limited to guarding the markets and preventing any interference with "economic laws." It was political democracy that remedied this situation. Suffrage was extended, and universal suffrage proved to be incompatible with sub-sistence wages, a high rate of unemployment, and unsafe and unsanitary working conditions. In short, the already existing democratic values gave rise to the welfare state, thereby ensuring that all the people benefited from industrialization. The lesson seems clear: Industrialization reinforces the polit-ical system and social structure in existence when the process of industrialization begins.

In Germany and Japan, the political orders in vogue when industrialization began were semi-absolutist feudal regimes. Industrialization was produced in both countries by what the Germans referred to as an alliance between iron and grain. The bourgeoisie was quite willing to allow the aristocracy to retain its grip on the levers of political power in return for a substantial degree of freedom in the economic sphere. But in return for surrendering its liberalism, the bourgeoisie demanded a nationalist foreign policy; the aris-tocracy, wishing to preserve its political monopoly, obliged. In Germany and Japan, industrialization therefore reinforced what were basically feudal systems. This is hardly surprising, since industrialists are concerned only with efficiency and production. If the political system provides them with a stable environment in which they can "produce," it fulfills its task. Industrialists are basically administrators or technicians. They are not political philosophers. If they do possess demo-cratic beliefs, this is a reflection of the strength of the society's social values. But industrialists have in the past adapted themselves to varying political frameworks.

Thus, if history is any guide, it can be safely predicted that industry will strengthen the Soviet political system, rather than weaken it and ultimately transform it into a pluralistic democracy. Indeed, Marx predicted this result. In describing capitalism, he said that those who control the means of production also control the power of the state. Improvement of the proletariat's lot was consequently im-possible, and basic reforms within the system were unfea-sible—revolution was thus the only recourse. Marx was, of course, wrong with regard to capitalism; the accompany-ing political process provided a channel through which social protest could be registered and popular grievances satisfied. But the political leaders also control the means of production in the Soviet Union; the political and economic spheres are thus in the grips of the same men. Soviet Communism has, in fact, taken on precisely the form of state capitalism that Marx so bitterly criticized. The political leaders determine both the nature of the economy and the purposes for which it is to be used; the economy does not function independently of the political sector in response to the consumer demand on the market. That is why the Soviet Union is usually referred to as a totalitarian state. The Communist Party controls all phases of life: economic, social, cultural, scientific, and spiritual. In this system, there are— as Marx foresaw—no political channels through which the subjected masses can seek amelioration of their political, economic, and social grievances. How ironic that the Soviet Union and Communist China should have molded themselves in Marx's image of capitalism! But the father of Communism also never pretended that a state that combined the political and economic spheres would change its essential nature from within. Marx condemned this as an illusion. Neither the Soviet state nor the Chinese state is, if Marx was right in this respect, likely to "wither away," lightening our foreign-policy burdens and minimizing our responsibilities. Indeed, the demands made upon the United States will remain heavy and continuous, particularly in the effort to help the new nations develop economically and modernize politically and culturally.

For the greater the diffusion of power and the larger the number of restraints present in the society of states, the lower international tensions are likely to be. The restraints engendered in NATO and the Sino-Soviet bloc by the diffusion of power within both alliance systems are most important. The leading power cannot pursue its policies quite as wholeheartedly or energetically if it must gain the support of reluctant or opposing allies; thus each will have to moderate its policies if it does not wish "to go it alone." It is in the interest of the United States, therefore, to increase the number of these restraints by encouraging the degree of independence that the former Soviet satellites have gained and, more important, by aiding the growth of the potentially more powerful new states. The greater the vested interest that the states of Eastern Europe have in their relations with the United States and Western Europe, particularly in the economic realm, the more reluctant they will be to jeopardize these relations and the more they will urge a policy of moderation and caution upon Moscow. And the sooner countries like India and Nigeria mature into modern nation-states, the sooner they will become the great powers to whom the other nations in their respective regions will be attracted. Above all, the nationalism of all the new states, once they see that they can lift themselves up by their "sandal straps" and gain a degree of self-confidence, will prove to be a resolute barrier to Communist expansion. The real surprise is not that the new states have been attracted to Russia and China but that, with the single exception of Cuba, none has actually gone Communist, despite their intense desire for rapid economic development. Although their leaders frequently talk in Marxist terms, especially on colonialism, although they call themselves socialists and believe in public ownership of the major sectors of the economy—hardly surprising since they identify capitalism with colonialism and its nineteenth-century image as a dog-eat-dog economic system—they are highly nationalistic; their primary emphasis is not on the class struggle, let alone an international bourgeois-proletariat struggle that can end only in victory with the destruction of the "world bourgeoisie." Rather, they keep a close watch on the local Communists, if they do not put them in jail or outlaw them. Nor is the fact that they take money from the Communists surprising for, being wooed by both sides in the cold war, they can maximize the aid they need for their economic growth. The crucial point is that new nations, having emerged from colonial subjection by the West, have no intention of being subordinated by Communist colonialism. When their positions on international issues seem to parallel those assumed by Russia or China or both, it is more likely to be the other way around—that is, the Soviets or Chinese may have attempted to identify with the positions of the underdeveloped nations.

It is the long-range impact of these developments on the Communist leadership itself which may be decisive for the future of the world. For only if the Communists' expectations for the political and economic collapse of the capitalist West fail to materialize, and only if their hopes that the new nations, eager for development, will go Communist are disappointed, may they at some future date realize that the ideological glasses through which they view the world give a distorted, if not false, picture. If the Communist leaders, whether Russian or Chinese, ever realize this, they may re-evaluate their ideology as a framework for anaysis and understanding, and bring it more nearly in line with "reality." Then, and only then, will there be the possibility for them to adopt a live-and-let-live attitude and become genuinely interested in a peaceful coexistence that is both genuinely peaceful and permanent. The United States, herself a pluralistic society, can live in a pluralistic international society. The Soviet Union and Communist China, as totalitarian states suppressing domestic pluralism, are not accustomed to living in a pluralistic world. Nevertheless, they must live in one and learn to cope with it. In turn, this pluralism poses obstacles to the attainment of the Communist world revolution; and sooner or later, the Russian and Chinese leaders may be compelled to re-evaluate their ideological outlook. Whether they will do so, and whether cold-war tensions will subsequently abate, will depend in good measure upon the ability of American foreign policy to frustrate Communist expectations of continued expansion via limited challenges. And it will depend in equal measure on America's contribution to the revolution of modernization that is raging throughout the underdeveloped world. This, then, is the challenge to the Johnson Administration as it confronts post-Khrushchev Russia and the world's newest atomic power, Communist China.

A SELECTIVE BIBLIOGRAPHY

An atlas is an indispensable companion for those who seek to understand international relations and wish to follow past and present events on the world scene. Perhaps the best "map book" and one that covers extremely well the history of the post-World War II period is Andrew Boyd's *An Atlas of World Affairs* * (5th rev. ed.; New York: Frederick A. Praeger, 1964).

American Society

ALMOND, GABRIEL A. *The American People and Foreign Policy.** New York: Harcourt, Brace & Co., 1950. Paperback ed.; New York: Frederick A. Praeger, 1960. This is a first-class analysis relating the "American character" to foreign policy.

BOORSTEIN, DANIEL J. *The Genius of American Politics.** Chicago: University of Chicago Press, 1953. As Hartz (see below) does, Boorstein emphasizes the unique nature and conformity of American society.

HARTZ, LOUIS. *The Liberal Tradition in America.** New York: Harcourt, Brace & Co., 1955. This is a brilliant analysis of America as a liberal society; it stresses heavily the absolutism of the American value system.

HERBERG, WILL. *Protestant, Catholic, and Jew.** New York: Doubleday & Co. (Anchor Books), 1960. This excellent and stimulating book clarifies beyond any doubt that "Americanism" is this country's real religion, and that Protestantism, Catholicism, and Judaism are merely three different expressions of the "American way of life."

POTTER, DAVID M. *The People of Plenty.** Chicago: University of Chicago Press, 1953. A very penetrating analysis of the concept of "national character" and of the impact of American abundance on American character and foreign policy.

American Foreign Policy

GILBERT, FELIX. *To the Farewell Address.* Princeton, N.J.: Princeton University Press, 1961. A discerning commentary on the conflict between "utopianism" and "realism" in early American foreign policy.

---

* Titles thus asterisked are available in paperback editions.

GRAEBNER, NORMAN A. *The New Isolationism*. New York: The Ronald Press Co., 1956. A good account of America's reluctant postwar adjustment to the world.

KENNAN, GEORGE. *American Diplomacy, 1900–1950*.* Chicago: University of Chicago Press, 1953. A brief analysis of this period in terms of what Kennan calls our "moral-legalistic" approach to foreign policy. The book contains Kennan's famous "Mr. X" article, "The Sources of Soviet Conduct" (originally published in *Foreign Affairs*), which was the basis for the containment policy.

LEFEVER, ERNEST. *Ethics and United States Foreign Policy*.* New York: Meridian Books, 1958. A first-rate discussion of American attitudes on such topics as diplomacy, propaganda, and the United Nations.

MORGENTHAU, HANS J. *In Defense of the National Interest*. New York: Alfred A. Knopf, 1951. A critique of U.S. postwar policy, particularly good for the barrage it levels against American "moralism," "sentimentalism," "utopianism," and "legalism" in foreign policy.

———. *The Purpose of American Politics*.* New York: Alfred A. Knopf, 1960. A withering attack on America's dedication to a sterile preservation of the political and material *status quo* and its lack of purpose in domestic and foreign policy during the late 1950's and early 1960's.

ROSTOW, W. W. *The United States in the World Arena*. New York: Harper & Brothers, 1960. A searching analysis of America's role in world affairs over the past twenty-five years, calling for major changes in our habits of dealing with international problems.

American Military Strategy

BRODIE, BERNARD. *Strategy in the Missile Age*.* Princeton, N.J.: Princeton University Press, 1959. Like all the author's writings, outstanding for the incisiveness of its thought and the freshness and candor of its insights into such problems as those of total war and limited nuclear war.

BUCHAN, ALASTAIR. *NATO in the 1960's*.* Rev. ed.; New York: Frederick A. Praeger, 1962. A good brief analysis of NATO's nuclear crisis.

KAHN, HERMAN. *On Escalation: Metaphors and Scenarios*. New York: Frederick A. Praeger, 1965. An analysis of the dynamics of escalation involved in limited conflicts.

———. *Thinking About the Unthinkable*.* New York: Horizon Press, 1962. A much condensed and more readable version of the author's famous *On Thermonuclear War*. Some of the topics covered are the different types of nuclear war, civil defense, and various types of deterrence.

KAUFMANN, WILLIAM W. (ed.). *Military Policy and National Security*. Princeton, N.J.: Princeton University Press, 1956. Contains Kaufmann's own perceptive analysis of American total- and limited-war strategy.

KISSINGER, HENRY A. "NATO's Nuclear Dilemma," *The Reporter*,

March 28, 1963. The single best presentation and critique of the U.S. position in the NATO crisis of the mid-1960's.

———. *The Necessity for Choice.** New York: Harper & Brothers, 1960. A critical analysis of American military policy during the 1950's, plus superb sections dealing with American attitudes toward negotiations, the underdeveloped nations, and the problems of policy formulation.

———. *Nuclear Weapons and Foreign Policy.** New York: Harper & Brothers, 1957. This is a trenchant critique of America's all-or-nothing strategy. It includes a controversial chapter on the use of tactical atomic weapons in limited wars.

MORGENSTERN, OSKAR. *The Question of National Defense.** New York: Random House, 1959. A comprehensive indictment of American military policy and other aspects of foreign policy.

OSGOOD, ROBERT E. *Limited War.* Chicago: University of Chicago Press, 1957. Excellent in its analysis of American postwar military policies and of the political and social conditions which prior to the twentieth century kept wars limited.

———. *NATO: The Entangling Alliance.* Chicago: University of Chicago Press, 1962. The best detailed historical analysis of the alliance since its inception. It stresses particularly the changing strategic and political factors that threaten to disentangle the cohesive bonds of NATO.

PARET, PETER, and SHY, JOHN W. *Guerrillas in the 1960's.** New York: Frederick A. Praeger, 1962. A concise analysis of guerrilla warfare.

TAYLOR, MAXWELL. *The Uncertain Trumpet.* New York: Harper & Brothers, 1960. The former Army Chief of Staff's account of the Eisenhower Administration's emphasis on massive retaliation and its economy-minded approach to the whole problem of defense.

THAYER, CHARLES W. *Guerrilla.** New York: Harper & Row, 1963. An excellent and very readable analysis of guerrilla warfare.

TURNER, GORDON B., and CHALLENER, RICHARD D. (eds.). *National Security in the Nuclear Age.** New York: Frederick A. Praeger, 1960. A series of articles dealing with foreign policy and military strategy.

WOLFERS, ARNOLD (ed.). *Alliance Policy in the Cold War.* Baltimore, Md.: The Johns Hopkins Press, 1959. An analysis of the manifold problems inherent in the relationship between American strategy and alliance systems during the first decade of containment.

American Policy in Postwar Europe

ACHESON, DEAN. "The Illusion of Disengagement," *Foreign Affairs,* April, 1958. A withering reply—but an eminently satisfactory one, in the author's opinion—to the disengagement proposals of Kennan and others.

DAVISON, W. PHILLIPS. *The Berlin Blockade.* Princeton, N.J.: Princeton

University Press, 1958. A detailed account of the first Berlin crisis.

HOLBORN, HAJO. *The Political Collapse of Europe.* New York: Alfred A. Knopf, 1951. This is a masterpiece of brevity and lucid analysis of the main political and social currents that have affected Europe's development since 1815.

HOWARD, MICHAEL. *Disengagement in Europe.** Baltimore: Penguin Books, 1958. A good discussion of the various disengagement proposals advocated for Europe.

JONES, JOSEPH. *The Fifteen Weeks.* New York: The Viking Press, 1955. This is the definitive account—and a very exciting one at that —of the formulation of the Truman Doctrine and the Marshall Plan.

KENNAN, GEORGE. *Russia, the Atom and the West.* New York: Harper & Brothers, 1957. Kennan's controversial lectures, originally delivered over the BBC, advocating disengagement in Europe.

KLEIMAN, ROBERT. *Atlantic Crisis.** New York: W. W. Norton & Company, 1964. An excellent analysis and indictment of the Kennedy Administration's inept attempts to implement its plan for Atlantic partnership. Kleiman shows quite clearly that the United States and Britain have themselves primarily to blame for De Gaulle's famous veto of January, 1963. Washington's concept of a "partnership" was one in which Europe would be kept in a subordinate nuclear and political status.

KNORR, KLAUS (ed.). *NATO and American Security.* Princeton, N.J.: Princeton University Press, 1959. A superb analysis of the many political and military dilemmas inherent in American strategy during the 1950's, and of the consequences it held for the Western alliance.

KRAFT, JOSEPH. *The Grand Design.* New York: Harper & Brothers, 1962. A fine presentation of the problems the new Europe posed for the United States in the early 1960's and the response of the Kennedy Administration in terms of an Atlantic partnership.

MANDER, JOHN. *Berlin, Hostage for the West.** Baltimore: Penguin Books, 1962. A first-rate brief analysis of the post-1958 Berlin crisis and Soviet nuclear-blackmail tactics.

ROYAL INSTITUTE OF INTERNATIONAL AFFAIRS. *Atlantic Alliance.* London: Oxford University Press, 1952. An account of the problems confronting NATO during its formative years.

SPEIER, HANS. *Divided Berlin.* New York: Frederick A. Praeger, 1960. A blow-by-blow account of the Berlin negotiations under the Soviet threat of war.

STEEL, RONALD. *The End of Alliance.* New York: The Viking Press, 1964. A good analysis of the impact of Europe's resurgence on European-American relations.

WHITE, THEODORE H. *Fire in the Ashes.* New York: William Sloane Associates, 1953. This sympathetic and beautifully written book remains by far the best general introduction to Europe after 1945 and to the role of the United States in rekindling the fire of the Old World.

France

EARLE, EDWARD M. *Modern France*. Princeton, N.J.: Princeton University Press, 1951. A first-rate introduction to modern France and its political, social, and economic problems.

FURNISS, EDGAR S. *France, Troubled Ally*.* New York: Harper & Brothers, 1960. Paperback ed.; New York: Frederick A. Praeger, 1960. A good comprehensive review of France's domestic and foreign policies from 1944 to the Fifth Republic.

HOFFMANN, STANLEY (ed.). *In Search of France*. Cambridge, Mass.: Harvard University Press, 1963. A searching analysis of the social and economic changes of postwar France.

LUETHY, HERBERT. *France Against Herself*.* New York: Frederick A. Praeger, 1955. An extremely well-written and informative analysis.

Britain

BLONDEL, J. *Voters, Parties and Leaders*.* Baltimore, Md.: Penguin Books, 1963. A very good analysis of Britain's postwar social fabric.

BOYD, FRANCIS. *British Politics in Transition*.* New York: Frederick A. Praeger, 1964. An examination of Britain's postwar social, economic, and political changes.

EDEN, ANTHONY. *Full Circle*. Boston: Houghton Mifflin Co., 1960. The former Prime Minister gives his views of the Suez War and of the events leading up to it.

EPSTEIN, LEON D. *Britain—Uneasy Ally*. Chicago: University of Chicago Press, 1954. A very fine analysis of British national and party responses to American cold-war policies.

MIDDLETON, DREW. *These Are the British*. New York: Alfred A. Knopf, 1957. A good introduction to Britain and her position in the world.

NORTHEDGE, F. S. *British Foreign Policy*. New York: Frederick A. Praeger, 1962. A historical account of British foreign policy since World War II.

ROYAL INSTITUTE OF INTERNATIONAL AFFAIRS. *Britain in Western Europe*. London: Oxford University Press, 1956. A good account of Britain's postwar commitments to Europe.

Germany

BÖLLING, KLAUS. *Republic in Suspense*. New York: Frederick A. Praeger, 1964. A critical evaluation of postwar Germany.

DAVISON, EUGENE. *The Death and Life of Germany*. New York: Alfred A. Knopf, 1959. A vivid and fluently written account of the American occupation of postwar Germany.

DEUTSCH, KARL W., and EDINGER, LEWIS J. *Germany Rejoins the Powers*. Stanford, Calif.: Stanford University Press, 1959. A first-rate analysis of the interrelationship between the various West German elites and foreign policy.

GROSSER, ALFRED. *The Federal Republic of Germany.** New York: Frederick A. Praeger, 1964. A concise history .

HORNE, ALISTAIR. *Return to Power.* New York: Frederick A. Praeger, 1956. A very good report on the early rebuilding of postwar Germany.

LOWENSTEIN, KARL. "Unity for Germany?" *Current History,* January, 1960. Some very pertinent comments on the problem of German reunification.

SPEIER, HANS, and DAVISON, W. PHILLIPS (eds.). *West German Leadership and Foreign Policy.* Evanston, Ill.: Row, Peterson & Co., 1957. An outstanding analysis of the attitudes of the different West German elite groups toward the country's many foreign-policy problems.

European Integration

GOORMAGHTIGH, JOHN. "European Coal and Steel Community," *International Conciliation,* May, 1955. A balanced evaluation of the Community.

HAAS, ERNST B. *The Uniting of Europe.* Stanford, Calif.: Stanford University Press, 1958. This case study of the European Coal and Steel Community is a masterpiece.

HURTIG, SERGE. "The European Common Market," *International Conciliation,* March, 1958. A good detailed analysis of the Market's prospects.

KITZINGER, U. W. *The Politics and Economics of European Integration.** New York: Frederick A. Praeger, 1963. One of the two best analyses of Common Market integration and the need for Britain to join Europe.

SHANKS, MICHAEL, and LAMBERT, JOHN. *The Common Market Today—and Tomorrow.** New York: Frederick A. Praeger, 1962. The other excellent analysis of the process of European integration and its impact on Britain.

American Policy in China, Korea, and Indochina

FALL, BERNARD B. *The Two Viet-Nams.* Rev. ed.; New York: Frederick A. Praeger, 1964. The single best analysis of the continuing guerrilla war, especially since 1957. Fall shows particularly well the difficulties confronting the United States in fighting anti-guerrilla warfare.

FEIS, HERBERT. *China Tangle.* Princeton, N.J.: Princeton University Press, 1953. A good account of American policy toward China during World War II.

HAMMER, ELLEN J. *The Struggle for Indochina.* Stanford, Calif.: Stanford University Press, 1954. This is the best volume on French policy in this area, providing background for the later American involvement.

Military Situation in the Far East. [The MacArthur] Hearings before the Committee on Armed Services and Foreign Relations, United

States Senate, 82nd Congress, 1st Session. 5 vols. Washington: Government Printing Office, 1951.

PAUKER, GUY J. "Southeast Asia as a Problem Area in the Next Decade," *World Politics*, April, 1959. An excellent analysis of the social and political forces which keep this area weak and a prey for Communist expansion.

ROBERTS, CHALMERS M. "The Day We Didn't Go to War." *The Reporter*, September 14, 1954. This is an apparently "inside" account of how the U.S. Government decided not to intervene in Indochina.

SPANIER, JOHN W. *The Truman-MacArthur Controversy and the Korean War.** Cambridge, Mass.: Harvard University Press, 1959. Rev. paperback ed.; New York: W. W. Norton & Company, 1965. A full-length study and analysis of the policies and events during this war which had such an overwhelming impact upon the United States after 1952.

TANHAM, GEORGE K. *Communist Revolutionary Warfare.* New York: Frederick A. Praeger, 1961. An analysis of the successful Vietminh guerrilla war against the French.

TSOU, TANG. *America's Failure in China, 1941–50.* Chicago: University of Chicago Press, 1963. The definitive analysis of this controversial subject.

VINACKE, HAROLD M. *The United States and the Far East, 1945–51.* Stanford, Calif.: Stanford University Press, 1952. Very good and, also to its advantage, quite short.

American Policy in the Other Underdeveloped Areas

BURKE, FRED G. *Africa's Quest for Order.* Englewood Cliffs, N.J.: Prentice-Hall, 1964. A fine analysis of African politics.

CAMPBELL, JOHN C. *Defense of the Middle East.** New York: Harper & Brothers, 1960. Paperback ed.; New York: Frederick A. Praeger, 1960. A first-rate study of America's postwar policy and problems in this area.

CREMEANS, CHARLES D. *The Arabs and the World.** New York: Frederick A. Praeger, 1963. A good analysis of Arab attitudes and policies in international affairs.

DEAN, VERA MICHELES. *The Nature of the Non-Western World.** New York: New American Library of World Literature, 1957. A valuable introduction.

DRAPER, THEODORE. *Castro's Revolution.** New York: Frederick A. Praeger, 1962. A fine analysis of Cuban-American relations since Castro's assumption of power.

EMERSON, RUPERT. *From Empire to Nation.** Cambridge, Mass.: Harvard University Press, 1960. The best single analysis of the manifold problems of the world's new nations as they emerge from colonial rule.

GOLDSCHMIDT, WALTER (ed.). *The United States and Africa.** New York: Frederick A. Praeger, 1963. An excellent introduction to Africa's polity, economy, and society.

KAUTSKY, JOHN H. (ed.). *Political Change in Underdeveloped Countries.** New York: John Wiley & Sons, 1962. A very good selection of articles on this topic, especially on the role of the intelligentsia in the new nations, the appeals of Communism, and the nature of non-Western nationalism.

— KIRK, GEORGE E. *A Short History of the Middle East.** 7th rev. ed.; New York: Frederick A. Praeger, 1964. Very good for background information.

LAQUEUR, WALTER Z. *The Soviet Union and the Middle East.* New York: Frederick A. Praeger, 1959. An excellent analysis of Russia's penetration of the Middle East. The author followed this book with two further articles on this subject: "Nasser and the Iraqi Communists" and "As Iraq Goes Communist," in *Commentary,* February and May, 1959, respectively.

MARTIN, LAURENCE W. (ed.). *Neutralism and Nonalignment.** New York: Frederick A. Praeger, 1962. This volume includes several excellent selections analyzing nation-building and non-alignment.

MENDEN, FRED VON DER. *Politics of the Developing Areas.** Englewood Cliffs, N.J.: Prentice-Hall, 1964. A good analysis of the new nations' colonial heritage, national cohesion, political parties and elites, and the role of the military.

MILLIKAN, MAX F., and BLACKMER, DONALD L. M. *The Emerging Nations.** Boston: Little Brown & Company, 1961. An excellent brief analysis of the process of transforming traditional societies into modern nation-states.

MILLS, C. WRIGHT. *Listen Yankee.* New York: Ballantine Books, 1961. An uncritical presentation of the Castro regime's attitudes and feelings; worth reading because its emotional tone apparently conveys well the regime's strongly held views.

MURKLAND, HARRY B. "Fidelism for Export," *Current History,* April, 1961. A very good evaluation of Castro's ability to do so.

ROSTOW, W. W. *The Stages of Economic Growth.** New York: Cambridge University Press, 1960. This analysis by a leading political economist is a must for those concerned with this aspect of American foreign policy.

———, and MILLIKAN, MAX W. "Foreign Aid: Next Phase," *Foreign Affairs,* April, 1958. A very fine article, with special emphasis on the need to aid India.

STALEY, EUGENE. *The Future of Underdeveloped Countries.** Rev. ed.; New York: Harper & Brothers, 1961. Paperback ed.; New York: Frederick A. Praeger, 1961. A fine book pointing to the need for a vast-scale American economic aid program and social politics.

STREIT, PEGGY and PIERRE. "Close-up of the Foreign Aid," *The New York Times Magazine,* April 13, 1958. A discerning article by two perspicacious observers emphasizing the difficulty, if not impossibility, of economic development which is unaccompanied by changes in the social structure.

SZULC, TAD. *The Winds of Revolution.** Rev. ed.; New York: Frederick A. Praeger, 1965. An incisive description of the nationalist and social revolution raging in America's own backyard.

Fulbright

montgomery

WARD, BARBARA. "Economic NATO for One Billion," *The New York Times Magazine*, October 19, 1958. A call for large-scale Western economic aid to underdeveloped areas.

———. *Five Ideas That Change the World.** New York: W. W. Norton & Company, 1959. An examination of the effects of nationalism, industrialism, colonialism, Communism, and internationalism on the modern world, particularly on the new nations.

———. "For a New Foreign Aid Concept," *The New York Times Magazine*, March 11, 1956. A brilliant article comparing Soviet and American aid programs. Miss Ward points to the urgent need for a political-ideological framework within which aid should be granted.

———. *The Rich Nations and the Poor Nations.** New York: W. W. Norton & Company, 1962. This excellent and highly readable book analyzes the impact of Western colonialism on the under-developed areas, as well as the economics and politics of development.

———. "To Widen the Base of World Wealth," *The New York Times Magazine*, March 14, 1954. In this article, Miss Ward shows the necessity for an international redistribution of the wealth, as this was necessary domestically in the nineteenth century, and she advocates that the means used should be an international income tax levied on the Western industrialized states.

WALLERSTEIN, IMMANUEL. *Africa: The Politics of Independence.** New York: Vintage Books, 1961. A perceptive analysis of Africa's new nations.

WINT, GUY, and CALVOCORESSI, PETER. *Middle East Crisis.** Baltimore: Penguin Books, 1957. A good analysis of the events leading up to the Suez War; focuses on British policy.

Memoirs and Biographies of American Statesmen and Administrations

BEAL, JOHN R. *John Foster Dulles.* New York: Harper & Brothers, 1956. Recounts the Secretary's policy of brinkmanship.

BUNDY, McGEORGE (ed.). *The Pattern of Responsibility.* Boston: Houghton Mifflin Co., 1952. A compilation of Secretary Acheson's speeches and Congressional testimony.

BYRNES, JAMES F. *Speaking Frankly.* New York: Harper & Brothers, 1947.

DONOVAN, ROBERT J. *Eisenhower: The Inside Story.* New York: Harper & Brothers, 1956. Apparently an "inside" account. (For a very fine evaluation of the Eisenhower Administration—one that is likely to stand for a long time—see William V. Shannon's "Eisenhower as President," in *Commentary*, November, 1958.)

EISENHOWER, DWIGHT D. *Mandate for Change.* New York: Doubleday & Co., 1963. The first volume in Eisenhower's narrative of his Presidential years.

TRUMAN, HARRY S. *Memoirs.* 2 vols. New York: Doubleday & Co., 1956. The President's account of the events which occurred during his stewardship.

The Sino-Soviet Bloc

BARNETT, A. DOAK. *Communist China and Asia.* New York: Harper & Brothers, 1960. The best detailed and balanced analysis yet of this new power's foreign policy.

BAUER, RAYMOND A.; INKELES, ALEX; and KLUCKHOHN, CLYDE. *How the Soviet System Works.* Cambridge, Mass.: Harvard University Press, 1956. This excellent book describes, analyzes, and evaluates the nature and operations of Soviet totalitarianism.

BERLINER, JOSEPH S. *Soviet Economic Aid.* New York: Frederick A. Praeger, 1959. A first-rate, balanced treatment of this increasingly important instrument of Soviet foreign policy.

BOORMAN, HOWARD, *et al. Moscow-Peking Axis: Strengths and Strains.* New York: Harper & Brothers, 1957. Concerned mainly with the strengths.

BRZEZINSKI, ZBIGNIEW K. *Ideology and Power in Soviet Politics.* New York: Frederick A. Praeger, 1962. Five essays linked by a common theme: the interrelationship of ideology and power in domestic and international Soviet politics.

————. *The Soviet Bloc.* Cambridge, Mass.: Harvard University Press, 1960. Rev. paperback ed.; New York: Frederick A. Praeger, 1961. A detailed analysis of the relationships among the Communist-bloc countries. In the paperback edition, a new chapter has been added on Sino-Soviet relations.

BROMKE, ADAM (ed.). *The Communist States at the Crossroads.* New York: Frederick A. Praeger, 1965. A comprehensive analysis of the changing relations between China and Russia, as well as Russia and her "satellites."

DALLIN, DAVID J. *Soviet Foreign Policy After Stalin.* Philadelphia: J. B. Lippincott Co., 1961. A history of Khrushchev's foreign policy.

DINERSTEIN, H. S. *War and the Soviet Union.* Rev. ed.; New York: Frederick A. Praeger, 1962. A good account of the changing nature of Soviet strategy, but it probably overemphasizes the role of "pre-emptive attack" in Russian military thinking.

FLOYD, DAVID. *Mao Against Khrushchev.* New York: Frederick A. Praeger, 1963. A good blow-by-blow account of the quarrel from 1956 to 1963.

GARTHOFF, RAYMOND L. *Soviet Strategy in the Nuclear Age.* Rev. ed.; New York: Frederick A. Praeger, 1962. An excellent analysis of this subject, showing how the Soviets have integrated nuclear weapons into their traditional notions of strategy.

HENDEL, SAMUEL L. (ed.). *The Soviet Crucible.* Princeton, N. J.: D. Van Nostrand Co., 1959. Contains selections on Communist ideology, the nature of Soviet totalitarianism, post-Stalin changes, and other highly relevant aspects of the Soviet political and social system.

MOSELY, PHILIP E. *The Kremlin and World Politics.* New York: Vintage Books, 1960. A collection of discerning and acute articles on the Soviet Union's foreign policy; written by one of the foremost authorities in the field.

STRAUSZ-HUPÉ, ROBERT, *et al. Protracted Conflict*. New York: Harper & Brothers, 1959. A good analysis of Communist tactics of expansion.

TUCKER, ROBERT C. "Russia, the West, and World Wonder," *World Politics,* October, 1959. This excellent article, which analyzes the Communist view of the global struggle, calls for a similar American comprehensive understanding of the world conflict and theory of foreign policy.

ULAM, ADAM B. *The Unfinished Revolution*. New York: Random House, 1960. A superb and original analysis of the relationship between Soviet domestic politics and foreign policy; highly critical of the thesis that the Soviet Union will become increasingly "liberal" at home and "peaceful" in her foreign relations.

WALKER, RICHARD L. *China Under Communism*. New Haven, Conn.: Yale University Press, 1955. Very good on both the domestic and foreign policies of Peking during its first years in power.

ZAGORIA, DONALD S. *The Sino-Soviet Conflict*. Princeton, N. J.: Princeton University Press, 1962. The definitive analysis of the origins and nature of this conflict.

INDEX